Young People's Educational Careers in England and Germany

Young People's Educational Careers in England and Germany

Integrating Survey and Interview Analysis via Qualitative Comparative Analysis

Judith Glaesser
Senior Lecturer in Education, Durham University, UK

palgrave
macmillan

First published 2015 by
PALGRAVE MACMILLAN

Palgrave Macmillan in the UK is an imprint of Macmillan Publishers Limited, registered in England, company number 785998, of Houndmills, Basingstoke, Hampshire RG21 6XS.

Palgrave Macmillan in the US is a division of St Martin's Press LLC, 175 Fifth Avenue, New York, NY 10010.

Palgrave Macmillan is the global academic imprint of the above companies and has companies and representatives throughout the world.

Palgrave® and Macmillan® are registered trademarks in the United States, the United Kingdom, Europe and other countries.

ISBN 978–1–137–35549–2

This book is printed on paper suitable for recycling and made from fully managed and sustained forest sources. Logging, pulping and manufacturing processes are expected to conform to the environmental regulations of the country of origin.

A catalogue record for this book is available from the British Library.

A catalog record for this book is available from the Library of Congress.

Typeset by MPS Limited, Chennai, India.

Contents

List of Figures, Tables and Boxes   viii

Acknowledgements   x

1   Introduction   1
    1.1   Substantive aims   1
    1.2   Methodological aims   4
    1.3   ESRC project   5
    1.4   Policy   5
    1.5   Structure of the book   6

2   Description and Explanation: Methodological Rationale   13
    2.1   Introduction   13
    2.2   Role and forms of description   13
    2.3   Theory, explanation and mechanisms   16
    2.4   Methods for establishing description and explanation   21

3   Qualitative Comparative Analysis   29

4   Overview of the Project   39
    4.1   Theoretical rationale   39
    4.2   Outcomes and explanatory factors   43
    4.3   Secondary schooling in England   44
    4.4   Secondary schooling in Germany   45
    4.5   Survey data   48
          4.5.1   England   48
          4.5.2   Germany   50
    4.6   Interviews   50
    4.7   Findings   56
          4.7.1   Flexibility in the selective German
                  secondary system   56
          4.7.2   GCSE success   60
          4.7.3   Comprehensive versus selective schooling   61

5   Which Young People in Germany Are in a Gymnasium
    at the Age of 17? A Typological Analysis   63
    5.1   QCA findings   63
    5.2   Classification and selection of typical, deviant
          and inconclusive cases   69

5.3	Typical cases	74
5.4	Deviant cases	78
5.5	Inconclusive cases	82
5.6	Lessons from the analysis of interviews	85
5.7	Conclusion	87

6 Secondary Schooling Careers in England — 89

6.1	QCA findings	89
	6.1.1 QCA without key stage 2 test, outcome 'in full-time education age 17'	90
	6.1.2 QCA without key stage 2 test, outcome 'HE likely age 17'	92
	6.1.3 QCA with key stage 2 test, outcome 'in full-time education age 17'	94
	6.1.4 QCA with key stage 2 test, outcome 'HE likely age 17'	97
	6.1.5 Necessity analyses	99
6.2	Classification and selection of typical, deviant and inconclusive cases	101
6.3	Typical cases	103
6.4	Deviant cases	107
	6.4.1 Deviant with regard to combinations of conditions and outcome – sufficiency	107
	6.4.2 Deviant with regard to combinations of conditions and outcome – necessity	110
	6.4.3 Deviant with regard to an outcome	112
6.5	Inconclusive cases	114
6.6	Lessons from the analysis of interviews	116
6.7	Conclusion	121

7 What Types of Young People Are Bound for Higher Education at the Age of 17? — 122

7.1	Germany and England: system differences and similarities	123
7.2	University aspirations in Germany	126
7.3	Analysis of interviews	128
	7.3.1 Country and system	128
	7.3.2 School influences	134
	7.3.3 Individual factors	138
7.4	Conclusion	141

8   Using In-Depth Case Studies to Explore Causal
Mechanisms in Detail   145
   8.1   Overdetermined outcomes   149
   8.2   Unexpected constellations and the role
       of contingency   151
      8.2.1   Unfavourable factors and positive outcome   151
      8.2.2   Favourable factors and unexpectedly low
          educational outcome   157
   8.3   Conclusion   162

9   Summary and Conclusions   164
   9.1   Substantive conclusions   164
   9.2   Methodological conclusions   167
   9.3   Implications for policy   170
   9.4   Concluding remarks   175

Notes   177

References   184

Index   192

List of Figures, Tables and Boxes

Figures

3.1	Sufficiency of condition A for outcome O	30
3.2	Necessity of condition A for outcome O	31
3.3	Venn diagram, two conditions	32

Tables

3.1	Ragin's Table 4.4: Cause Is Sufficient but Not Necessary	31
3.2	Ragin's Table 4.3: Cause Is Necessary but Not Sufficient	32
3.3	Crosstabulation, three conditions	33
3.4	Truth table, three conditions	34
3.5	Example truth table, three conditions	35
4.1	LSYPE sample description ($n = 4972$)	51
4.2	SOEP sample description ($n = 790$)	52
4.3	German interviewees	54
4.4	English interviewees	55
4.5	Truth table, outcome moving up from Hauptschule	58
5.1	Truth table, outcome in Gymnasium at age 17	65
5.2	Analysis of necessary conditions, outcome variable: GY17	67
5.3	Types of configuration with names of interviewees	72
6.1	Truth table, outcome full-time education age 17, three conditions	91
6.2	Truth table, outcome HE expectation age 17, three conditions	93
6.3	Truth table, outcome full-time education age 17, four conditions	95
6.4	Truth table, outcome HE expectation age 17, four conditions	98
6.5	Test of necessity, outcome in full-time education age 17	100

6.6   Test of necessity, outcome HE likely age 17   100

6.7   Types of configuration with names of interviewees   103

6.8   Truth table, outcome HE expectation age 17,
      four conditions including school type   118

6.9   Truth table, outcome HE expectation age 17,
      three conditions including school type   119

7.1   Truth table, German young people's HE intention   127

Boxes

3.1   Three solutions for Table 3.5: Example truth table,
      three conditions   36

4.1   Solutions for Table 4.5, outcome moving up from
      Hauptschule   59

5.1   Solutions for Table 5.1, outcome in Gymnasium
      at age 17   66

6.1   Solutions for Table 6.1, outcome full-time education
      age 17, three conditions   91

6.2   Solutions for Table 6.2, outcome HE expectation
      age 17, three conditions   93

6.3   Solutions for Table 6.3, outcome full-time
      education age 17, four conditions   94

6.4   Solutions for Table 6.4, outcome HE expectation
      age 17, four conditions   99

6.5   Solution for Table 6.9, outcome HE expectation
      age 17, three conditions including school type   120

Acknowledgements

First of all, my warmest thanks to Barry Cooper who has supported me throughout the work on this book, from when I was designing the underlying research project to the final writing stages. He also first introduced me to Qualitative Comparative Analysis (QCA). I have bene-fited hugely from my discussions with him and I am very grateful for all his advice, thoughts and support.

I would like to thank the young people who took part in the inter-views and shared some of their thoughts and experiences with me. I am also very grateful to the teachers and schools who helped me organise the interviews and found me some space in which to conduct them.

Thanks are due to the Deutsches Institut für Wirtschaftsforschung (DIW) for supplying the Socio-Economic Panel (SOEP) data, to the Department for Education for supplying the Longitudinal Study of Young People in England (LSYPE) data, to the Centre for Evaluation and Monitoring (CEM) centre for the Yellis data and the Centre for Longitudinal Studies for the National Child Development Study (NCDS) data.

Finally, I would like to thank the Economic and Social Research Council (ESRC) for their financial support for this project.

1
Introduction

The motivation for this book is twofold. One aim is to contribute to sociological research concerning young people's educational careers and the interconnected roles of individual characteristics, home, school, and educational system. The other is to contribute to methodological development in the social sciences by describing how a combination of large n based cross-case configurational analysis with in-depth interviews in two countries can contribute to theoretical development as well as being able to provide explanations for the outcomes of individual cases.

In this introductory chapter, I will briefly comment on the background to both these aims before describing the project funded by the Economic and Social Research Council (ESRC) which underpins the research for this book. Since the research presented in this book potentially has policy implications, this will be followed by some comments on policy. The chapter closes with a summary of the book's remaining chapters.

1.1 Substantive aims

Education forms a central part of young people's lives. While gaining an education has intrinsic value, leading to a fulfilling life, it is also often seen, more extrinsically, as a means to a rewarding occupation. For this reason, it is often a topic for public debate. Some of the issues discussed are social inequality in education (in other words, the extent to which educational opportunities and achievements are linked to social background), the way an educational system should be organised, a country's educational performance compared with others in terms of economic competitiveness, education and employment chances, and migrants' chances in their new country's education system, to name but

1

a few. Some of these topics have been debated for some considerable time, but interest in them remains high, especially in the face of social change and associated new challenges for all education systems. In this book, I focus on just some of these issues, in particular on the links between social background and educational opportunities and achievements. Some of the other points will be shown to have a bearing on these. I draw on empirical data from two countries, England[1] and Germany. While these two countries share many characteristics, their education systems differ in important ways, and this will enable me to study to what extent these system differences shape educational outcomes, and to what extent social processes override any system differences and shape outcomes regardless of these.

The phrase 'social mobility' is frequently used in Britain in the media and by politicians as a shorthand way of describing the idea that people should have equal life chances regardless of social background, and that people from the bottom of the social hierarchy should be able to move up, given appropriate qualifications and skills.[2] Education is commonly assumed to have a key part to play in making social mobility possible. However, while both social class of origin and social class destination have been linked to education for the individual (for example Goldthorpe, 2003), it does not follow that simply improving individual young people's educational outcomes will improve social mobility rates for the whole society (Goldthorpe, 2013).[3] This claim is based on the observation that the increase in absolute social mobility, that is, the improved chances of attaining a high social class position, observed during the period following the Second World War, was largely the result of a change in occupational structure. More jobs became available in higher social class positions during this period, but the strength of the connection between educational qualification and social class position hardly changed. It is true that over this period, more people achieved higher qualifications, and were therefore able to obtain higher social class positions, but this was 'demand driven: that is, by the growth of professional and managerial employment that far outstripped the supply of highly qualified personnel' (Goldthorpe, 2013, p. 442) and not the result of educational reform. So, for an individual, higher qualifications do increase the chances of obtaining a higher social class position, but within the population, an increase in the rate of high qualifications will not, on its own, necessarily lead to an increase in the overall rates of mobility (absolute or relative). Nevertheless, the aim of improving social mobility is often used as a justification for school reforms and an interest in outcomes and educational targets in England.

Likewise, there is a concern with the link between social background and educational outcomes in public debates in Germany, as can be seen, for example, from the debate regarding Germany's performance in the first Programme for International Student Assessment (PISA) study (Baumert & Schümer, 2001). While this debate was largely focussed on Germany's performance in the mid-range of participating countries (rather than near the top, as had been hoped for and expected both by politicians and the general public), another significant part of the discussion concerned the finding that in Germany, social background and immigration seemed to have a particularly strong influence on performance. Various reasons were suggested for this finding, among them the existence of a selective tripartite secondary school system. Criticism of selection at the end of primary school has been a feature of educational debates since well before the PISA studies, as is evident, for example, from the debates regarding comprehensive schooling in the 1970s and the introduction of comprehensive schools in some parts of Germany around that time. While comprehensive schools did not become the norm, debates concerning the ideal secondary school system have continued to this day, along with ongoing reforms in all of Germany's 16 federal states (Länder). A particular concern is with the fate of children who attend Hauptschule, the least academic of the three hierarchically ordered types of secondary school. Originally, this was the most commonly attended type of school, offering a qualification which enabled pupils to take up an apprenticeship. Now, it is attended by around 10 per cent of a cohort, and the prospects of its school leavers are much worse than those of any other school type.[4] This has led to the Hauptschule being called the 'Restschule', or the school for leftovers. This rather cynical term is used to indicate a concern with the social problems that can be present in a Hauptschule and that may be created by a school type whose intake largely consists of young people who are not seen as academically able or motivated, many of whom are immigrants whose knowledge of German varies considerably, and whose parents either cannot or will not seek a 'better' type of school for their children.

These brief sketches of some of the debates in the two countries illustrate that the concern with the link between social background and education is widespread. I discuss the sociological, theoretical background to this debate in Chapter 4. Here, I merely gave a flavour of some of the issues debated in both countries which drive both educational policy and individual decision-making.

1.2   Methodological aims

The previous section explained the substantive background to this book. I now turn to the second set of aims, that of illustrating the usefulness of a particular methodological approach. At the core of the project described in this book is a concern with describing and explaining social phenomena and confirming and developing relevant explanatory theory. Causal explanation is a difficult and contentious aim in the social sciences (more on this in Chapter 2). Some argue that only cross-case analyses using large samples, statistical testing and control variables can establish causal models and provide a basis for generalisation, whereas others would see such models as a form of sophisticated description and suggest, alternatively, a stress on the understanding of generative or causal mechanisms based on theoretical knowledge and the in-depth analysis of a small number of cases.[5] My view is that, on its own, either approach falls short of being able to provide causal explanation, and I therefore combine cross-case analysis of survey data with in-depth case studies in order to gain deeper insights than would be possible from either form of analysis on its own.

My method of choice for analysing survey data is Charles Ragin's increasingly popular *Qualitative Comparative Analysis* (QCA) (Ragin, 1987, 2000, 2008) which I introduce in Chapter 3. QCA is a conjunctural method which relies on Boolean algebra and set theory. It aims to preserve the case as a configuration of characteristics as the basis of analysis rather than analysing variables as if they could be treated almost as actors and their effects on some outcome could be identified net of that of other influences. The configurational context of any factors under study can therefore be taken into account. As well as for the cross-case analyses, I use QCA to inform the selection of cases, via a typological analysis, for interviewing. Subsequently, the results of the analysis of these interviews enabled me to refine some of the QCA analyses.

Another feature of the research design is the use of two comparison countries, England and Germany. Given that, among other things, the organisation of secondary schooling and higher education in the two countries is different, the international comparison will allow a deeper understanding of adolescents' careers through the analysis of cross-national similarities and differences. It will be possible to identify mechanisms and processes that are shaped by organisational features specific to one country, as well as those that are more universally applicable.

1.3 ESRC project

The research reported in this book was made possible through an ESRC-funded research fellowship I held from 2009 to 2011. It arose from joint work I had been undertaking with Barry Cooper (who also was my mentor during the fellowship) on QCA and large *n* analysis applied to British secondary survey data, with a substantive interest in the sociology of education (see for example Cooper & Glaesser, 2008; Glaesser, 2008). I sought the ESRC's support because I wished to take this work further and gain deeper insights into sociological processes by combining QCA with process-tracing interviews (George & Bennett, 2005). To this end, I identified appropriate existing survey data from both England and Germany (for details see Chapter 4) and I undertook 79 interviews with 16 to 18 year olds in both countries (43 in Germany and 36 in England). As noted above, choosing to study two countries was done for both substantive and methodological reasons. In addition, I have some knowledge of both countries which I was able to draw on. I am German and, having received my own schooling and university education in Germany as well as having studied educational careers in Germany for my PhD thesis, I was able to draw on relevant contextual knowledge in devising the interview schedule for the semi-structured interviews and in responding to points raised by the interviewees. Likewise, I was familiar with the English system, having lived in England for five years by the time I undertook the interviews, and having worked in an education department in an English university (Durham) during this period.

1.4 Policy

My key concern in this book is with gaining methodological understanding, that is, an understanding of how causal knowledge may be acquired by social scientists, as well as substantive, sociological insights. I do not undertake any policy evaluation as such. However, I expect some of my findings to be of potential use to policymakers, in particular regarding the set-up of a school system and the implications of a system's properties for social processes and outcomes. As indicated above, the debate on selective versus comprehensive schooling has been going on in the two countries under study (as well as many others) for some time and shows no signs of being resolved. The comparison I undertake might therefore prove useful to those having to make decisions in this respect. Such comparisons between the educational systems of different countries with the aim of learning from a different system are not a new idea; policy-borrowing has a long history. Phillips (2000), for example, points out that comparative research has frequently formed the basis for implementing some aspects of another country's educational policy or system. However, it can be risky merely to pick and choose isolated elements of another system since the various elements act in conjunction with others. They have also developed in the context of a particular society and culture, which means that a single policy or aspect of a school system cannot always be imported easily. Politicians also occasionally make reference to another country's system by way of justification of their own preferred policies, but this is not always based on sound empirical evidence (Morris, 2012; Phillips, 2000). My findings compile the sort of empirical evidence that would be suitable to inform policy decisions regarding the selectivity or otherwise of secondary schools, and might have something to offer for teacher education and professionals working in careers advice services. I explain why in Chapter 9. Policy evaluation and policy recommendations frequently make use of randomised controlled trials (RCTs) and other forms of experimental research. I briefly discuss these methods in Chapter 2.

1.5   Structure of the book

In the remainder of this chapter, I summarise each subsequent chapter briefly. In addition to giving an overview of the structure of the book, this is intended particularly for the benefit of those readers who may not wish to read the whole book, but who prefer to focus on particular aspects. For those particularly interested in the *methodological* approach, I suggest reading Chapters 2, 3 and 9, and possibly one of the substantive Chapters 5 to 7 for an illustration. For those who are mainly interested in the *substantive, sociological* findings, it is possible to skip Chapters 2 and 3, especially if they have some prior knowledge of QCA. Chapter 4 introduces the theoretical background to Chapters 5 to 8, so should be read regardless of the particular substantive focus of interest. Chapters 5 to 8 then each have their own particular substantive focus and it is possible to read just one or all of them. I suggest reading Chapter 9 for a summarising overview, conclusions and discussion of policy implications, regardless of the particular substantive point of interest.

Chapter 2 outlines my view of the relationships between description, causal explanation and theory, building on the assumption that causal mechanisms generate observed empirical regularities. Good description can be important and useful in its own right, but it is also required for successful explanation, the aim of much of social science. This sounds obvious, as Merton (1987) notes: 'In the abstract, it need hardly be said that before one proceeds to explain or to interpret a phenomenon, it is advisable to establish that the phenomenon actually exists, that it is enough of a regularity to require and to allow explanation.' In this chapter, I suggest that statistical models, for example those based on regression analysis, can describe such regularities, or 'establish the phenomenon' (see also Goldthorpe, 2001), but that other forms of sophisticated description can be provided by configurational methods such as QCA. Pawson (2008) suggests that both regression-based and configurational models fall short of providing knowledge of generative or causal mechanisms. While I agree with this view, I also suggest that QCA as a configurational method is better suited to describing the complex cross-case regularities that characterise social life than regression-based analyses. I then show, drawing on other studies as examples, how various methods can and should be used together to analyse generative mechanisms.

Drawing on some key publications (Cooper & Glaesser, 2011; Ragin, 1987, 2000, 2006b, 2008), *Chapter 3* provides an introduction to the central features of QCA. QCA is the core method employed throughout the book for the cross-case analyses and to construct the typologies of cases from which interviewees are chosen for in-depth study. This typological approach allows me to integrate quantitative and qualitative approaches.

QCA draws on set theory, Boolean algebra and the concepts of necessary and sufficient conditions. Sufficiency and necessity involve subsethood relations. If a condition is sufficient for an outcome to occur, the set of cases with the condition is a subset of the set of cases with the outcome. Conversely, if a condition is necessary for some outcome, the set of cases with the outcome is a subset of the set of cases with the condition. Ragin (2006b) has developed measures of quasi-sufficiency and quasi-necessity, in other words, an index of how close a relationship between condition(s) and outcome is to perfect sufficiency/necessity. This is important given the fact that social relationships are not usually perfect, that is, without exceptions to general patterns, so the notions of quasi-sufficiency and quasi-necessity are useful. Likewise, conditions often do not act in isolation, but in conjunction with other conditions. QCA is able to describe the complex regularities that arise from such conjunctural causal relationships. Boolean notation is used, where capital letters stand for the presence of a condition and lower case letters for its absence, or logical NOT. The * symbol represents logical AND, the + logical OR. An illustrative example of a QCA model from my Chapter 6 is ALEVEL_1P*SC_1P + male*SC_1P => FT_EDU17. This may be read as indicating that the configuration 'having at least one parent with A-levels' AND 'having at least one parent in the service class' OR 'being female [=NOT MALE]' AND 'having at least one parent in the service class' is sufficient for 'being in full-time education at the age of 17'. Such a model, or 'solution', to use the proper term, is identified on the basis of a so-called truth table which maps out all the possible combinations of conditions and the relationship of these configurations with the outcome. All these concepts and technical details are explained in Chapter 3.

Chapter 4 gives an overview of the design of the study on which this book is based. It starts by explaining its theoretical background which draws on *rational action theory (RAT)* (Boudon, 1974; Breen & Goldthorpe, 1997; Goldthorpe, 1996b) and Bourdieu's concepts of *habitus* and *cultural capital* (Bourdieu, 1977, 1986). All these have been used by sociologists to explain social inequality in education. They are sometimes seen as contradictory or mutually exclusive, but I will argue that they can be fruitfully employed together (Glaesser & Cooper, 2014; Vester, 2006). I then explain the rationale for the choice of the explanatory factors and outcomes analysed throughout the book. Explanatory factors include parental social class and education, the young person's prior attainment where possible, and gender. The outcomes are, for Germany, whether the young person was in a Gymnasium (the most selective German school type) at the age of 17, and for England, whether the young person was or would be in full-time education at the age of 17, and, in addition, for both countries, whether the young person intended to go to university.

This is followed by an overview of the secondary school systems in the two countries. Next, I describe my data, beginning with the survey data used for Germany, the Socio-Economic Panel (SOEP), and those for England, the Longitudinal Study of Young People in England (LSYPE), including details of my samples. Regarding the interview data, I explain how I selected the cases for interview in both countries, and I describe the resulting samples. The chapter closes with summaries of some of the findings from the ESRC project that have been reported elsewhere (Glaesser & Cooper, 2011b, 2012a, b).

Chapter 5 analyses the outcome of attending a German Gymnasium, the most academic type of secondary school, at the age of 17. I first describe the situation, drawing on a QCA analysis of SOEP data which shows that having received a recommendation in primary school for entering the Gymnasium has to be combined with having at least one parent with the Abitur (equivalent of A-levels) or, for boys, with having at least one parent in the service class. The recommendation, which is used as an indicator of academic ability as well as usually being a prerequisite for entering the Gymnasium straight after primary school, is shown to be a quasi-necessary condition, too. I discuss implications of these findings before moving on to developing a classification of cases, based on the QCA results, as 'typical', 'deviant' or 'inconclusive' with regard to expected outcomes. This classification forms the basis of the selection of cases for subsequent interview analysis. I am able to show that the cases classified as 'typical' are indeed those that follow theoretical expectations, based on the theories described in Chapter 4, but that the summarising nature of the QCA results also masked some interesting differences between these cases regarding the relevant causal mechanisms. Similarly, for 'deviant' cases, the analyses show that these differ in relevant ways from cases that shared the same configuration of conditions in the initial analysis. For example, in these 'deviant' cases, other factors were able to compensate for the lack of the recommendation which meant that they attended a Gymnasium at the age of 17 despite not having had the quasi-necessary condition of the recommendation. Finally, 'inconclusive' cases were those where QCA showed that there was no clear expectation to be derived from the analysis with regard to their receiving the outcome or not, in other words, that there was no clear tendency for cases of their type. I conclude that presence or absence of ambition and talent in the young people themselves coupled with institutional arrangements that made a later transition to the Gymnasium possible were able to explain why they did or did not attend the Gymnasium aged 17.

Chapter 6 has a similar structure to Chapter 5. It starts with a QCA analysis of LSYPE data to analyse the outcomes of being in full-time education after the end of compulsory schooling, that is, at the age of 17, and of expecting, at that age, to enter higher education later on. For both outcomes, having at least one parent with A-levels and having at least one parent in the service class had to be combined. Since the LSYPE data contain a measure of prior attainment, a test taken at key stage 2 (that is, at age 11), I added this to the analyses. With one exception, having done well in this test was not a sufficient condition on its own for obtaining either of the two outcomes; it had to be combined with the parental background measures in all of the analyses. As with the German analyses, I discuss the fit of these findings with theoretical expectations before classifying the cases on the basis of the QCA results into 'typical', 'deviant' or 'inconclusive' with regard to whether they were likely to enter higher education. In addition, I identify a further group of 'deviant' cases: it is fairly unusual not be in full-time education at the age of 17 in England, and so it seemed to me that it was worth investigating who belonged to this unusual group of young people.

In England, schools are not as easily classified into types with regard to their academic orientation as they are in the largely hierarchically ordered German system, but I argue that some schools are nevertheless more likely to encourage staying on in education and to prepare for higher education than others, effectively acting as sponsors (Turner, 1960) for those who have entered them. This applies to academically selective schools in particular, but also to some comprehensives. This assumption is borne out by the evidence from the interviews. Such schools form part of the mechanism that leads to young people's either leaving education or staying on and expecting to go to university. With one exception, all the 'typical' interviewees attended such schools, and this, coupled with their favourable social background, explained their wish to obtain higher education. Likewise, I was able to explain the outcomes of 'deviant' cases by showing that they lacked the support of a suitable school or a suitable social environment, despite the fact that the individual's social background as measured by simple indicators related to parental education and social class suggested that their home environment should lead to the expectation of going to university. Once again, this illustrates the additional insights to be gained by employing in-depth case studies to overcome the shortcomings of summarising factors and models. In other 'deviant' cases, suitable schools, coupled with individual ambition and talent, acted as effective substitutes in cases where the social background would not have led to the expectation that the young person would develop higher education aspirations. These were also key factors for the 'inconclusive' cases.

Chapter 7 focusses on the question of what types of young people from both countries are bound for higher education at the age of 17. I begin by noting the difference between the two countries in the proportion of young people who intend to attend a higher education institution. This proportion is 34 per cent in Germany, based on SOEP data, and 65 per cent in England, based on LSYPE data. Given this, my next step is to describe and discuss differences between school systems as well as higher and further education sectors in both countries which may be connected to this gap. I then use QCA in a cross-case analysis of the SOEP data to investigate higher education aspirations in Germany (the parallel analysis for England using LSYPE data is presented and discussed in Chapter 6). QCA uses so-called truth tables to map out all the possible constellations of explanatory factors and their relationship with the outcome, and to identify factors or configurations of factors that are (quasi-)sufficient for obtaining the outcome (this is explained in detail in Chapter 3). The analysis of the SOEP-based truth table does not identify any configuration of factors (or individual factor) quasi-sufficient for the outcome of higher education aspirations. However, this truth table itself yields some interesting findings, showing that configurations comprising factors that indicate social advantage are considerably above the grand mean of 34 per cent with respect to the outcome.

I then analyse the interviews focussing on three areas and their influence on the development of higher education aspirations or otherwise: country or system differences, school influences, and individual factors. While it is helpful to discuss these three areas separately, they are obviously interrelated, and I identify some of the ways in which they are. For example, both school type and the particular constellation of home background factors can influence, jointly or separately, how a young person relates to England's hierarchical higher education system. In the conclusion, I note that the young people themselves explain their preferences for higher education or other routes by reference to their talents and interests. While these are clearly important, my QCA and cross-case interview analyses help identify, in addition, broader social processes which shape the young people's preferences and decision-making.

In *Chapter 8*, I focus on explaining *individual* cases' educational pathways and outcomes. To do so, I draw on existing theory and combine this with knowledge of factors covered by the theory *and* knowledge of additional, specific factors of a particular case, making use of Lieberson's (1997, p. 376; Lieberson & Silverman, 1965) framework of 'underlying causal conditions' and 'immediate precipitants' to explain specific events. Lieberson applied this approach in the context of explaining the occurrence of race riots. Unlike educational pathways and outcomes, race riots are relatively rare events, but I show how Lieberson's ideas can be applied in my context. Underlying causal conditions in my study are the individual and social background factors discussed in the previous chapters, i.e. type of school system and type of school, social background, and early academic achievement. Knowledge of the constellation of these factors helps predict for an individual case whether certain outcomes are more or less likely. Immediate precipitants then are events or idiosyncrasies which lead to an individual's either following the expected path and gaining the outcome, or deviating from this path. To begin with, I return to some of the 'typical' cases from previous chapters to demonstrate that for them, there is less scope for contingency or unexpected events to have a significant impact on these individuals' educational pathways. The 'underlying causal conditions' alone can explain their outcomes. The greater part of the chapter is then devoted to unexpected cases, in other words, those where there is a mismatch between causal factors and outcome. Here, 'immediate precipitants' have a greater role to play.

Chapter 9 offers a brief summary of the findings alongside substantive and methodological conclusions and a discussion of the findings with regard to implications for policy. For the substantive findings, RAT as well as Bourdieu's habitus and cultural capital prove to be appropriate explanatory concepts. In developing explanations, a key point was that I was able to show that the joint presence of many advantageous factors was the surest route to educational success. The comparison of two countries is also briefly discussed and shown to have provided additional insights. Methodologically, I discuss in this chapter how my particular approach of combining various sources of evidence was useful in obtaining descriptive and explanatory knowledge. Using QCA to inform the choice of cases for subsequent interviews also proves to be very fruitful. In the discussion of policy issues, I suggest that school system itself – whether selective or comprehensive – does not appear to be as important for most individual outcomes as might be assumed, though it does have a bearing on the shape young people's careers take. More generally, I also discuss the limitations of any policy given the influences of home background and wider social network. I note that teachers in particular may benefit from sociological knowledge of the sort discussed in this book.

2
Description and Explanation: Methodological Rationale

2.1 Introduction

This chapter sets out the methodological basis for the work reported in the book and provides my perspective on the topics of description, explanation and causation. Social science research, explicitly or implicitly, often aims to provide causal explanations. In other words, it is often concerned with 'why' questions, for example, why do people go to university? Why did Finland often come out top in international studies on educational performance? Why do women earn less than men? In this chapter, I discuss how social scientists attempt to provide causal explanations of the sort required to answer such questions.

2.2 Role and forms of description

A necessary first step on the way to providing explanations is to describe the phenomenon or phenomena under study. Merton (1987, p. 2) notes that 'in the abstract, it need hardly be said that before one proceeds to explain or to interpret a phenomenon, it is advisable to establish that the phenomenon actually exists, that it is enough of a regularity to require and to allow explanation.' He goes on to discuss instances where, contrary to this advice, researchers have developed plausible explanatory accounts of apparent phenomena or events which had not actually taken place.

The three questions listed in the introduction to this chapter all refer to some established phenomenon. We already know that some people, but not others, go to university, but this alone does not tell us why they do or do not do so. Before it is possible to explain this, it is imperative to describe this phenomenon in as much detail and precision as possible.

For example, it would probably be helpful to establish the proportion of young people going to university, whether there have been changes over time, whether differences with regard to higher education entry exist between countries, between people of different social classes of origin, ethnic background and gender, what the employment prospects of graduates versus non-graduates are and so on. Such description is theoretically informed in the sense that the categories used to organise the description, such as social class, will already reflect the researcher's belief that some factors rather than others are likely to explain attendance or non-attendance. Theoretically informed description then makes it possible to analyse potential explanations. Similarly, on the question regarding women's pay, it is important first to establish the size of any gender pay gap, and then to investigate matters such as equality legislation, changes and trends over time, differences between public and private sector, career point, part-time versus full-time workers, to name but a few potentially relevant issues.

These examples are intended to illustrate what good description might entail, and, in addition, how such useful description relies on ideas about potentially explanatory factors. For example, among the factors I listed which might be relevant to describing who goes to university, I omitted eye colour. It does not seem plausible that this would be a relevant explanatory factor, and it can therefore be safely left off any description of the composition of the group of university applicants compared with that of non-applicants. Class, on the other hand, seems a possible candidate for an explanatory factor,[1] and therefore its inclusion in the description seems justified. However, it is not always easy or indeed possible to know which factors should be included, and which can safely be left out. The choice of factors can have implications not only for the description, but also for any explanation which might be attempted subsequently. In addition, the purpose of the description and/or explanation can have a bearing on what factors are chosen. Research funders may have their own agendas, for example.

Similarly, Ragin (2004) notes that defining the population to which an explanation is to be applied is an important and potentially difficult part of the analytic process. Applied to my example, the explanations of why individuals do or do not attend university are likely to vary depending on whether the population to be considered is the group of school-leavers in one particular year or from one particular school, from one country, all of the Western world and so on.

Description can be important, interesting and useful in its own right as well as being a prerequisite for successful explanation (Collier, 2011).

Before moving on to explanation in the next section, I will discuss various forms of description in some more detail here. It will become obvious throughout that it is not actually possible to separate description and explanation; description contains elements of explanation and/or is quite often undertaken with the aim of explaining, while explanation has to refer to description. Nevertheless, I will treat the two separately to begin with.

Regression analysis and its variants are thought of by some as capable of providing causal models, at least in ideal circumstances and when properly specified (Pearl, 1999, for example). Very briefly, the logic is that such models establish the effect of some target variable on some outcome, holding other potentially confounding variables constant. The target variable is thought to be the cause, and the size of its effect on the outcome can be quantified. Other authors – including many statisticians and quantitative researchers – are not convinced that these models are actually able to provide causal explanation by themselves (Freedman, 1991, 1997a, 2005; Goldthorpe, 2001, 2007b). Goldthorpe (2001) notes that sociologists' explananda are social regularities of some sort, and that statistical models are useful for establishing such regularities, especially in cases where the regularities are not readily observable and sophisticated statistical analyses are necessary. However, such models are descriptive, though they may suggest causal accounts. Explanatory hypotheses as to their underlying generative mechanisms have to be developed and tested in a further step. If the hypothesised underlying processes are directly observable, then this will allow a direct test of the hypothesis, but if they are not, indirect tests have to be undertaken. This can involve specifying other effects the underlying process would be expected to have, and testing whether they do indeed arise. This testing may be based on further statistical models, so from this perspective, these have a role where causal explanation is concerned, over and above providing the initial sophisticated description.

Pawson (2008) agrees with the view that regression-based research and experimental research on their own fall short of providing causal explanations. Such research is sometimes described as variable-based, in contrast with case-based research. Pawson's preferred term for these variable-based models is 'successionist' because they aim to establish a causal chain. By contrast, he describes certain forms of case-based research as configurationist to indicate that their aim is to identify configurations of factors which are causally linked to an outcome. The most prominent among these methods is Ragin's Qualitative Comparative Analysis (QCA) (Ragin, 1987, 2000, 2008), the method I draw on throughout this book for cross-case analyses. Again, Pawson notes that such configurational models in themselves cannot provide causal explanations. A similar point is made in Cooper and Glaesser (2012a), where we explored the way in which the summarising nature of some of these models might obscure important causal mechanisms. Nevertheless, I believe that QCA and related methods have a greater affinity with many social phenomena than regression-based models, both in terms of the configurational descriptions they can provide and as a potential basis for explanation. I will explain why in more detail below.

2.3   Theory, explanation and mechanisms

As noted, good description can be an important research goal in its own right as well as being the prerequisite for explanation. Goldthorpe (2007b) argues that statistical analysis of large-scale data sets can provide a form of sophisticated description which serves to 'establish the phenomenon', using Merton's (1987) phrase. Goldthorpe's preferred form of empirical evidence of relationships between factors found via empirical research comes from large *n* survey analysis, and he stresses the crucial role of theory in providing explanations of these relationships. However, the generative processes which produce observable relationships between factors and outcomes cannot be inferred solely from statistical analysis or other forms of sophisticated description. Theory provides an account of such generative mechanisms. Pawson (1989, p. 130), drawing on Bhaskar's critical realism, notes that a generative mechanism is not simply an additional variable in some model describing an empirical regularity, but 'an *account* of the constitution and behaviour of those things that are responsible for the manifest regularity'. He concludes that social research with the goal of providing explanation has to explore underlying mechanisms which link events in a regular fashion (1989, p. 157). Within a given context, the mechanism provides the explanation for the outcome (Pawson, 2006, see figure 2.1, p. 22). Pawson stresses that the realist generative model of causation does not rely on establishing causation on the basis of the regularity alone, and a generative process can be assumed even in the face of some irregularity. An irregularity in itself does not make the assumption of the mechanism invalid (Pawson, 2006, p. 20–21).

I will illustrate this view of causation as a generative mechanism by taking up my earlier example. Let us assume that we have established that some young people go to university, and we have carefully described those who do and do not choose to do so with regard to their social and ethnic backgrounds, academic achievement, aspirations and other factors that seemed relevant based on theoretical and other forms of prior knowledge. A pattern may have emerged, showing, among other things, that young people from the highest social classes are twice as likely to apply to university as those from the lowest, given the same level of qualifications. This is the description, an empirical regularity. To explain it, we have to identify an underlying generative mechanism. The finding that young people from a high social class background are more likely to go to university is not in itself a mechanism, although many people would find it easy enough to propose a mechanism that could explain this finding. This could be that those privileged young people have had better schooling to prepare them for university, or that they are more familiar, through social networks, with university life and therefore feel more comfortable applying to and attending university, or that they are better aware of a degree's value in the labour market and so on. These are the potential mechanisms that produce the regularity,[2] but they are not so easily observable empirically. There is no simple recipe for establishing generative mechanisms. One way of doing so, in Goldthorpe's view, is the use of qualitative work to suggest plausible mechanisms that have generated the regularities established via the analysis of survey data (Goldthorpe, 2007b, chapter 4). I noted above that theory can also suggest generative mechanisms. How, then, do we build theories? Where do they come from and what is their role? A quote from Hammersley (2012) captures well different roles of theory and how it relates to explanation. According to him, there is a

> distinction between case studies that focus on 'explaining' and those that are concerned with 'theorizing' [...]. To underline the difference, the first aims to account for why some particular event or set of events, of intrinsic interest, happened, when and where they did, and in the ways that they did; or what consequences of interest have followed from some earlier event or set of events. The second activity aims at producing a theory about what types of factor tend to produce a particular type of outcome, or what type of outcome is generally the product of a particular type of prior event. Of course, when we explain particular events we draw on general ideas, in other words on explanatory theories of some sort, about what tends to cause what, but here we are using these theories as tools, rather than developing them and testing their validity; and we may well use more than one explanatory theory simultaneously to illuminate a single case. (p. 398)

Hammersley discusses theory in the context of case study research (hence the reference to case studies), but his remarks apply more generally to the relationship between theory and explanation, and different forms of theory. Before discussing theory in more detail, a few comments on explanation. One instance of Hammersley's first 'activity', explanation, is historical explanation (for example Mahoney et al., 2009), that is, the attempt to identify the causes of specific outcomes. George and Bennett (2005), like Hammersley, describe how historical explanation of a particular case can draw on more general theory to explain some outcome. They note that their process-tracing method has much affinity with historians' work. However, process-tracing is not only applied to historical events, but can also be used to explain individuals' pathways to various outcomes. Collecting individuals' life stories can also help explain social relations (Bertaux, 1981). Bertaux suggests that these are better suited than survey-based research to explaining social structures. An example from his own research, together with Isabelle Wiame-Bertaux, is the use of bakers' life stories (Bertaux & Bertaux-Wiame, 1981) to study social class relations in France in the wake of the 1968 social movements. They showed why it was that (at the time of the study; things have changed in the meantime) most of the bread sold in France came from small independent shops, despite changes in the food industry which had already affected most other foodstuffs. The life stories Bertaux and Bertaux-Wiame collected illustrated the underlying social processes and how the structure of the baking trade affected the everyday lives of workers and bakery owners.

One difficulty in explaining particular outcomes is that there is a danger of providing explanations post-hoc which may happen to fit the particular case, but it is not easy to know whether they are valid. George and Bennett (2005) point to the danger of neglecting potential alternative hypotheses to the one studied: 'Too often, researchers focus great attention on the process-tracing evidence on the hypothesis that interests them most, while giving the process-tracing evidence that bears on alternative explanations little attention or using it only to explain variance that is not adequately explained by the hypothesis of interest. This can create a strong confirmation bias, and it can overstate the causal weight that should be accorded to the hypothesis of interest' (p. 217).

In contrast to specific explanations, explanatory *theories* are those that can be applied in a general way to all cases fulfilling the scope conditions specified. One way of developing such explanatory theories is inductively on the basis of empirically observed regularities. Again, I assume that regularity alone does not constitute an explanatory theory;

rather, it is the regularity *plus* the subsequent postulation of plausible mechanisms that do so. A regularity thus forms the starting point for an explanatory theory. Pawson's (1989) example is that of social mobility research. He refers to findings by Goldthorpe (1985) which show that rates of mobility into the service class in mid-20th-century Britain were relatively high. This empirical regularity is then interpreted by Goldthorpe by reference to economic and technical change which took place during that period and which, given the resulting greater need for skilled workers, formed the mechanism for the increase in upward social mobility. Goldthorpe applied what Pawson terms 'powerful and astute' theorising (Pawson, 1989, p. 166). However, this theorising is undertaken post-hoc, and it is therefore necessary to check any hypothesised mechanism against new evidence or evidence from other sources, making sure that theory is compatible with the data (Pawson, 1989, p. 166–167). This inductive process therefore can pose difficulties in the same way as historical and individual explanations. 'The first difficulty of such inductive strategies is that any regularity will normally lend itself to any number of interpretations and without more specifically constructed data no further adjudication between competing theories is possible' (Pawson, 1989, p. 166).

Such additional data or evidence can take different forms. It may be further statistical modelling, refining the original model and applying it to new data, supplementing this by adding qualitative evidence of different kinds, and/or the study of historical comparisons and of additional cases that are similar to those already studied. Freedman (1991) describes this sort of evidence gathering in his article 'Statistical models and shoe leather' using the example of John Snow's development of an explanatory theory of how people become infected with cholera. At the time, in the 1850s, it was received wisdom that cholera is caused by poison particles in the air (the miasma theory). Snow collected a large variety of data, based on quantitative comparisons, case studies, and the application of the treatment methods based on his theory to show that cholera is actually a waterborne disease. Any one piece of evidence might have been compatible with different theories, but Snow's approach of assembling different forms of relevant evidence and his line of reasoning developed from it showed his theory to be correct, and, incidentally, saved many lives by applying precautions such as boiling drinking water and isolating sick individuals. Ideally, tests of new theories should rule out any competing theories, no matter how plausible they are. They therefore have to take account of the particulars of the predictions of each theory and develop appropriate ways of investigating the circumstances under which the theory predicts correctly. Mahoney (2012) describes such tests and classifies them according to whether they can confirm or eliminate a hypothesis.

This section has outlined my view of description, explanation and theorising which clearly rests on a particular model of causality. This view is based on the notion that observable relationships between factors or causes on the one hand and outcomes or effects on the other are the result of generative mechanisms. Throughout this book, I engage in description, explanation and theorising. *Description* here takes the form of using QCA to establish patterns, but also summarising interview findings to describe educational trajectories and individuals' ways of reasoning. *Explanation* is undertaken of individual cases' outcomes, drawing on their interview responses and referring to existing theory. *Theorising* takes the form of testing the validity of existing theories, drawing on both QCA and interview analyses, and of developing existing theory further.

A final point I would like to add concerns the distinction between deterministic and probabilistic causation, since this also affects what may be regarded as useful explanation. I briefly hinted at this point in note 2 (this chapter) where I noted Baumgartner's objection to probabilistic accounts of causation. A probabilistic account of causation may, however, be adopted for two reasons: firstly, it might be assumed that there is genuine randomness in the world, as one would find with a lottery, and that events can therefore never be perfectly predicted, but only probabilistically. Secondly, there may or may not be deterministic causation in the world, but since the number of potentially causal factors is too large and the relationships between them too complex for them ever to be modelled appropriately, the assumption of probabilistic causation is a useful approximation (Lieberson, 1997, especially pp. 364–365 and pp. 374–375), an idea captured by the term pseudo-indeterministic processes (Baumgartner, 2007), that is, 'processes whose indeterminacy is merely due to incomplete knowledge of or control over the involved factors' (p. 18–19). Because of the impossibility of adequately modelling such processes, Lieberson suggests that probabilistic models are more appropriate than deterministic accounts (see also Collier et al., 2004, p. 24).

My own view is that both deterministic and probabilistic causal processes may exist in the social world, and I share Lieberson's view that given the difficulties of modelling many deterministic processes, probabilistic accounts are preferable. In addition, a further source of complication regarding the question of determinism versus randomness is that causal models tend to be situated within a particular causal field, but factors from outside this causal field can have a bearing on the outcome under study nevertheless. Consider a causal account of an educational outcome by way of example. The potentially causal factors under study might concern parental education, individual cognitive ability, and peer groups. But specific life events such as an illness can also influence educational outcomes. Such life events might seem like random events within the educational model, but in a medical context it might be possible to model the causes of the illness without referring (much) to randomness, for example by studying genetic causes or infection. This is a matter of perspective, or, in other words, what the causal field is taken to be in a given study.

2.4 Methods for establishing description and explanation

As noted, a regression model is frequently thought of as a causal model. While I agree that regression models can point to potential underlying causal factors, I will explain here why I believe that in some sense, the result of a regression analysis is closer to being description (albeit often of a sophisticated kind). Regression models, in their simplest form, look like this:

$$Y = b_1X_1 + b_2X_2 + e \qquad \text{(Equation 1)}$$

where Y is the outcome, X_1 and X_2 the potentially causal factors, and e an error term. Without further information, it is not possible to see from this equation whether X_1, X_2, or both exert causal force. It may be, for example, that X_1 is merely correlated with Y and the relationship between them is due to an external factor, X_3. In addition, even where we are convinced that X_1 causes changes in Y, we may still be interested in going beyond the regression equation to establish the mechanism through which X_1 causes these changes in Y. Obviously, regression models are usually more sophisticated than this example with just two independent variables with their additive effects. But the basic point remains the same.

I have mentioned Ragin's Qualitative Comparative Analysis (QCA) as another form of sophisticated description. I will introduce this method in more detail in Chapter 3. For now, here is an example of a simple Boolean equation representing a QCA solution:

$$A + B*C*D => Y \qquad \text{(Equation 2)}$$

QCA solutions use Boolean notation where * represents logical AND and + represents logical OR. Equation 2 describes a situation where the presence of factor A is sufficient for Y, or alternatively where the joint presence of factors B, C and D is sufficient for Y (or where A and B and C and D are jointly present and are sufficient for Y). Let us assume that Y is educational attainment again, A is high cognitive ability, B is at least moderate cognitive ability, C is effort and D is a flexible school system. The model then describes a situation where high cognitive ability alone will lead to high educational attainment, but where, for those lacking high cognitive ability, at least moderate cognitive ability coupled with effort and the possibility to stay on in school offered by a flexible school system, will also lead to such attainment. Again, as in the regression example, the factors seem plausible explanatory factors, but we cannot be sure, on the basis of the model alone, of whether they actually are causal factors. At best, they are shorthand for underlying causal processes. 'Moderate cognitive ability plus effort plus school system', for example, summarises a causal chain where hard work, coupled with at least moderate cognitive ability, produces enough academic success to make staying on in school a realistic option, and where individuals' choices then have to be made to actually stay on in school and where, finally, this staying on will lead to subsequent higher educational attainment. Again, this simple example is intended to illustrate the basic principle. QCA models are often more complex than this.

Both regression and QCA formalise their models by using algebraic terms and operators to specify relationships, with regression relying on linear algebra and QCA on Boolean algebra. Description can also take the form of verbal accounts of a case or several cases. Many qualitative researchers aiming to undertake description refer to Geertz's notion of thick description (Geertz, 1973). He suggests that thick description is the ethnographer's task, and that what is often referred to as 'data' inevitably already reflects the ethnographer's selection of relevant contextual information and his or her construction of meaning. Thus, ethnography is not as purely descriptive as it is sometimes made out to be. Hammersley, for example, (2008, chapter 3), in discussing Geertz' (1973) essay, notes the ways in which thick description contains both description and elements of explanation.

All the forms of description discussed, regression, QCA and verbal description, have something in common. They can provide either a starting point – the phenomenon to be explained – or a piece of evidence required for causal explanation, as used by John Snow in his work on cholera. What is more, they are developed on the basis of theoretical or common sense expectations with regard to causal processes; none of them is free of theory and/or preconceived ideas and expectations. However, while there is no single method which is always (or never) capable of providing such descriptions, I suggest that among the methods used in cross-case analysis, QCA has more affinity with the forms of causation thought to be operating in the social world than regression-based methods. Sociological theories often refer to contexts and/or configurational causal claims, and some specify quasi-necessary and/or quasi-sufficient conditions. The following examples of such theories are taken from Cooper & Glaesser (2012b):

- Boudon (1974) accounts for the social distribution of educational achievement in terms of the primary and secondary effects of stratification. The primary effects of social class create some part of the differences in measured achievement early in a child's career while secondary effects, arising from the ways in which the perceived costs and benefits of subsequent educational decisions vary by class origin, lead to further class differentiation of outcomes, even amongst those with similar levels of early achievement. This account has a clear affinity with a description of the form, 'a high level of achievement in early episodes of assessment, e.g. at the end of elementary school, is necessary but not sufficient for a high level in assessments later in an individual's educational career.'
- Bourdieu's theory of capitals has included, at various times, the claim that academic capital, 'a converted form of cultural capital' (Bourdieu, 1974), has to be combined with other forms of capital to receive its full economic and social return. Here, academic capital in the form of diplomas is not sufficient for certain outcomes unless conjoined with other forms such as social capital (Bourdieu, 1974).
- Lacey's (1970) *Hightown Grammar* included the claim that the reaction of boys to their being ranked in the pressurised academic environment of the grammar school was a function of their class origin and relevant family resources rather than simply linear. (Cooper & Glaesser, 2012b, pp. 174–175)

None of the authors in this list, of course, have used QCA; it didn't exist when they carried out their work. Instead, they have used a variety of methods to develop their theories. My point is simply that the way we often think about the social world can be captured well by the kinds of configurational description QCA can provide. For this reason, I have chosen QCA over regression analysis for the cross-case analyses of large *n* data in this study. As I explain in Chapter 4, I combine this with process-tracing interviews to provide another element of the evidence needed to develop explanations of the regularities documented by the descriptive analysis.

Moving on to methods of explanation, process-tracing has been suggested by various authors as a means of obtaining causal explanations (for example Cartwright & Hardie, 2012; Collier, 2011; George & Bennett, 2005; Mahoney, 2012). It is the examination of evidence pointing to generative mechanisms which have led to the outcome under study: 'The process-tracing method attempts to identify the intervening causal process – the causal chain and causal mechanism – between an independent variable (or variables) and the outcome of the dependent variable' (George & Bennett, 2005, p. 206). Given that different kinds of causal processes exist, the form process-tracing takes has to be adapted depending on the process (George & Bennett, 2005, chapter 10). George and Bennett distinguish processes where the outcome is the result of a *linear* chain of events, where there is *convergence* of several conditions, where there are *interacting* causal variables, and where it is *path-dependent*, in other words, the outcome is the result of 'a sequence of events, some of which foreclose certain paths in the development and steer the outcome in other directions' (p. 212). It is a challenge for the researcher to choose the appropriate form of process-tracing. While process-tracing has its roots in qualitative research and is related to historians' development of historical explanations, process-tracing may focus on both qualitative and quantitative data. Collier (2011), for example, notes that the kinds of evidence which together can form the proposed chain of events used to explain an outcome may also contain quantitative data. He cites a study by Lerner on modernisation in a Turkish village by way of example. Lerner analysed demographic characteristics as one element in his process-tracing study. Such demographic characteristics are clearly something that relies on numerical indicators.

In Section 2.3, I discussed the relationship of explanation and theory. Theoretical knowledge, theory-led description, theory confirming and theory developing case studies using process-tracing to identify generative mechanisms all should be used together, as summed up by Freedman (2005): 'causal inference seems to require an enormous investment of skill, intelligence, and hard work. Many convergent lines of evidence must be developed' (see also Freedman, 1997a, 1997b).

Theory testing and theory development are different, though related, goals, and therefore the kinds of cases to be studied may differ. A challenge here is the selection of relevant cases. In the same way that the form of process-tracing undertaken should match the causal process under study, the selection of cases should match the goal of a study, which may be description, explanation, theory testing or theory development. George and Bennett stress the importance of deviant cases for heuristic purposes (2005, p. 75, see also p. 252) and for developing '*contingent generalizations* that identify the conditions under which alternative outcomes occur' (p. 216). Generalisation can be based on two different approaches. The first is generally thought to require a large sample to be taken so as to be representative of the population of interest. Findings based on statistical analyses of the sample can then be generalised to the population, on the grounds that it does not differ in relevant ways from the population. The second approach, which does not require a large sample, is described by Hammersley who notes that a similar rationale is given for some forms of ethnographic research where generalisations from cases are permissible on the grounds that the cases are chosen to be typical for the population to which findings are to be applied. He terms this 'theoretical inference'. Here, 'the setting is taken as a critical case which establishes the validity of a theory that applies to all cases of the same type' (Hammersley, 1991, p. 82). The assumption is that, once the typicality of a case has been established, any findings from this case will apply to ones it is taken to be typical of.

There is also a view (particularly in policy studies) that the only way to establish causation is by conducting randomised controlled trials (RCTs) and other forms of experimentation. Put simply, in an RCT, participants are selected and allocated randomly to either an experimental or a control group. An intervention is then administered to the experimental group. Outcomes for both groups are then compared to assess whether the intervention had an effect on the outcome. Proponents of this method assume that experiments are the best – or indeed the only – way of gaining causal knowledge concerning which intervention or policy has the desired effect. However, there are reasons to doubt this assumption. Experiments by their nature tend not to be able to take context into account, making it hard to know whether what has been shown to work in a particular classroom, school or region will also work in a different setting, given that the focus is on success of an intervention rather than the underlying causal mechanism that led to this success. This raises questions about external validity. There are also numerous research problems that cannot be investigated experimentally, for ethical or practical reasons (for example, the effect of divorce on children). Cartwright and Hardie (2012) therefore suggest that RCTs should form only one of several components of evidence in making policy decisions, discussing in detail why RCTs may not be adequate as the sole source of evidence. Among other things, they argue that an understanding of causal mechanisms is essential for anyone wishing to assess whether some policy, intervention or reform is likely to be successful in a particular context and at a particular point in time. In my view, their arguments apply more generally, not just in a policy context, and this is why I believe that various forms of evidence can and should be used together in developing an understanding of causal mechanisms.

Systematic reviews are another potential source of information on causal mechanisms for policymakers. Hammersley (2001) raises some important critical points regarding the assumption that systematic reviews are superior to other forms of literature review, among them the criteria for studies to be included and excluded in a systematic review. Scholars undertaking systematic reviews generally consider RCTs to be the gold standard, but Hammersley notes that research design alone cannot be a criterion of whether a study is valid and useful: 'Now, it is certainly true that research designs have different general advantages and disadvantages in relation to threats to validity. However, it is not the case, even in abstract terms, that some designs have all the advantages and others have none. Advantage in one respect is usually bought at the expense of disadvantage in another' (p. 547). Again, in my view this point applies more generally to social science research designs.

Clearly, it is not possible to point to any one research method that can provide completely secure explanation and/or theory development and testing. Explanation is a complex undertaking which relies on different activities, and each phenomenon or case to be explained may require a different approach, as do the different goals of a theory-focussed study. By way of example, I now briefly describe a study through which a new explanatory theory on the basis of different forms of evidence was developed. I have already mentioned Freedman's account of John Snow's discovery of the cause of cholera (Freedman, 1991) as providing such an example. This was taken from the field of public health, and I now wish to add an instructive example from the sociology of education, Colin Lacey's (1970) Hightown Grammar mentioned above.[3] Lacey studied a boys' grammar school. All the boys who entered the school were officially the most academically able in their primary schools, having passed the selective eleven plus examination. They all arrived at the grammar school highly motivated and with an image of themselves as being high performers. Lacey observed that in the course of their schooling, some boys continued to be motivated and to perform well, whereas others rejected the school's values, their performance dropped, and some left school early. This is the phenomenon Lacey wished to explain. He spent a considerable amount of time in the school doing participant observation, and he collected a large amount of data on attainment, samples of pupils' work, social background data, symptoms of emotional upheaval and the like. From his observations and existing theory, he developed his differentiation-polarisation model to explain why some boys succeeded academically and behaviourally, while others – who had arrived with similar academic credentials and self-perception – did not. In his theoretical model, differentiation is the process whereby pupils are ranked in the course of their school careers according to academic criteria, and polarisation refers to the separation of boys into separate subcultures, including an anti-school culture influenced by societal and cultural forces outside the school. Lacey's model thus stresses the social relations *within the school* and how these interact with the relationship *between home and school* and with processes taking place in the family of origin.

I have described Lacey's study here because it encompasses many of the elements of good description, explanation and theorising I have discussed in this chapter. He uses various methods to establish the phenomenon he wishes to explain, and he proceeds to undertake this explanation drawing on a wide range of evidence – both qualitative and quantitative – from several sources. His theoretical model is capable of explaining all these findings, and it has more general applicability because, while it was developed in just one school, the processes and mechanisms described can also be found in other contexts.

Some readers may wonder why I have not described the research approach I propose to use as a 'mixed methods' design. After all, according to one definition, '[mixed] methods research is formally defined here as the class of research where the researcher mixes or combines quantitative and qualitative research techniques, methods, approaches, concepts or language into a single study' (Johnson & Onwuegbuzie, 2004, p. 17), and this seems to capture my proposed approach. The reason I am reluctant to use the term is that I do not consider it a particularly helpful label. Methods can be mixed in so many ways that mixed methods studies do not necessarily have much in common. It is also not new to use a variety of methods to approach a single research problem. Lacey's study described above is one such example, and it was undertaken well before the term mixed methods was in use. In addition, it seems to me that mixing methods does not in itself make a study a better piece of research. As always, the required approach depends on the problem to be studied, and some research problems can be studied perfectly well using just one method of analysis. Much also depends on the way in which the various methods are combined. Both Pawson (2006) and Hammersley (2001) note (though in the context of undertaking systematic reviews) that merely adding evidence from various studies does not in itself improve understanding. Synthesis is required, with a proper understanding of what aspect of the research problem the different studies or elements of a study are able to offer (see also Tarrow, 2004). I aim to show that, for my research problem, QCA can provide a useful framework for the fruitful synthesis of quantitative and qualitative data (see also Cooper et al., 2012).

3
Qualitative Comparative Analysis

Qualitative Comparative Analysis (QCA) is the core method employed throughout this book, both in the cross-case analysis of large *n* data sets and as the basis of the construction of the typologies of cases from which interviewees were chosen for in-depth study. It was developed by Charles Ragin (Ragin, 1987, 2000, 2008), with one of its first applied fields being political sciences, and it has since been used in other social science contexts. Originally mainly used with small to medium *n* samples, it has been usefully employed with large *n* (for example, Cooper, 2005; Fiss, 2011; Glaesser, 2008; Glaesser & Cooper, 2011b; Ragin, 2006a). Drawing on set theory, Boolean logic and algebra and the concepts of necessary and sufficient conditions, QCA offers a systematic way of analysing small to medium *n* data, and it can provide an alternative to regression-based methods for large *n* analysis. In regression approaches, the focus is on estimating the net effects of independent variables, while controlling for others (Ragin, 2006a). QCA, rather than focussing on net effects, explores the various ways in which the factors under study combine to produce some outcome. QCA is well suited to analysing such conjunctions of conditions and, in addition, to situations where there are several pathways to the outcome.

QCA uses Boolean notation. Consider the following equation, taken from Mahoney and Goertz (2006) and reproduced in a modified form:

$$A*B*c + A*C*D*E => Y \qquad \text{(Equation 3)}$$

Here, capital letters stand for the presence of a condition, lower case letters for its absence, or logical NOT. The * symbol represents logical AND (denoting set intersection), the + logical OR (denoting set union). This equation therefore shows two alternative pathways as sufficient for the outcome Y to occur: one is the combination of the presence of A and B with the absence of C; the other is the presence of all of A, C, D and E. Either pathway is sufficient for the outcome, but neither is necessary, given that the other exists. To capture such causal complexity, Mackie (1974) developed the concept of an INUS condition, which was taken up by Ragin (1987). An INUS condition is an insufficient but necessary part of a condition which is itself unnecessary but sufficient. In Equation 3, B provides an example of an INUS condition because it is itself insufficient (A and the absence of C are also required), but is a necessary part of the conjunction of conditions A*B*c which is sufficient for the outcome, but not necessary given A*C*D*E exists.

I begin by introducing the use of the concepts of sufficiency and necessity with just one condition, and I then explain their application in situations with several explanatory conditions. Sufficiency and necessity involve subsethood relations. If a condition is sufficient for an outcome to occur, the set of cases with the condition is a subset of the set of cases with the outcome. This relationship is reflected in the Venn diagram to the left of Figure 3.1. Here, condition A (which can also be a conjunction of conditions) is sufficient but not necessary for outcome O: whenever A occurs, O will occur. In the real world, relations are usually less than perfect and we tend to find situations such as the one represented to the right of Figure 3.1, where most but not all cases with condition A also have outcome O. This situation of near sufficiency is often termed quasi-sufficiency. The proportion of cases with the condition that also have the outcome can be taken as a measure of the degree of consistency with sufficiency (Ragin, 2006b).[1] Usually, values of around 0.8 or above and no less than 0.7 are considered to indicate quasi-sufficiency.

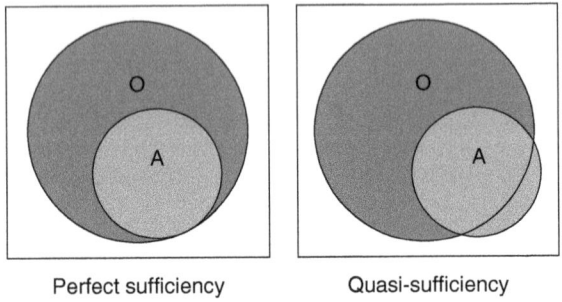

Perfect sufficiency   Quasi-sufficiency

Figure 3.1   Sufficiency of condition A for outcome O

Venn diagrams may also be used to introduce explanatory 'coverage'. In a similar way to 'variance explained' in regression analysis, coverage indicates how important a condition or, typically, a conjunction of conditions is with respect to predicting and/or explaining the outcome. In Figure 3.1, we can see that there must be other (conjunctions of) conditions which also lead to the outcome, since a substantial proportion of the outcome set, O, is not covered by the condition set, A. Numerically, coverage is expressed as the proportion of cases with the outcome that also have the condition(s).[2]

Parallel arguments apply to necessity and quasi-necessity, where the outcome set has to be a subset of the condition set. Figure 3.2 illustrates a necessity relationship. In the left-hand panel, outcome O is a perfect subset of condition A, making A a necessary, but not sufficient, condition for O. O cannot occur without A being present, but even if A is present, O will not always occur. In the right-hand panel, there is an example of a quasi-necessary condition with most but not all cases in O being a subset of A. Consistency with necessity is assessed by calculating the proportion of cases with the outcome that also have the condition.

Consider Table 3.1 and Table 3.2, taken from Ragin (2000, p. 98), for another way of describing the relationships of sufficiency and necessity.

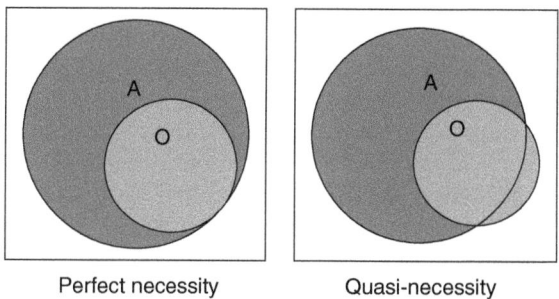

Perfect necessity   Quasi-necessity

Figure 3.2   Necessity of condition A for outcome O

Table 3.1   Ragin's Table 4.4: Cause Is Sufficient but Not Necessary

Outcome	Cause absent	Cause present
Present	[Cell 1] not relevant	[Cell 2] cases
Absent	[Cell 3] not relevant	[Cell 4] no cases

Table 3.2   Ragin's Table 4.3: Cause Is Necessary but Not Sufficient

Outcome	Cause absent	Cause present
Present	[Cell 1] no cases	[Cell 2] cases
Absent	[Cell 3] not relevant	[Cell 4] not relevant

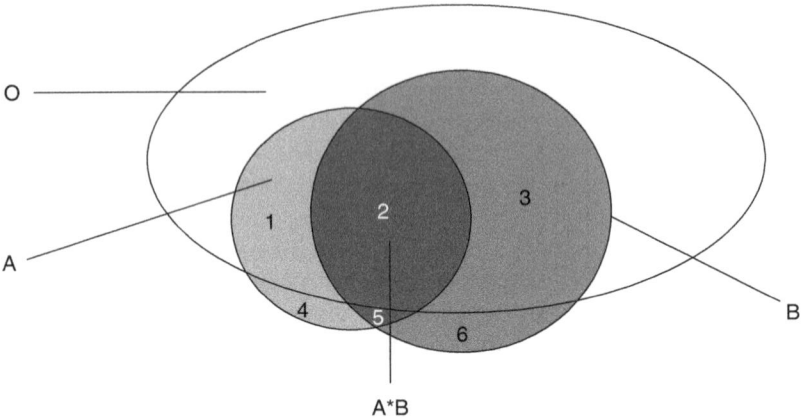

Figure 3.3   Venn diagram, two conditions

The cells to be inspected in order to assess sufficiency and necessity are not the same. They are cells 2 and 4 for sufficiency and cells 1 and 2 for necessity. An analysis of a correlational relationship, by contrast, would take account of all four cells, expecting there to be cases in cells 2 and 3 and none in cells 1 and 4 (or far fewer than in cells 2 and 3) for there to be a positive correlation.

I now turn to how QCA deals with more than just one condition, that is, the sort of more complex situation social science researchers generally find interesting. Figure 3.3 illustrates how two conditions, A and B, are associated with outcome O. They are quasi-sufficient conditions because they are near subsets of O, but they are not necessary, either individually or jointly, given that there are parts of O not covered by either A or B. The intersection A*B (areas 2 and 5 in the diagram) comprises cases which have both conditions. The union A + B contains all those cases who have condition A or condition B (or both), represented by the three shaded areas, areas 1–6, in the diagram (Figure 3.3).

Explanatory coverage can be split into two parts whenever there are at least two conditions linked by logical OR. The unique coverage due to a condition is that part of O which is only covered by that condition and not by any other sufficient condition(s). In this diagram (Figure 3.3), the unique coverage of A is the proportion of the outcome set covered by area 1. A's raw coverage is the proportion of O covered by both A and the overlap, so here for condition A it is the proportion represented by areas 1 and 2 taken together.

If the unique coverage figure for a condition is lower than its raw coverage figure, this indicates that there is some overlap between cases' membership in the condition sets. In fact, a large degree of overlap is not empirically unusual. For example, we know that parents' education as well as parents' social class are associated with their child's educational attainment, and also that high parental education is usually associated with high parental social class. Figure 3.3 illustrates such a situation: the majority of cases in set A are also in set B. This is one of the issues that QCA is well suited to addressing, since such an overlap is made explicit and treated as an important feature of the putatively causal process, rather than addressed in terms of the larger net effect of one or the other condition.

I now explain QCA's data analysis procedure, using an invented data set with three conditions, A, B and C, and some outcome O. Table 3.3 is a crosstabulation of the three conditions, A, B and C, with cells showing the percentage of each combination of factors that also have outcome O. I have used upper and lower case notation in Table 3.3: capital letters indicate presence of a factor, lower case letters its absence.

In order to undertake QCA, the same information is laid out differently, in a so-called truth table. In a truth table, rows represent combinations or configurations of conditions. Table 3.4 is the truth table containing the same information as that presented in Table 3.3. Here, a '1' is entered to indicate presence of a factor, '0' to indicate absence. Row 1 then contains all cases in sets A and B and C, in other words, it represents the set intersection of sets A, B and C. The column 'number' gives 'the total number of cases' in this particular configuration, whether or not they have the outcome. The last column gives the

Table 3.3   Crosstabulation, three conditions

		C	c
A	B	96.7%	83.3%
	b	40.0%	47.6%
a	B	70.9%	77.8%
	b	33.3%	10.0%

Table 3.4   Truth table, three conditions

A	B	C	Number	O	Consistency
1	1	1	90		0.967
1	1	0	24		0.833
0	1	0	252		0.778
0	1	1	55		0.709
1	0	0	21		0.476
1	0	1	10		0.4
0	0	1	108		0.333
0	0	0	200		0.1

consistency with sufficiency for each configuration. Remember that for crisp data, that is, those where a factor or a condition is simply either present or absent, this is the proportion of cases with the conjunction of conditions which display the outcome of interest. Rows are usually ordered in descending order of consistency, so that rows highest in quasi-sufficiency are at the top of the table.

It can be informative to inspect the truth table itself to obtain an overview of any relationships in the data. For example, in this truth table, all the rows containing condition B are in the top half of the table. Given that the rows are ordered by consistency, we can see that the presence of B is associated with higher frequencies of the outcome, but that the extent to which this is the case depends on which other factors B is combined with. We can also see that cases are distributed very unevenly across the rows, indicating that not all combinations of factors are equally common. Empirically, this is often the case since potentially causal conditions are often related. This may result in some rows having only a few cases. This latter phenomenon is termed limited diversity, and I discuss it in more detail below.

The next step, after obtaining the truth table, is to obtain a minimised Boolean solution. This involves setting a threshold above which consistency is considered high enough to indicate quasi-sufficiency. It is common to choose a threshold of around 0.8, and usually no lower than 0.7, while taking into account any jumps in consistency from one row to the next of the table.[3] A useful approach is also to work through various levels of consistency (for example Cooper, 2005), since this gives a more detailed picture of the relationships between conditions and outcome and makes the process more transparent by demonstrating to the reader how results vary depending on the chosen threshold. I will demonstrate this approach here, and also use it to illustrate the concepts of raw and unique coverage and to explain Boolean minimisation.

Table 3.5 Example truth table, three conditions

A	B	C	Number	O	Consistency
1	1	1	90	1	0.967
1	1	0	24	0	0.833
0	1	0	252	0	0.778
0	1	1	55	0	0.709
1	0	0	21	0	0.476
1	0	1	10	0	0.4
0	0	1	108	0	0.333
0	0	0	200	0	0.1

To begin the process for our example, a threshold of 0.9 was chosen. This is reflected in the 1s and 0s entered into the outcome column 'O' in Table 3.5.

At this threshold, just the first row is considered a quasi-sufficient configuration of factors for outcome O, and the Boolean solution is A*B*C. If more than one row passes the chosen level of consistency, the next step is to examine the rows that pass and, if possible, subject them to Boolean minimisation. Its purpose is to simplify an otherwise potentially complex expression through a process of logical minimisation. Continuing our example, we next take a threshold of 0.8. This results in the first two rows entering the minimisation process. The Boolean solution, prior to minimisation, is now A*B*C + A*B*c. This expression can be simplified to A*B: the presence or absence of condition C, given our setting of the threshold at 0.8, makes no relevant difference.

Setting the threshold at 0.75 results in the first three rows entering the Boolean minimisation process, producing the solution of A*B*C + A*B*c + a*B*c which can be simplified to A*B + B*c in the following way: A*B is obtained by combining A*B*C and A*B*c as before. B*c is obtained by combining A*B*c and a*B*c: condition A makes no difference here, so the two expressions can be collapsed to give B*c.

With just two or three expressions as in this example, it is possible to carry out the minimisation by hand, but with more conditions, this becomes increasingly complex so that it is advisable to use appropriate software. For the analyses presented in this book, I have used fs/QCA (Ragin et al., 2009) and the QCA package available in R (Duşa & Thiem, 2013). The software output not only gives the minimised overall solution, but also the overall consistency and coverage figures as well as raw and unique coverage.

Box 3.1 shows the software output (obtained from fs/QCA in this case) for our example for all three thresholds:

Box 3.1   Three solutions for Table 3.5: Example truth table, three conditions

Solution 1: 0.9 threshold

	Raw Coverage	Unique Coverage	Consistency
A*B*C	0.211	0.211	0.967

Solution coverage: 0.211
Solution consistency: 0.967

Solution 2: 0.8 threshold

	Raw Coverage	Unique Coverage	Consistency
A*B	0.26	0.26	0.939

Solution coverage: 0.26
Solution consistency: 0.939

Solution 3: 0.75 threshold

	Raw Coverage	Unique Coverage	Consistency
A*B+	0.26	0.211	0.939
B*c	0.524	0.476	0.783

Solution coverage: 0.735
Solution consistency: 0.828

Lowering the threshold increases coverage by adding cases to earlier solutions which had been obtained using a higher threshold. For example, comparing solutions 1 and 2, we can see that overall coverage has increased. The set forming the solution is larger in solution 2: as well as comprising A*B*C (solution 1), it also comprises A*B*c.

Solutions 1 and 2 have only one element each; there is only one 'causal' pathway leading to the outcome. The situation in solution 3 is different: here, we find two pathways linked by logical OR. They have different consistency figures, and the consistency for the whole solution is different again. They each describe a different set and these have different proportions of cases showing the outcome, hence the differing consistency figures. The two pathways in solution 3 are partly overlapping: the set ABc is contained in both AB and Bc. The effects of this can be seen in the raw and unique coverage figures: if the unique coverage for a term in the solution is lower than its raw coverage, this indicates that there is some overlap between cases' membership in the terms in the solution.[4] As noted earlier, it is quite common to find some degree of overlap, since it is empirically not unusual for potentially causal conditions to be related.

Solutions 1–3 illustrate a further point: there is usually some trade-off between consistency and coverage. Lowering the consistency level produces solutions with higher coverage.[5] This means that more of the outcome set is 'covered', or explained, by the solution term(s), but at the same time their consistency with sufficiency is lower, that is, there is a higher proportion of cases in the solution which do not actually have the outcome. Moving through different levels of consistency illustrates this trade-off, and it can be an informative strategy to obtain solutions for different levels of consistency.

QCA may be used with more than two or three conditions. However, the number of truth table rows grows exponentially with more conditions added, so using four conditions results in a truth table of $2^4 = 16$ rows, five conditions generate $2^5 = 32$ rows and so on. It is therefore important for the researcher to pay attention to the number of cases in their sample and how they are distributed across the rows. Even with large data sets, but in particular with small to medium data sets, it is possible for some truth table rows to have very few or no cases, a phenomenon described by Ragin as limited diversity (Ragin, 2008; Ragin & Sonnett, 2005). Certain analytical difficulties arise in the case of limited diversity. This is not a major problem in the analyses presented in this book, however, so I do not discuss it further here but refer the reader to the publications mentioned.

Likewise, I do not discuss fuzzy sets in great detail since I do not use fuzzy set analysis in this book. But their use constitutes an important development of crisp set QCA, and I therefore describe them briefly. Ragin developed QCA to incorporate fuzzy sets in order to address the fact that crisp sets can only deal with dichotomous factors (Ragin, 2000). This limitation of crisp set analysis has attracted some criticism, for example from Goldthorpe who also has other reservations with regard to QCA (Goldthorpe, 2007b, Chapter 3). Fuzzy sets, by contrast, allow for partial membership of a set. Fuzzy membership scores run from 0 (completely out of the set) to 1 (fully in the set), with 0.5 being the crossover point at which a case is as much in as out of the set. Allocation of set membership is straightforward for many crisp sets such as 'female' or 'university graduate' (assuming that there is no ambiguity over which higher education institutions are regarded as universities), but it is less clear for other conditions. The case of adulthood is frequently used to illustrate this problem. A 30-year-old is clearly a full member of the set of adults, and a ten-year-old clearly is not. But what about an 18-year-old? We might allocate a fuzzy membership score of, say, 0.8, based on our knowledge of what adulthood means and what 18-year-olds are like. There are various techniques for allocating fuzzy membership scores to cases, a process known as calibration (Ragin, 2008). Fuzzy consistency and coverage may then be calculated using indices of fuzzy subset relations (Ragin, 2006b).

While fuzzy sets constitute a very useful addition to the set analytic repertoire, their use is not without problems (for example Cooper & Glaesser, 2011). Partly for this reason, I employ crisp sets only in this book. Another reason for my decision is the fact that many of the factors I am interested in typically exist in binary form, for example sex. In addition, it is possible to overcome the shortcomings of crisp set QCA to some extent by using dummy variables. For example, a social class variable which is coded into three categories, service, intermediate and working class, can be recoded into three[6] dummy variables to indicate whether or not a case is in the service, intermediate or working class. These dummies can then be employed in the analysis. Most of the factors used throughout this book can be coded in this way without loss of information.

This use of dummies, as well as the principles of QCA explained above, will be illustrated further in Chapter 4 where I summarise earlier project findings from our papers using QCA, and in Chapters 5–7 where I conduct QCA analyses using real data.

4
Overview of the Project

As noted, this book is largely based on the Economic and Social Research Council (ESRC)-funded project 'Exploring and evaluating the use of configurational methods in large *n* contexts: transitions in the English and German educational systems'. This chapter gives an overview of the design of this project and summarises some of its findings which have been published elsewhere to inform the reader of the background to the book. After briefly explaining the theoretical rationale on which the choice of potential explanatory factors included in the study is based (sections 4.1 and 4.2), I describe the relevant aspects of school systems in the two countries under study, England (4.3) and Germany (4.4). I will then describe the large *n* data sets used from both countries (4.5), followed by an account of the sample selection for the interviews (4.6). The chapter ends with a summary of some of the previously published project findings (4.7).

4.1 Theoretical rationale

As noted in Chapters 1 and 2, a concern with describing and explaining underpins this project. Large *n*, cross-case analysis using QCA serves to 'establish the phenomenon' to be explained (Merton, 1987), that is, to show the configurations of factors associated with particular outcomes. I discuss these potentially causal relationships in the light of existing theory. The configurations are then used to identify relevant cases for further in-depth study. The purposes of these in-depth case studies based on interviews are to develop existing theory and explore the mechanisms generating outcomes, and to explain *individual* outcomes by reference to the cross-case analysis, existing theory and cases' own particular circumstances.

The phenomenon studied in this book is the differential distribution of young people across educational pathways and their aspirations for future study. I describe it with reference to factors such as social background (indicated by parental social class and educational attainment) and gender, as well as academic achievement wherever possible. I then attempt to explain it drawing on these factors and their interrelationships at the individual, social and systemic levels alongside theoretical expectations, potential causal mechanisms and findings from in-depth interviews.

A large amount of research is concerned with social inequality in education (for example, Ambler & Neathery, 1999; Boudon, 1974; Bourdieu, 1974; Breen & Goldthorpe, 1997; Goldthorpe, 2007a; Lareau, 2003). Authors largely agree that social class of origin and parental education are linked to educational outcomes over and above differences that can be explained by reference to the way cognitive ability differs by social class (for example Bourdieu, 1974; Breen & Goldthorpe, 2001; Goldthorpe, 1996a; Goldthorpe, 2005; Reay et al., 2005, though for an alternative view see, for example, Saunders, 1997). Various explanations of this link have been offered. One main theoretical strand is *rational choice* or *rational action theory (RAT)* (Boudon, 1974; Breen & Goldthorpe, 1997; Goldthorpe, 1996b), another comprises explanations based on Bourdieu's concepts of *habitus* and *cultural capital* (Bourdieu, 1977, 1986), and I will now briefly outline each of these in turn.

Rational action theory (RAT) explains actions by assuming that actors undertake a cost-benefit analysis before acting. Applied to educational decision-making, this implies that parents and/or their children consider the costs of staying in education (foregone earnings as well as the direct costs of education), weighing them against expected benefits such as expected higher earnings. Costs can include non-monetary costs such as the danger of alienation from one's background of origin. Risks attached to a particular course of action, for example dropping out of education before a qualification is obtained, are also considered (Breen & Goldthorpe, 1997). The perceived costs, benefits and risks depend partly on the family's social background. According to Goldthorpe (2007c), an important motive is at least to maintain one's socio-occupational status relative to the family of origin. Given the well-known relationship between level of education and occupation, this in itself leads to social classes having different educational goals. Boudon (1974) also drew on RAT to develop his well-known model of primary and secondary effects to explain social inequality in education. Briefly, primary effects refer to class differences in academic achievement early in a child's career. Then, even given similar levels of initial achievement, secondary effects, resulting from differences in destination goals and perceived costs and benefits between children from different social class origins, lead students to choose educational pathways differing in prestige and levels of possible qualifications. Thus, secondary effects result from RAT-type decision-making in the context of particular class circumstances.

The concept of *habitus* was developed by Bourdieu (1977, 1986; Bourdieu & Passeron, 1977, 1979). Habitus is a system of lasting dispositions acquired through past experiences. These cognitive and normative predispositions vary systematically between individuals from different social classes, since 'the material conditions of existence characteristic of a class condition' (Bourdieu, 1977, p. 72) are part of the environment which produces habitus. These deeply ingrained dispositions influence, among other things, individuals' attitudes towards curriculum, pedagogy and assessment, and, importantly, also influence how schools behave towards children from different class backgrounds. For Bourdieu, this explains why working-class children often struggle in schools. Because their habitus aligns less well with the school's assumptions, requirements and values, they are less likely to succeed. Actions constrained or enabled by habitus have their roots in an individual's past experiences, thereby allowing the latter to shape expectations. Habitus has an influence on which goals are considered desirable or achievable per se. In addition, whether a particular course of action is chosen depends partly on the subjective estimation of its likelihood of success. Such estimations reflect previous collective experience within the class of origin. For example, a bright working-class child may have reached a level of attainment which would, all else being equal, more or less guarantee that he or she can secure a place at university and graduate successfully. Objectively, this would suggest to an outsider observer that securing a place at university and graduating successfully is more or less guaranteed. However, the subjective estimation is based on previous experiences in the immediate environment, and these may imply that 'people like us' do not go to university in the first place or, if they do, they are bound to struggle and fail eventually. Whether this particular child will attempt to go to university therefore depends not only on the objective likelihood of success, but also on these subjective experiences and expectations formed early on.

Cultural capital is a concept developed by Bourdieu (1986) in order to help explain the transmission of social class advantages from parents to children. He notes that academic success or failure is not merely due to natural talent and parental economic capital. The latter may be spent directly on children's education. In addition, educational advantages are gained through the hereditary transmission of cultural capital. Cultural capital can take three forms: embodied, objectified and institutionalised cultural capital. *Embodied* cultural capital refers to characteristics acquired in the family of origin such as accent. Bourdieu notes that it is acquired unconsciously over a long period of time from an early age, that is, it cannot be transmitted instantaneously, and he suggests that 'the link between economic and cultural capital is established through the mediation of the time needed for acquisition'. Its value lies in its relative scarcity. *Objectified* cultural capital refers to possessions such as books and objects of art. Bourdieu suggests that strengths and profits derive from the mastery of objectified cultural capital within the field of social class struggles. *Institutionalised* cultural capital includes educational credentials. Like the other forms of cultural capital, its value partly derives from its relative scarcity:

> Because the material and symbolic profits which the academic qualification guarantees also depend on its scarcity, the investments made (in time and effort) may turn out to be less profitable than was anticipated when they were made (there having been a de facto change in the conversion rate between academic capital and economic capital). The strategies for converting economic capital into cultural capital, which are among the short-term factors of the schooling explosion and the inflation of qualifications, are governed by changes in the structure of the chances of profit offered by the different types of capital.
>
> (Bourdieu, 1986, p. 248)

In summary, families rich in cultural capital are able to pass this on to their children and thus convert it into educational advantages.

Bourdieu's concepts and RAT are often seen as being in conflict, but, as Vester (2006) has argued, they can also fruitfully be used together. For example, there is a view that primary effects as developed by Boudon have some affinity with the idea of cultural capital: the family's cultural capital provides children with the kind of knowledge and approach to the world helpful for early success in school.

Swartz (1981) similarly argues that while there are important differences between the two approaches, they have much in common, including their attention to socio-economic structure, their focus on individual actors and the ways in which interacting factors produce social phenomena. Throughout this book, I take the position that both families of theories, Bourdieu's habitus and cultural capital theories on the one hand and RAT-based explanations on the other hand, can be helpful for explaining the outcomes under study, and I therefore draw on both. This position is strengthened by preliminary analyses of interviews for the project on which this book is based (published as Glaesser & Cooper, 2014). To summarise briefly, we came to the conclusion that young people both in England and Germany talk about their educational choices in ways which fit RAT accounts. However, their class-based habitus often provides upper and lower boundaries for their aspirations, thus conditioning the nature of the cost-benefit analysis entering into decision-making.

4.2 Outcomes and explanatory factors

As noted at the beginning of this chapter, the research presented in this book aims to describe and explain the differential distribution of individuals across educational careers. The specific *outcomes* under study comprise type of secondary school attended, whether the individual was in full-time education at the age of 17, and higher education aspirations.

The previous section made it clear that social background as indicated by parental social class and parental level of education are key *explanatory factors* for both Bourdieu's theories and RAT approaches. I therefore include social background factors in all the analyses in this book. In addition, potential gender differences in educational careers will be examined. There is considerable evidence that girls perform better at school than boys in most industrialised societies (for example, Buchmann et al., 2008; Ofsted, 2003). They obtain higher marks in tests early in their educational careers as well as reaching higher qualifications than boys (Buchmann & DiPrete, 2006; Buchmann et al., 2008, see also Glaesser & Cooper, 2012b).

In addition to such ascriptive factors (social background and gender), which can explain individuals' careers once the associated mechanisms are spelt out, academic ability is obviously linked to educational outcomes. Whenever the data allow, I have therefore included this, as indicated by prior academic achievement, as a further *explanatory factor*. The qualitative data provided by the interviews (see below) enabled me to study in greater detail how these explanatory factors have their effects.

Finally, I will study factors on the systemic level. The way in which the secondary school systems are organised in the two countries under study, England and Germany, provides the structure of constraints and opportunities within which social actors operate and I therefore describe these organisational features in the following sections. These features form the framework in which the individual factors under study operate in an interactive way.

4.3   Secondary schooling in England

The state secondary school system in England is largely comprehensive, in other words, schools do not usually select pupils for admission based on academic ability, though many schools use some form of internal stratification (so-called streaming or setting), that is, pupils are allocated to and taught in groups of children of similar ability. Alongside comprehensive schools, grammar schools which do select pupils by academic ability exist in some areas, and there is a private sector comprising both academically selective and non-selective schools.

In the state sector, parents are able to apply for a place for their child at their preferred secondary school. When schools have more applications than places, they allocate places according to various criteria such as how close the family live to the school and whether there are siblings already at the school. Given this, some parents choose to move to a particular area because of the reputation of a particular school. In effect, this leads to socio-economic selection via house prices to some extent, since house prices tend to be higher near 'desirable' schools. Specialist schools may select a proportion of up to 10 per cent of their intake based on aptitude in a particular subject such as sports or languages. Faith schools may give preference to members of a particular faith as long as this does not contradict other existing legislation (Eurydice, 2013c). Again, given that some faith schools have a good reputation for academic achievement, some parents emphasise their commitment to a particular faith in order to gain a place for their child at such a school.

There are a few regions in England where secondary schools are formally selective rather than comprehensive. Kent is such an area. Here, children sit an exam, the eleven plus, during their last year of primary school. This is not compulsory, but a pass in the eleven plus (or the Kent test, as it is sometimes called) is required for admission to grammar school. Grammar schools in other regions have the same entry requirement, the difference being that grammar schools are less common in these areas, therefore comprehensive schooling is the norm there.

The situation in Kent and the other selective areas reflects the history of secondary schooling. The 1944 Education Act introduced free universal secondary education within a tripartite system. The three school types were grammar schools, technical grammar schools (whose number remained very low) and secondary modern schools. The latter were attended by those who had failed the eleven plus. This comprised the majority of children. Depending on region, around 20 per cent of children attended a grammar school. One aim of the 1944 Act had been to ensure greater ease of access to post-compulsory education for able working-class children, but evidence as to whether this was successful is mixed (Halsey et al., 1980). Working-class children were less likely to enter grammar schools than middle-class children in the first place and more likely to drop out if they did enter, even given similar levels of ability (Halsey et al., 1980; Ministry of Education, 1954). From the 1960s onwards, comprehensive schools were gradually introduced, partly to address the concerns regarding social inequality and working-class children's access to post-compulsory and higher education. However, it is not clear whether comprehensivisation really led to greater access to post-compulsory education for all (for example, Heath & Jacobs, 1999).

Finally, independent schools (sometimes termed public schools) exist alongside the state comprehensive, grammar and secondary modern schools. They are funded largely through fees paid by parents (Eurydice, 2013d). They are subject to less regulation than state schools. Around 7 per cent of all children in England are educated privately (http://www.isc.co.uk/research/Publications/fact-sheets/independent-schools-an-integral-part-of-education-uk). The figure is higher for secondary pupils.

Clearly, there is scope for parental choice in England (though this may be more restricted in rural areas), given these characteristics of the school system. Independent schools are often seen as offering a better education than state schools, but access to them is usually limited to those whose parents have the financial means to pay the fees, although some means-tested bursaries exist. Grammar schools, where they exist, are an option for academically able children, regardless of their parents' financial means. Among the state comprehensive schools, some schools are oversubscribed because they offer particular subject specialisms, or their reputation for academic excellence or a particular ethos make them particularly attractive for parents. In various ways, though, choice is constrained, especially for those unable to move house to be in the catchment area of a 'good' school.

4.4 Secondary schooling in Germany

Education in Germany is the responsibility of the federal states, or Länder (singular: Land). This means that the systems vary to some degree, but they also have much in common. In the following, I will discuss differences between the Länder insofar as they are relevant for the design of the study and as analytic tools, but otherwise I will focus on commonalities across Germany.

A key characteristic of the German secondary school system is stratification. At the end of primary school,[1] children receive a 'recommendation' based on their academic attainment from their primary school for one of three hierarchically ordered types of school, Hauptschule, Realschule or Gymnasium, each offering a particular qualification. The qualification offered at a Hauptschule is Hauptschulabschluss, normally obtained at the age of 15. It is the most basic qualification intended as preparation for skilled manual work, serving as a prerequisite to obtaining an apprenticeship of this sort. At a Realschule, pupils obtain the intermediate qualification Realschulabschluss, which enables them to access most types of apprenticeship and training short of university. At some Hauptschulen, it is possible for pupils who perform well to obtain the Realschulabschluss through spending an extra year at school. Some of the most able Realschule pupils stay in education for longer in order to obtain the highest possible qualification, the Abitur which is the prerequisite for university entry. Those that do so most commonly attend a Berufliches Gymnasium (Vocational Gymnasium) to gain their Abitur. These Berufliche Gymnasien have a specialism such as nutrition or health and social care and a stronger focus on applied subjects than traditional Gymnasien, but the Abitur obtained from a Berufliches Gymnasium is equivalent to that obtained at a traditional Gymnasium, with both allowing university access to study any subject. As well as being an option for able Realschule leavers, they also attract pupils who attend a traditional Gymnasium up to year 10 and then wish to specialise in more vocationally oriented areas such as nutritional science or technology.

The traditional Gymnasium is for the most academically able children who leave at the age of 18 or 19[2] with the Abitur. Leaving the Gymnasium after having successfully completed year 9 is equivalent to a Hauptschulabschluss and leaving Gymnasium after having successfully completed year 10 is equivalent to a Realschulabschluss. The former happens rarely, but the latter is not unusual. In some Länder, Gesamtschulen (comprehensive schools) exist alongside the tripartite system (Eurydice, 2013b). All three types of qualification are on offer at Gesamtschulen.

The recommendation made by the primary school is binding in some Länder but not in others.[3] Where it is binding, parents have various ways of challenging it if they wish to enrol their child in a type of school further up the hierarchy than that recommended, either by having the child assessed by specialised teachers who can recommend a different school type, or by the child's passing an entrance exam for the school type they wish to attend. In addition, parents are always free to choose a lower type of school than that recommended. Clearly, there is some scope for parental choice even in those Länder where the recommendation is binding. However, there is some evidence that parents from lower social classes are more likely not to enrol their children in the Gymnasium even given the required recommendation while parents from higher social classes are more likely to appeal against a recommendation they are not happy with (Ditton & Krüsken, 2009).

Private schools have to be approved by the state to ensure that educational provision is adequate (Eurydice, 2013a). The proportion of pupils attending a private school varies considerably between Länder: in 2011/2012, the range was from 3.9 per cent in Schleswig-Holstein to 13.8 per cent in Saxony. Overall, the proportion is around 8 per cent. Of all pupils attending private schools, 38.2 per cent attend a Gymnasium, 15.6 per cent a Realschule, 11.6 per cent a primary school and 11.2 per cent a Steiner school (known in Germany as Waldorfschule), with the rest attending other types of school, for example comprehensive or special needs schools (Statistisches Bundesamt, 2012). Private secondary schools largely follow the tripartite structure of the state schools. Waldorfschulen only exist in a private form. The role of private schools is somewhat different from the private sector in Britain: they are not necessarily expected to provide a better academic education than state schools, but they tend to be chosen by parents who are dissatisfied with the state system for other reasons. The ethos of private schools can be different, for example in the case of church-run schools, or they may offer smaller class sizes and/or more extracurricular activities and after-school care. By contrast, in England, private schools are often seen as offering a more academically oriented education to a child who would not have access to it otherwise (for example because of a lack of places at academically oriented schools in the area, or a lack of such schools altogether), and there is a tradition for the elite to use private schools for their children, with the tradition of attending a particular school sometimes running in families. German private schools rely on the same information such as recommendation and prior academic performance as do state schools when they admit pupils and the education on offer is also similar to that of state schools with respect to academic rigour, expectations and outcomes.

I will discuss the social selectivity in Germany and underlying mechanisms in more detail in Chapter 5. Here, I wish to stress some characteristics of the English and German systems which make them useful case studies for the purposes of my study. The most salient difference between the two countries is that England's system is largely comprehensive and Germany's academically selective. One reason for comprehensivisation in England was the expectation that it would lead to a less socially selective system. I shall therefore explore mechanisms of social selectivity in both countries with the German selective system providing a useful contrast to the English nominally largely comprehensive one. Rational action theory might predict that there should be lower social selectivity under a comprehensive system: there are fewer branching points and therefore fewer decisions have to be taken, resulting in reduced selectivity by social background given that cost-benefit analyses and primary and secondary effects have less opportunity to come into play. Bourdieu's habitus and cultural capital theories, on the other hand, would lead us to expect comprehensive schools to perform much in the same way as selective schools insofar as they attempt to offer the same education to everyone while not everyone has an equally relevant socio-cultural background. In such circumstances, children from a privileged background will tend to benefit more from the education on offer. In practice, however, not all comprehensive schools in England actually are the same: as described above, schools vary in their emphasis and success with regard to those forms of academic achievement favoured by the higher status universities, and specialist and faith schools exist, all within the comprehensive sector. Privileged social classes are more likely to gain access for their children to the most prestigious 'comprehensive' schools, and given the higher academic ability, on average, of such children, this in turn helps the success of these schools. In addition, there are alternatives given the existence of academically selective state schools (the grammar schools) and the private sector. Indeed, there is evidence to show that comprehensivisation has not reduced social selectivity (Bynner & Joshi, 2002; Galindo-Rueda & Vignoles, 2005; Glaesser & Cooper, 2012a). Against this background, it will be interesting to analyse and assess the mechanisms generating socially selective educational outcomes under two differing systems.

In the next section, I describe the data sets used for the cross-case analyses.

4.5   Survey data

4.5.1   England

For the cross-case analyses in England, I drew on two different data sources throughout the project and I have drawn on a further one for the new analyses presented in this book.

One set of data used for the cross-case analyses for England was from Durham University's Centre for Evaluation and Monitoring (CEM). CEM conducts large-scale educational monitoring studies whose main purpose is to provide feedback to schools on pupils' performance. In addition to performance indicators, background data are collected (for an overview of CEM's work, see Tymms & Coe, 2003 and http://www.cem.org/).

While the CEM centre data are contemporary, the other survey data set used, the National Child Development Study (NCDS), reflect an earlier period. The NCDS is a longitudinal study covering all children born during one week in March 1958 (Centre for Longitudinal Studies, 2008). It contains data on family of origin, schooling, cognitive ability, educational and occupational outcomes and many other topics. The cohort members entered secondary school in 1969, when they were 11 years old. This was the period of comprehensive reorganisation (see Section 4.3), with some regions having completed the transition to comprehensive secondary schools and others not even having started. This made it a useful data set to study with respect to the effects of secondary school organisation, given that there were effectively two systems within one country during this period.

The findings summarised in this chapter (below) are based on CEM centre and NCDS data. However, for analyses pertaining to England new to this book, the Longitudinal Study of Young People in England (LSYPE) (Department for Education and National Centre for Social Research, 2012) was used. This is a panel study of young people, commissioned by the Department for Children, Schools and Families (DCSF) (formerly the Department for Education and Skills (DfES) and currently the Department for Education (DfE)). It began in 2004 when 15,770 young people (then aged between 13 and 14) were interviewed along with their parents. Through annual interviews, information is obtained from the young person, and additional information is gained through interviews with the parents. For parental education, I report the categories degree, A-levels, GCSE, and below GCSE/no qualification. GCSE (General Certificate of Secondary Education) is the qualification obtained at the end of compulsory schooling, at the age of 16. A-levels (Advanced levels) are taken at the age of 18, usually in three or four subjects, and they form a prerequisite for university admission. Parental class in the LSYPE data is coded following the NS_SEC scheme which is a development of the Erikson-Goldthorpe class scheme (Erikson & Goldthorpe, 1993). I have recoded the class categories into just three social class groups: service, intermediate and working class.

Independent schools are underrepresented in the study: while the response rate at school level was 73 per cent overall, it was only 57 per cent for independent schools (DfE, 2011). The proportion of selective schools is fairly low, too, at around 4 per cent. Table 4.1 gives an overview of some of the characteristics of the sample used in Chapter 6 of this book. This sample comprises all the cases from seven LSYPE waves with no missing data[4] on any of the variables of interest.

4.5.2   Germany

The German data used here are from the German Socio-Economic Panel (SOEP).[5] The SOEP is a representative household panel study which has been conducted annually since 1984 in West Germany. East German households were added in 1990. There are separate questionnaires for each household and for each individual living there. Parents are asked to give information on their children up to and including the age of 16. At age 17, the young people fill in a specific youth questionnaire, and the adult questionnaire from the age of 18. They remain in the study even if they move out of their parental home, in which case their new household is added to the study. The last wave I am using is from 2007. My sample (*n* = 790) consists of all those born between 1986 and 1990 who filled in a questionnaire at the age of 17 with no missing information[6] on the variables used in this study, using all the SOEP samples including refreshment as well as high-income samples.[7] Parental class here is coded following the Erikson-Goldthorpe scheme (Erikson & Goldthorpe, 1993), and as with the LSYPE data, I have recoded class into the three categories service, intermediate and working class (Table 4.2).

4.6   Interviews

The previous section described the data sets used for the cross-case analyses. The purpose of the interviews described in this section was to supplement the insights gained via large *n* QCA cross-case analyses with within-case process-tracing case studies (George & Bennett, 2005), with the aim of exploring mechanisms that generate the regularities described by the QCA.

As noted in Chapter 2, George and Bennett (2005) stress the importance of careful case selection as a key element of process-tracing, and that the selection of cases has to match the goal of a study. I undertook the selection of cases for interview and analysis in two steps: (1) the selection of the whole sample of cases through a process of theoretical sampling, and (2) from this sample subsequent selections of cases for particular purposes.

(1) In selecting the whole sample of interviewees, I aimed to ensure, as far as possible, a spread of cases across the different combinations of factors identified as theoretically relevant, i.e. gender, parental

Table 4.1 LSYPE sample description (*n* = 4,972)

Factor	Values	*n* (per cent of total)
Gender	Male	2,502 (50.3)
	Female	2,470 (49.7)
Father's highest qualification	Degree	799 (16.1)
	A-levels	1,589 (32.0)
	GCSE	1,355 (27.3)
	Below GCSE/no qualification	1,229 (24.7)
Mother's highest qualification	Degree	607 (12.2)
	A-levels	1,488 (29.9)
	GCSE	1,626 (32.7)
	Below GCSE/no qualification	1,251 (25.2)
Father's social class	Service class	2,160 (43.4)
	Intermediate class	1,824 (36.7)
	Working class	988 (19.9)
Mother's social class	Service class	1,610 (32.4)
	Intermediate class	1,662 (33.4)
	Working class	1,700 (34.2)
Young person is in full-time education age 17	Yes	3,891 (78.3)
	No	1,081 (21.7)
Young person's current or last type of school	Comprehensive	4,693 (94.4)
	Selective	279 (5.6)
Young person is expecting to go to university ('likely' or 'very likely')	Yes	3,231 (65.0)
	No	1,741 (35.0)
Key stage 2* test results	Mean	27.99
	Median	28.48
	Standard deviation	3.605
	Minimum	15.00
	Maximum	36.00
High performer on key stage 2 test[+]	Yes	3,037 (61.1)
	No	1,935 (38.9)

* 'The national curriculum is organised into blocks of years called "key stages" (KS). At the end of each key stage, your child's teacher will formally assess their performance to measure your child's progress' (https://www.gov.uk/national-curriculum/overview). Key stage 2 comprises years 3–6, with a test taken at the end when children are aged 11.
[+] This is based on splitting the sample at the median for the full sample (*n* = 14,420) which was 27.4. Due to dropout, the resulting split for my sample is not at the sample median of 28.48.

Table 4.2   SOEP sample description (*n* = 790)

Factor	Values	*n* (per cent of total)
Gender	Male	395 (50.0)
	Female	395 (50.0)
Father's highest academic qualification	Degree	263 (33.3)
	Abitur	49 (5.2)
	Realschule	246 (31.1)
	Hauptschule	224 (28.4)
	No qualification	8 (1.0)
Mother's highest academic qualification	Degree	224 (28.4)
	Abitur	51 (6.4)
	Realschule	338 (42.8)
	Hauptschule	169 (21.4)
	No qualification	8 (1.0)
Father's social class	Service class	335 (42.4)
	Intermediate class	154 (19.5)
	Working class	301 (38.1)
Mother's social class	Service class	252 (31.9)
	Intermediate class	341 (43.2)
	Working class	197 (24.9)
Young person's secondary school recommendation	Gymnasium	433 (54.8)
	Realschule	259 (32.8)
	Hauptschule	98 (12.4)
Young person's current type of school	Not in education	19 (2.4)
	Hauptschule	44 (5.5)
	Realschule	202 (25.6)
	Gesamtschule	38 (4.8)
	Gymnasium	382 (48.4)
	Vocational training	105 (13.3)
Young person is expecting to go to university ('likely' or 'very likely')	Yes	269 (34.1)
	No	521 (65.9)

background factors and school types. Another criterion was to include interviewees in both England and Germany from regions and schools which are different from the system in the rest of each country. The rationale for this was as follows: one of the aims of this study was to investigate whether and to what extent the school system forms part of the constellation of factors influencing educational outcomes. It can therefore be fruitful to study countries with different systems. However, this leaves open the question of whether any differences in outcomes to be found are due to the differences between the school systems, or to some cultural differences between the countries. For this reason, I studied within-country differences concerning the organisation of the school system in addition to between-country differences. For example, for England, I conducted interviews with pupils attending a grammar school and a secondary modern school in Kent. The reason for choosing Kent rather than selecting some grammar school in a different part of the country was that Kent, unlike other regions, is almost purely selective. If a grammar school exists in a largely comprehensive region, the choices to be made by parents and their children are less restricted than if selection is the only system on offer. In Germany, I interviewed pupils at two Gesamtschulen (comprehensive schools) in Nordrhein-Westfalen. While there is no purely comprehensive region in Germany, Nordrhein-Westfalen has a large enough number of Gesamtschulen to make this a real option for many parents. The other interviews took place in purely comprehensive areas in England (South East and North East of England) and purely selective areas in Germany (Baden-Württemberg).

The interviewees were drawn from 15 schools altogether, nine in Germany (three Hauptschulen and two each of Realschulen, Gymnasien and Gesamtschulen) and six in England (comprehensive with sixth form, comprehensive without sixth form, voluntary aided comprehensive,[8] grammar school in Kent, secondary modern school in Kent, independent school). The interviewees were chosen based on information given on a short form that pupils had completed, giving details of parents' education and occupation and, for German interviewees, of the recommendation received at the end of primary school. The interview transcripts are available to researchers via the UK data archive (http:// reshare.ukdataservice.ac.uk/851503/).

(2) In a second step, I employed QCA to analyse which configurations of factors were quasi-sufficient or quasi-necessary for obtaining specific educational outcomes, drawing on the SOEP and LSYPE data.[9] The factors again included parental education, parental occupation, the pupil's sex and, for Germany, academic achievement as indicated by the recommendation (I did not use the academic achievement measure from the LSYPE data because I did not have an achievement measure for the English interviewees), and the school type attended at the age of 15 or 16, i.e. towards the end of compulsory schooling. On the basis of these analyses, I classified cases as typical, deviant and inconclusive with regard to necessity and sufficiency and chose cases relevant for a particular analytic purpose from these categories (for details see Chapters 5 and 6).

The interview sample comprised 79 cases in total. 43 interviews were conducted in Germany and 36 in England. The cases are described as configurations of factors in the following tables (Tables 4.3 and 4.4).

Table 4.3 German interviewees

Parents' education	Parents' social class	School type	Cases (pseudonyms)
One or both at least Abitur	One or both service class	Gymnasium	Alina, Anna, Ludwig ($n = 3$)
None at least Abitur	One or both service class	Gymnasium	Jonas ($n = 1$)
One or both at least Abitur	None service class	Gymnasium	Lena, Roman, Sibel ($n = 3$)
None at least Abitur	None service class	Gymnasium	Diana, Jessica, Magdalena, Marina, Marko, Sebastian ($n = 6$)
One or both at least Abitur	One or both service class	Realschule	Andreas, Nicole ($n = 2$)
None at least Abitur	One or both service class	Realschule	No cases
One or both at least Abitur	None service class	Realschule	Martina, Sabrina, Samuel ($n = 3$)
None at least Abitur	None service class	Realschule	Gabriele, Katrin, Kevin, Nadine, Patrick, Tanja, Tobias ($n = 7$)
One or both at least Abitur	One or both service class	Hauptschule	Michael, Sarah, Tim ($n = 3$)
None at least Abitur	One or both service class	Hauptschule	Mike ($n = 1$)
One or both at least Abitur	None service class	Hauptschule	Elena, Katja, Philipp ($n = 3$)
None at least Abitur	None service class	Hauptschule	Natascha, Peter, Vera, Yvonne ($n = 4$)
One or both at least Abitur	One or both service class	Gesamtschule	Daniela, Julia ($n = 2$)
None at least Abitur	One or both service class	Gesamtschule	Christian ($n = 1$)
One or both at least Abitur	None service class	Gesamtschule	Aynur ($n = 1$)
None at least Abitur	None service class	Gesamtschule	Orhan, Tessa, Vanessa ($n = 3$)

Table 4.4 English interviewees

Parents' education	Parents' social class	School type	Cases (pseudonyms)
One or both at least A-levels	One or both service class	Independent school	Charlotte, Kalvinder, Saskia, Vicky ($n = 4$)
None at least A-levels	One or both service class	Independent school	Deborah ($n = 1$)
One or both at least A-levels	None service class	Independent school	Hannah ($n = 1$)
None at least A-levels	None service class	Independent school	no cases
One or both at least A-levels	One or both service class	Grammar school	Philippa ($n = 1$)
None at least A-levels	One or both service class	Grammar school	Emily, Rosie ($n = 2$)
One or both at least A-levels	None service class	Grammar school	Lauren, Patricia, Ruth ($n = 3$)
None at least A-levels	None service class	Grammar school	no cases
One or both at least A-levels	One or both service class	Secondary modern school in Kent	Marcus ($n = 1$)
None at least A-levels	One or both service class	Secondary modern school in Kent	no cases
One or both at least A-levels	None service class	Secondary modern school in Kent	no cases
None at least A-levels	None service class	Secondary modern school in Kent	Amy, Harry, Kim, Leanne, Paul, Zoe ($n = 6$)
One or both at least A-levels	One or both service class	Voluntary aided comprehensive	Benjamin, Beth, Denise, William ($n = 4$)
None at least A-levels	One or both service class	Voluntary aided comprehensive	no cases
One or both at least A-levels	None service class	Voluntary aided comprehensive	Matthew, Samantha ($n = 2$)
None at least A-levels	None service class	Voluntary aided comprehensive	no cases
One or both at least A-levels	One or both service class	Comprehensive with sixth form	Georgia, Helen, Maya, Thomas ($n = 4$)
None at least A-levels	One or both service class	Comprehensive with sixth form	no cases
One or both at least A-levels	None service class	Comprehensive with sixth form	Alexandra ($n = 1$)
None at least A-levels	None service class	Comprehensive with sixth form	no cases
One or both at least A-levels	One or both service class	Comprehensive without sixth form	David, Kelly ($n = 2$)
None at least A-levels	One or both service class	Comprehensive without sixth form	no cases
One or both at least A-levels	None service class	Comprehensive without sixth form	no cases
None at least A-levels	None service class	Comprehensive without sixth form	Duncan, Michelle, Susan, Wayne ($n = 4$)

Clearly, even with 79 interviews, it is difficult to cover all the theoretically potentially relevant cases, and so some cells in Table 4.3 and Table 4.4 have no cases at all, while the others have just one or a few cases. This problem, often ignored by some who claim to be able to explore the effects of many factors with few cases, becomes obvious when types of cases are set out in a truth table representing the relevant property space or attribute space (Becker, 1998, Chapter 5; Lazarsfeld, 1937). These small case numbers reflect the fact that I was only able to conduct a limited number of interviews, but they also point to the phenomenon termed limited diversity (Ragin & Sonnett, 2005): not all combinations occur with equal frequency in the world because the factors themselves are related. For example, some of the empty cells are ones where there would be a mismatch between parental qualifications and social class. Level of qualification and occupational status are often related, and so it is not surprising that there are fewer cases where one but not the other is high. Similarly, it is not surprising that there are no cases of young people in the independent school where parents neither have high qualifications nor occupy service class positions. Such parents are less likely to hold either the economic or the cultural capital required to enable their children's attendance at such a school.

I should also note that both the independent and the grammar school in my sample were girls' schools. This reflects the fact that I wasn't able to gain access to mixed or boys' schools of either type.

4.7   Findings

Some findings from this project have already been published elsewhere. Since these have informed the analyses reported in this book, it may be helpful for the reader to be aware of their broad findings. I will therefore briefly summarise three earlier papers here. I will also use this opportunity, in summarising the first paper, to demonstrate some of the insights a QCA analysis has to offer. This first paper concerned Germany, with a focus on whether or not young people's schooling careers were stable or not; the second focussed on GCSE success in England today, taking account of gender, parental education and cognitive ability. The third paper also deals with educational success or otherwise in England, but with a special interest in school systems. All three papers use the large *n* data sets described above.

4.7.1   Flexibility in the selective German secondary system

As noted above, the German secondary school system is selective and stratified, but it also allows for changes between tracks. The paper summarised here (Glaesser & Cooper, 2011b) used SOEP data, firstly, to investigate, descriptively, the amount of flexibility in the system and, secondly, to analyse who experiences this flexibility. The descriptive part consisted of comparing the first type of secondary school attended after primary school with the one the young person attended age 17 (or, if they had already left school, the last one they attended). The majority of cases are in the same type of school at the beginning and towards the end of their secondary schooling careers, indicating a certain level of stability of German secondary school careers, but there are notable exceptions. Over 40 per cent of Hauptschule pupils move to a higher type of school or to a Gesamtschule. There is more movement up than down from the Realschule, with around 6 per cent of cases going to Hauptschule and 19 per cent to Gymnasium. The Gymnasium itself provides a fairly secure route to the Abitur: around 90 per cent of those who enter it age 10 are still in a Gymnasium age 17.

Our next step was to analyse whether there was any social selectivity in the way the young people moved between tracks. Using QCA, we were able to show that both moving up from Hauptschule and dropping out of the Gymnasium were associated with combinations of conditions comprising the recommendation received at the end of primary school, as well as parental education and/or social class. Following the more abstract introduction to QCA in Chapter 3, I will now use the first of these two analyses to illustrate both the issue of limited diversity and of the substantive interpretation of QCA findings. The outcome here is attending or having successfully completed a higher type of school than Hauptschule at the age of 17 ('HS_UP') if the first secondary school attended had been a Hauptschule. The conditions are gender ('MALE', coded 1 = male, 0 = female), whether at least one parent is in the service class ('SC_1P'), whether at least one parent holds at least Realschulabschluss as their highest school qualification ('RS_1P') and whether the young person had received a recommendation for the Hauptschule at the end of primary school ('HS_REC'). Table 4.5 is the relevant truth table.

All the rows have at least one case, so strictly speaking there is no limited diversity. However, Ragin (2008) notes that, particularly with large *n* analyses where the researcher lacks detailed case knowledge, there is a danger of measurement or coding error, and he recommends using a frequency threshold for the Boolean minimisation process so as not to include rows where the empirical evidence is not strong. In this particular analysis, the rows with particularly low *n* happen to fall below any reasonable threshold for consistency with sufficiency

Table 4.5   Truth table, outcome moving up from Hauptschule

Row no.	MALE	SC_1P	RS_1P	HS_REC	Number	HS_UP	Consistency
1	0	1	1	0	9		0.889
2	0	0	1	0	15		0.867
3	1	1	1	0	15		0.8
4	1	0	1	0	17		0.765
5	1	1	0	0	3		0.667
6	1	1	0	1	2		0.5
7	0	0	0	0	8		0.5
8	1	0	0	0	7		0.429
9	0	0	0	1	15		0.4
10	1	1	1	1	8		0.375
11	1	0	0	1	17		0.294
12	0	0	1	1	11		0.273
13	1	0	1	1	13		0.231
14	0	1	1	1	6		0.167
15	0	1	0	1	2		0
16	0	1	0	0	1		0

anyway, so a frequency threshold was not applied.[10] It would be a different matter if we intended to analyse the negated outcome, 'not moving up from Hauptschule'. This would entail entering the bottom rows into the process of Boolean minimisation, and they have very low *n* indeed.

Another point to note concerning limited diversity in this table is the fact that the rows with particularly low *n* tend to be those where there is a mismatch between the conditions. For example, rows 5 and 6 comprise cases where at least one parent is in the service class, but neither parent holds a qualification above Hauptschulabschluss. Given the relationship between qualification and social class, it is not surprising that such constellations are less common than those where qualification and social class match. Limited diversity often has its roots in the realities of the social world; it is not the result of a purely random process.

In the paper, we applied three different consistency thresholds, 0.85, 0.8 and 0.75, to explore what solutions are produced when the requirements for consistency with sufficiency move from strict to less strict. The solutions are reproduced in Box 4.1.

At the least demanding level of consistency with sufficiency (solution 3), the solution comprises just one pathway: the combination of having at least one parent who holds at least Realschulabschluss with the young person's having received a recommendation for at least Realschule at the end of primary school. Higher levels of consistency mean that more

Box 4.1 Solutions for Table 4.5, outcome moving up from Hauptschule

---

Solution 1 (0.85 consistency threshold)

	Raw Coverage	Unique Coverage	Consistency
male*RS_1P*hs_rec	0.273	0.273	0.875

Solution coverage: 0.273
Solution consistency: 0.875

Solution 2 (0.80 consistency threshold)

	Raw Coverage	Unique Coverage	Consistency
male*RS_1P*hs_rec+	0.273	0.169	0.875
SC_1P*RS_1P*hs_rec	0.260	0.156	0.833

Solution coverage: 0.429
Solution consistency: 0.846

Solution 3 (0.75 consistency threshold)

	Raw Coverage	Unique Coverage	Consistency
RS_1P*hs_rec	0.597	0.597	0.821

Solution coverage: 0.597
Solution consistency: 0.821

---

conditions have to be combined with this. In solution 2, they are having at least one parent in the service class *or* being female. In solution 1, at the most demanding consistency level of 0.85, having a parent in the service class does not feature and only being female, in combination with the other two conditions, constitutes a sufficient pathway to obtaining the outcome. The recommendation is clearly an important element, but it is equally clear that it is not sufficient on its own. Having had a higher recommendation than for the Hauptschule has to be combined with particular social background factors for someone to be able to move up from the Hauptschule.

Some brief remarks on boys: there is no quasi-sufficient pathway for boys at the highest level of consistency, 0.85 (solution 1 in Box 4.1). At the next level of 0.8, there is a sufficient pathway containing boys, but it comprises only those whose parents are in the service class *and* who hold at least the Realschulabschluss qualification themselves. Without further analyses, it is not easy to know why parental education was sufficient for girls, but for boys it had to be combined with parental social background at the 0.8 consistency level, and why there was no sufficient pathway for boys at all at the 0.85 level. This does, however, point to there being some difference in how boys and girls fare which is worth investigating further.

In Chapter 5, I will show how the interviews enabled me to explore further the roles of social background and the recommendation in shaping young people's educational pathways in Germany and therefore to make explanatory sense of these findings.

4.7.2   GCSE success

Moving to England, another set of findings concerns the significance of configurations comprising gender, ability and parental education in the prediction of success in obtaining good GCSEs (Glaesser & Cooper, 2012b). One disadvantage of the German SOEP data is that there is no ability measure. The data for England used in the paper summarised here are CEM centre data, and they do contain an ability measure based on a cognitive ability test taken during year 11, that is, at the age of 15/16. Using QCA, we conducted separate analyses for cases in non-selective and selective schools. We were able to show that while a minimum level of cognitive ability was part of all the configurations we identified as quasi-sufficient for obtaining good GCSEs, it was not sufficient on its own except for cases with very high ability, defined as being in the top quartile of the ability distribution. For cases with ability in the second quartile, being female and/or being from a family with high parental education had to be part of the configurations. In other words, for girls, cognitive ability above the median was sufficient for obtaining good GCSEs, regardless of family background. Boys of the same level of ability had to have two parents with degrees for this to be a sufficient configuration.

We concluded that 'boys suffer more from lack of cultural capital, as indicated by parental education, with regard to educational attainment at GCSE' and that

> we have been able, if not to confirm conclusively that a particular mechanism is operating, then at least to provide evidence which is in line with the theory claiming that the class/gender interaction is brought about by the greater compatibility both of girls' behaviour and of middle-class values and culture with school culture (p. 476).

There are two reasons why we use parental education in the analyses but then refer to class in the conclusion. The first is that parental education seemed a better proxy for cultural capital, which is the basis of much of the theoretical discussion in this area; the other is that the social class measure available in the Yellis data is not of a standard sociological form. However, we repeated our analyses using this social class measure and the results were similar, so we felt it was justified to refer to social class. I explore further the question of middle-class culture and its role in achieving educational success in particular throughout this book.

4.7.3 Comprehensive versus selective schooling

While comprehensive secondary schooling is now the dominant system in England, a selective system was the norm until the 1970s. Given the ongoing debate about forms of schooling in many countries, the next findings I report here are those based on an analysis of NCDS data and concern educational outcomes experienced by individuals born in 1958 (Glaesser & Cooper, 2012a). We made use of the fact that during the 1970s, there was a period where selective and comprehensive systems were in place in different areas. Not surprisingly, we found that, again, high social class of origin and high cognitive ability were associated with higher educational attainment, but we also showed that, contrary to expectations held both by some proponents and critics of comprehensivisation, the young people's experience in both systems was remarkably similar, with one exception. For the configuration non-service class boys with high cognitive ability, growing up in an area with selective schooling forms one element of a quasi-sufficient pathway to the outcome 'obtaining at least A-level qualifications'. Institutional arrangements did not form part of any of the other configurations that were quasi-sufficient for the outcome, with the consistency threshold set at 0.79 (there were a number of truth table rows very close to either side of 0.8, but then a huge jump, which is why we decided to include all the rows with consistencies above 0.79 in the Boolean minimisation process). This indicates that for most people, whether they grew up in a comprehensive or selective area did not greatly affect their educational outcomes. In addition to the Boolean truth table analysis, we also undertook pairwise comparisons of some relevant rows which led us to come to the same conclusion of the relative unimportance of school system.

This book, particularly through the analyses reported in Chapters 5–8, intends to contribute further to this debate by exploring selective and comprehensive schooling in England and Germany. I begin in the next chapter by analysing young people's educational careers in the largely selective German secondary school system.

5
Which Young People in Germany are in a Gymnasium at the Age of 17? A Typological Analysis

The Gymnasium is the most academically selective and the most prestigious among the types of secondary school in Germany (see Chapter 4). While attending a Gymnasium is not the only way to obtain the Abitur, the prerequisite for university access, it is the most common and straightforward way. Many parents therefore wish for their children to enter this type of school. In this chapter, I present and discuss findings both from Qualitative Comparative Analysis (QCA) analyses of German Socio-Economic Panel (SOEP) data (see Chapter 4) and in-depth analyses of my interviews to describe and explain Gymnasium attendance to age 17. Since some young people leave the Gymnasium at the age of 16 with the intermediate qualification of Realschulabschluss, staying on to 17 is a clearer indicator of being en route to obtaining the Abitur than merely entering the Gymnasium would be.

5.1 QCA findings

For this QCA analysis, the outcome focussed upon is whether the young person was in a Gymnasium at the age of 17, 'GY17'. The four conditions considered are (1) gender ('MALE', coded 1 = male, 0 = female), (2) parental qualification ('ABI_1P', coded 1 = one or both parents have Abitur, 0 = neither parent has Abitur), (3) parental social class ('SC_1P', coded 1 = one or both parents are in the service class, 0 = neither parent is in the service class) and the recommendation received at the end of primary school, 'GY_REC' (1 = recommendation was for Gymnasium, 0 = recommendation was for Realschule or Hauptschule). The recommendation is a fairly complex measure. It captures academic ability, given that it is based on performance in the last year in primary school, but it is also connected to social background since academic performance at this stage of development has been shown to be linked to this. In addition, teachers may be aware of a child's social background and use it to predict whether or not he/she will succeed or struggle in the Gymnasium. Another complicating factor concerning the recommendation, in addition to its reflecting ability as well as social background, lies in the formal properties of the school system: the recommendation is binding in some Länder which makes it very hard for children to enter the Gymnasium if the recommendation is for a lower type of school. Where it isn't binding, parents may be reluctant to override it to send their child to a higher type of school than that recommended, especially those from a less well-educated background (Ditton & Krüsken, 2009).[1] In summary, the recommendation can be expected to be a fairly good predictor of type of school attended, although this is likely to be for a variety of reasons.

Table 5.1 is the truth table setting out the configurations and their consistency with the outcome.

As recommended in Chapter 3, I begin by inspecting the truth table itself. Not surprisingly, given the key role of the recommendation, the top half of the table comprises all eight configurations containing the cases where the recommendation for the Gymnasium was present. There is then a noticeable drop in consistency, from 0.639 to 0.429, between rows 8 and 9.

Another point to note is the unequal distribution of cases across the rows. Parental education and parental social class are correlated, as expected. This is evident from the fact that rows where both social class and education are high as well as those where both are low tend to have more cases than rows where class and education are not so typically aligned.[2]

In the next step, I have obtained Boolean solutions for three thresholds of consistency:

Using a strict threshold of 0.9 results in just one truth table row entering the solution. Belonging to the configuration 'girls from the most privileged background who had received the recommendation for the Gymnasium' is a quasi-sufficient condition for attending a Gymnasium at age 17. Lowering the threshold slightly to include the next truth table row results in a solution with slightly lower consistency but more than double coverage to give all cases, male and female, from a privileged social background who had received the Gymnasium recommendation. Consistency for solution 3, employing a threshold of 0.75, is slightly lower again, but still fairly high, both for the solution as a whole and for each pathway in the solution. The two (partly overlapping) pathways to the outcome here are: ABI_1P*GY_REC + MALE*SC_1P*GY_REC, linked by logical OR, that is, the combination of having at least one parent

Table 5.1 Truth table, outcome in Gymnasium at age 17

Row no.	Male	At least one parent with Abitur	At least one parent in the service class	Recommendation was for Gymnasium	Number	In Gymnasium at age 17	Consistency
1	0	1	1	1	96		0.917
2	1	1	1	1	111		0.847
3	1	0	1	1	39		0.795
4	1	1	0	1	19		0.789
5	0	0	0	1	18		0.778
6	0	0	1	1	42		0.667
7	1	0	0	1	47		0.660
8	0	0	0	1	61		0.639
9	0	1	0	0	7		0.429
10	0	1	1	0	34		0.382
11	1	1	1	0	28		0.321
12	0	0	1	0	44		0.114
13	0	0	0	0	93		0.075
14	1	0	0	0	99		0.040
15	1	0	1	0	41		0.02
16	1	1	0	0	11		0

Box 5.1   Solutions for Table 5.1, outcome in Gymnasium at age 17

Solution 1: 0.9 threshold

	Raw coverage	Unique coverage	Consistency
male*ABI_1P*SC_1P*GY_REC	0.230	0.230	0.917

Solution coverage: 0.230
Solution consistency: 0.917

Solution 2: 0.8 threshold

	Raw coverage	Unique coverage	Consistency
ABI_1P*SC_1P*GY_REC	0.476	0.476	0.879

Solution coverage: 0.476
Solution consistency: 0.879

Solution 3: 0.75 threshold

	Raw coverage	Unique coverage	Consistency
ABI_1P*GY_REC+	0.552	0.306	0.865
MALE*SC_1P*GY_REC	0.327	0.081	0.833

Solution coverage: 0.634
Solution consistency: 0.855

with the Abitur and having received a recommendation for Gymnasium at the end of primary school, *or*, for males only, the combination of having had that recommendation coupled with having at least one parent in the service class. The first of these elements, ABI_1P*GY_REC, comprises the first two and the fourth and fifth truth table rows, i.e. the combinations 0111, 1111, 1101 and 0101 (where the 1s and 0s refer to the entry against the respective conditions). The second element, MALE*SC_1P*GY_REC, comprises the combinations 1111 and 1011. Combination 1111 is the overlap.

Coverage for the solution as a whole is fairly high, but not so high as to indicate that these two are the only pathways leading to the outcome. It is worth noting that the unique coverage of the second pathway is fairly low which indicates that most of the set representing this pathway overlaps the set representing the other pathway.[3] In other words, many cases who have the conditions indicated by the second pathway will also have those of the first. This is exactly the sort of situation where case studies of processes are required in order to move to any causal understanding: such case studies can be used to analyse whether the same causal processes characterise the cases belonging only to the first, only to the second pathway or to the overlap.

The recommendation for Gymnasium is part of both pathways in solution 3, and also part of solutions 1 and 2. In spite of the overall solution coverage figures not being high enough to indicate quasi-necessity of any of the solutions taken as a whole, a separate check showed the recommendation on its own to be a quasi-necessary condition, with a consistency with necessity of 0.890 (see Table 5.2).[4] (For a discussion of the relation between coverage of the solution as a whole and the quasi-necessity of the constituting conditions, see Glaesser & Cooper, 2010.) Solution 3 highlights another feature of QCA which can make it a fruitful basis for case selection. It is the finding that there are two quasi-sufficient pathways leading to the outcome, pointing to there being more than one type of typical case to explore. Regression analysts, insofar as they focus on a simple onlier/outlier distinction (where onlier refers to a low-residual case and outlier to a high-residual case), will tend to miss such causal complexity.[5]

The fact that the recommendation formed part of all the solutions meant that analysing its consistency with necessity was particularly important. In addition, I analysed the necessity of each condition (Table 5.2).[6]

Table 5.2 Analysis of necessary conditions, outcome variable: GY17

Condition	Consistency with necessity	Coverage for necessity
MALE	0.484	0.468
GY_REC	0.890	0.785
ABI_1P	0.618	0.728
SC_1P	0.704	0.618

Parental social class comes close to being a quasi-necessary condition, but with a consistency with necessity of 0.704, it falls slightly short of this. Put differently, nearly 30 per cent of cases who attend a Gymnasium at age 17 do not have a parent in the service class. Clearly, it is possible to be in a Gymnasium aged 17 without this social class background. Some other factor, in these 30 per cent of cases, may be operating as an alternative source of support. By contrast, only 11 per cent of cases in the Gymnasium had not received the recommendation for Gymnasium at the end of primary school, making the recommendation much more clearly a quasi-necessary condition.

Before moving on to the classification of cases as typical, deviant and inconclusive and the subsequent analyses of such types via my interviews, I will briefly discuss the implications of the QCA results.

The results are consistent with theoretical expectations: both parental social class and parental education have been shown to be associated with positive educational outcomes in many contexts. Plausible explanatory mechanisms can be suggested by referring to the appropriate theories (see Chapter 4): according to Bourdieu, parents from a high social class background will have the necessary cultural capital and habitus to support their children in performing well in primary school and thus gaining a recommendation for the Gymnasium. It is also possible to draw on Boudon's primary and secondary effects to explain these findings: children from these backgrounds perform better, on average, than their less privileged peers, and they therefore receive the recommendation for the Gymnasium – the primary effect – and they are subsequently more likely to actually attend the Gymnasium, given the recommendation, than other children – the secondary effect (for example Baumert et al., 2003).

The key role of the recommendation became evident in that it is an element of all the quasi-sufficient pathways and that it is, in addition, a quasi-necessary condition on its own. This also fits expectations, given its threefold nature as a proxy for academic ability, social background and system requirement.

However, notwithstanding the theoretical plausibility of these results, questions remain. For one thing, it is important to bear in mind that I have mainly discussed (quasi-)sufficient configurations of conditions so far. Such configurations of sufficient conditions can help explain why cases with certain characteristics obtain the outcome, but given that these configurations of conditions are mostly not (quasi-)necessary (see the coverage figures in Box 5.1), we know that some cases not in these configurations will also achieve Gymnasium entry. In addition, not all the cases showing the configurations of conditions identified as quasi-sufficient actually display the outcome. Finally, there are some configurations where there is no clear trend with regard to whether or not they are associated with the outcome. The next section describes how cases can be classified as typical, deviant and inconclusive on the basis of the results discussed so far, for the purpose of further theoretical exploration.

5.2 Classification and selection of typical, deviant and inconclusive cases

I now explore further the questions that remain following the QCA analysis, using within-case analysis of interview data. QCA has identified some quasi-sufficient pathways to the outcome consistent with theoretical expectations. These are not necessary conjunctions of conditions, however, indicating that many more cases will obtain the outcome than are captured by these (quasi-)sufficient[7] pathways. In addition, given that I have analysed quasi-sufficiency rather than strict sufficiency, there will be some cases that have a conjunction of quasi-sufficient conditions who do not obtain the outcome.

A strictly deterministic model might look like this: CONFIGURATION1 + CONFIGURATION2 + CONFIGURATION3 ⇔ OUTCOME (solution consistency = 1, solution coverage = 1), where the double arrow indicates that the solution is both sufficient and necessary. As we have seen, however, most solutions – including the ones I have found – are less perfect than this, with both consistency and coverage indices below 1. In my earlier discussion of Lieberson's (1997, especially pp. 364–365 and pp. 374–375) understanding of the role of probability in social analyses (end of Section 2.3), I noted that such less than perfect indices might result from true randomness or from less than complete model specification. It is unlikely, of course, that I have included in my models every factor relevant to explaining every individual's outcome. For this reason alone, it could be expected that there would be some cases which deviate from the outcome expected on the basis of quasi-sufficiency and quasi-necessity analyses, and these warrant further investigation, in order to be able to identify additional factors which are associated with the outcome. I extend this approach to those cases found in a number of truth table rows where consistency is not high enough to make them (quasi-)sufficient configurations, but high enough nevertheless that it is not very unusual for the cases described by them to obtain the outcome (for example the configuration male*abi_1p*sc_1p*GY_REC – girls with a Gymnasium recommendation whose parents neither hold the Abitur nor have service class occupations: consistency with sufficiency is 0.639 which means that 63.9 per cent of such cases will attend a Gymnasium aged 17. While this cannot be described as a quasi-sufficient condition, this proportion is higher than the grand mean of 48.4 per cent attending Gymnasium). Such cases can be harder to explain through cross-case large *n* analysis (though it can be possible *if* appropriate variables happen to exist in the data set), both with regard to obtaining and not obtaining the outcome.

My necessity analysis led to the identification of a condition – the recommendation – which was present in most but not all cases. It is to be expected that cases without the recommendation will not be in a Gymnasium at the age of 17, so cases that are in Gymnasium nevertheless are therefore particularly interesting for further analysis, since they have achieved an outcome without having a condition identified as quasi-necessary. Note that the converse is not true to the same extent: while we would normally expect cases with the recommendation to be in the Gymnasium, this outcome does not follow from their having this condition alone,[8] given that it is quasi-necessary but not (quasi-) sufficient (see Figure 3.2 and the associated discussion).

The in-depth case studies presented below are intended to shed some light on the generative mechanisms which led to unexpected pathways. They can also help explore additional pathways which can lead to the outcome and to explain why some cases do not follow the pathways identified via QCA. The next step is therefore to identify typical and deviant cases with regard to the outcome of being in Gymnasium at the age of 17.

George and Bennett (2005), who argue for within-case process-tracing as a route to causal understanding, classify types of cases in terms of their potential value for explaining outcomes, as part of what they term 'typological theorising'. They discuss, among others, deviant, most likely, least likely and crucial cases each of which can play a specific role in confirming or disconfirming the existence of some hypothesised causal pathway. Seawright and Gerring (2008) use a similar categorisation of cases, relying on forms of regression analysis to analyse large data sets and basing subsequent case selection on the pattern of results. Depending on the goal of the analysis, different kinds of cases may be selected. They discuss seven procedures for selecting cases. In keeping with the underlying regression paradigm, a key criterion is whether a case is an 'onlier' (a low-residual case) or an 'outlier' (high-residual). The former is regarded as *typical* for the phenomenon under study, the latter as *deviant*.[9]

For my purposes, the most relevant of these authors' suggestions are to classify cases merely as typical and deviant. In addition, I use a third category which I have termed inconclusive. Before allocating my specific cases to the three categories, I now explain which constellations of conditions and outcome can in principle be classified as typical or deviant, and which constellations are neither, making them inconclusive. By constellations I refer here to the way in which any given configuration of conditions is combined with either presence or absence of the outcome: a constellation can be both conditions and outcome present, conditions absent and outcome present, conditions present and outcome absent and both conditions and outcome absent.

I call cases showing the constellation *presence* of quasi-sufficient combinations of conditions with *presence* of the outcome '*typical with regard to sufficiency*'. Cases combining *presence* of such conditions with *absence* of the outcome, I term '*deviant with regard to sufficiency*'. Concerning necessity, again, cases combining *presence* of a quasi-necessary condition with *presence* of the outcome are '*typical with regard to necessity*'. Cases who are '*deviant with regard to necessity*' combine *absence* of a quasi-necessary condition with *presence* of the outcome (for a more detailed discussion of how cases may be classified as typical and deviant, see Glaesser & Cooper, 2011a).

Inconclusive cases, with or without the outcome, are all those contained within a configuration of conditions which is not (quasi-)sufficient for the outcome, but with a consistency which is higher than the grand mean. In Table 5.1, this comprises truth table rows 6–8. I do not have any cases in my interview sample corresponding to row 6, but I do have cases for rows 7 and 8 which can be summarised as abi_1p*sc_1p*GY_REC (males and females with the recommendation for the Gymnasium whose parents do not have the Abitur and who are not in the service class). My inconclusive category thus only refers to sufficiency; I have not analysed cases that are inconclusive with regard to necessity. The question of particular interest for inconclusive cases is whether, in further analyses, it is possible systematically to identify expanded configurations of conditions that are sufficient for all the inconclusive cases with a particular constellation through more in-depth analysis, in other words, to obtain a model where more truth table rows are close to 1 or 0. Alternatively, it is possible that there is no such shared configuration of conditions that would help explain the outcome, and each case's individual history has to be examined to explain presence or absence of the outcome.

Table 5.3 illustrates which cases were classified as typical, deviant and inconclusive based on the QCA solution and the truth table, and which

Table 5.3 Types of configuration with names of interviewees

Configuration	Outcome	Types of cases	Interviewees (pseudonyms)
ABI_1P*GY_REC	Present	Typical with regard to sufficiency	Alina, Anna, Daniela*, Lena, Ludwig+, Roman, Nicole ($n = 7$)
MALE*SC_1P*GY_REC	Present	Typical with regard to sufficiency	Jonas, Ludwig+ ($n = 2$)
ABI_1P*GY_REC	Absent	Deviant with regard to sufficiency	Samuel ($n = 1$)
MALE*SC_1P*GY_REC	Absent	Deviant with regard to sufficiency	No cases
gy_rec	Present	Deviant with regard to necessity	Sibel, Andreas, Julia*, Christian*, Aynur*, Tessa* ($n = 6$)
male*abi_1p*SC_1P*GY_REC	Present/ Absent	Inconclusive with regard to sufficiency, with or without outcome	No cases
abi_1p*sc_1p*GY_REC	Present	Inconclusive with regard to sufficiency, with outcome	Diana, Jessica, Magdalena, Marina, Marko, Peter, Sebastian, Vanessa* ($n = 8$)
abi_1p*sc_1p*GY_REC	Absent	Inconclusive with regard to sufficiency, without outcome	Kevin, Nadine, Patrick ($n = 3$)

*Daniela, Julia, Christian, Aynur, Tessa and Vanessa are on the Gymnasium route within Gesamtschulen.
+Ludwig appears twice in this table because his constellation of factors is MALE* ABI_1P*SC_1P*GY_REC which is the overlap of the two sufficient pathways ABI_1P*GY_REC and MALE*SC_1P*GY_REC.

interviewees from the full interview sample matched the classification. Note that cases that are typical with regard to necessity (those who have the condition of Gymnasium recommendation and the outcome of being in Gymnasium) are not listed because there are so many of them (though some of them are captured by the typical with regard to sufficiency category given that these all had the recommendation). Likewise, I have only listed the configurations captured by truth table rows 6–8 as inconclusive even though rows 9–11 also have consistencies far away from 1 or 0. I chose to focus on those where there is an absence of particularly favourable parental background conditions coupled with the presence of the recommendation (rows 7 and 8), because I was interested in what makes it possible for some but not others to use the opportunity given by the recommendation to overcome their potential social disadvantage. In addition, as noted above, I chose to focus on configurations with consistencies above the grand mean of 48.5 per cent achieving the outcome of being in Gymnasium.

I drew on solution 3 (Box 5.1) and the necessity analyses from the QCA described above (Table 5.2) as the basis of my classification of typical and deviant cases; and on the truth table itself (Table 5.1) for my classification of inconclusive cases. Recall that solution 3 contained two pathways to the outcome: GY17 = ABI_1P*GY_REC + MALE*SC_1P*GY_REC. Comparing this with solutions 1 and 2 in Box 5.1, we can see that solution 3 is a superset of solutions 1 and 2. This arises because the threshold for consistency used to generate solution 3 was the lowest of the three, which means that it contains all the rows in solutions 1 and 2 as well as some more in addition. In using solution 3 as the basis of my classification, I have chosen the most comprehensive solution rather than privileging one over the others.

I had originally entered some of the interviewees in Table 5.3 under a different school type (see Table 4.3), but they had to be reallocated following the interviews: Daniela, Julia, Christian, Aynur and Tessa are in year 10 in Gesamtschulen, which is where I had entered them originally, but within their Gesamtschule, they are on the Gymnasium track, and their marks are good enough for them to be certain that they will be able to stay on, and they are planning to do so. They are therefore in the same situation as any Gymnasium pupil in year 10 in the sense that they know they will stay on in education post-16 on a track that leads to the Abitur. The same applies to Nicole and Andreas: while they were in year 10 of a Realschule at the time of the interview, they already had a place at a Gymnasium for the following year. Similarly, Peter was chosen on the basis of his having been in the Hauptschule at the start of his secondary schooling, but at the time of the interview, he already attended a Technical Gymnasium. In Table 5.3, I have therefore listed all these cases as having the outcome, attending a Gymnasium at the age of 17. In Table 4.3 in Chapter 4, all these cases are listed under the type of school they initially attended. This reflects the fact that at the time of selecting interviewees, it was not possible for me to be aware of these trajectories; these only became apparent during the interview.

The numbers here are small, not least because out of 43 interviewees, only 26 appear in Table 5.3. This is because the others do not belong to any of the configurations of conditions which form part of the solution of the QCA or to the inconclusive constellations identified as interesting from the truth table, and they therefore cannot be identified as typical, deviant or inconclusive with regard to this particular outcome, being in Gymnasium at the age of 17. Clearly, given a different theoretical focus, analyses of conditions leading to other outcomes or leading to the absence of the outcome studied here could have been undertaken, and I would have identified other conditions and/or configurations of conditions to select these case studies.

In Chapter 2, I noted that description is a crucial step on the way to establishing phenomena that can subsequently be explained. The results of the QCA analyses presented above describe the phenomenon, and they suggest plausible causal processes on the basis of theory and substantive knowledge of the German school system. I will now first explain trajectories and outcomes of *individual* cases and types of cases by referring to the QCA models and existing theory in order to undertake process-tracing and then use the insights from these individual explanations to draw some more *general* lessons wherever possible.

5.3   Typical cases

In this section, I discuss all the cases that are typical with regard to sufficiency because they follow one of the pathways, having at least one parent with the Abitur and having received a recommendation for the Gymnasium (ABI_1P*GY_REC), or being male, having at least one parent in the service class and having received a recommendation for the Gymnasium (MALE*SC_1P*GY_REC). Alina, Anna, Daniela, Lena, Roman and Nicole are on the first pathway, Jonas is on the second, and Ludwig on both.

In Chapter 4, I discussed two competing but compatible theories, rational action theory (RAT) and Bourdieu's habitus theory, which are often used to explain educational outcomes. Glaesser and Cooper

(2014), drawing on interview data from the project which forms the basis of this book, showed how these two theories can be used together. Indeed, the cases identified above as typical behave as expected on the basis of both theories. They have in common that they have a fairly privileged social background, given their parents' high level of education or social class (or both). They also share the recommendation for the Gymnasium which, as discussed above, can be expected to be associated with Gymnasium attendance.

In all their accounts, there is some evidence of RAT-type reasoning with a view to status maintenance or – if possible – upwards mobility, relative to their family of origin. Roman for example, when asked why he was so keen to attend the Gymnasium once he had received the recommendation, reasons: 'ich wollt einfach mich gut bilden, um damit besser einen guten Beruf auszuüben und damit einfach nicht so tätige Arbeit zu tun, also so körperliche Anstrengungen wie bei meinem Vater, der ist Handwerker und bei dem merk ich dann schon, dass er ziemlich angeschlagen ist nach der Arbeit.' ('I just wanted to educate myself well so that I could have a better occupation which wouldn't involve physical work, I mean, physical labour like my father, he's a mechanic and I can see that he's pretty worn out after work.') His view of education sounds fairly instrumental: the benefit of having an eventual better job is worth the effort of staying in a Gymnasium. He also notes that the reason why his parents came to Germany from Poland was to give him and his brother a better life.

Branching points or decision points are of particular importance for RAT theorists[10] given that this is when cost-benefit analyses have to be undertaken. After the transition from primary to secondary school, the next branching point is the decision regarding whether to stay in the Gymnasium, or whether to leave it with the intermediate qualification to enter an apprenticeship. None of the interviewees discussed in this section left the Gymnasium at this point. For most, this didn't even seem like an active decision to be made; they simply stayed on their trajectory. If they do discuss it – whether in relation to themselves or to classmates – it is sometimes with a view to going on to a Technical Gymnasium, so a specialisation on the same level rather than a step down from the current trajectory.

They are now nearing the next branching point in their careers, the decision regarding higher education. Lena for example talks about a mix of motives: she wants to do something that interests her, but also mentions having to choose her degree subject not only on the basis of interest but also with a view of what job it might lead to, and studying abroad to increase her chances of a good job (for a detailed discussion of the transition to higher education, see Chapter 7).

Given that rational decision-making seemed to be a common strategy among the young people in this study (Glaesser & Cooper, 2014), it is not surprising that this was evident in these 'typical' cases, too, regardless of their particular configuration of conditions. However, it is important to bear in mind that the configurations I identified as typical cases are actually summarising descriptions with some configurations collapsed together to create simplified expressions. This is a useful strategy for prediction, but when it comes to undertaking causal explanation on the basis of these types, it is worth bearing in mind that these can contain different configurations (Cooper & Glaesser, 2012a). The configuration ABI_1P*GY_REC, for example, can comprise parents who are or aren't in the service class. In addition, there are some cases in my interview sample who have attended a Gymnasium throughout their secondary schooling career to date, and others who are either in a Gesamtschule or who came to the Gymnasium later on after having attended Realschule initially. These differences may be particularly important with regard to Bourdieu's habitus theory (Bourdieu, 1977): according to habitus theory, we should expect to find that young people act in line with a set of behaviours and dispositions which is common in their family of origin. These dispositions may differ to some degree among the cases discussed here, even though they are categorised together as typical. Alina, Anna and Ludwig[11] come from families where not only at least one parent has the Abitur, but where both parents actually hold degrees and where both parents are members of the service class. These families are also rich in cultural capital (Bourdieu, 1986); literature, classical music, museums and theatre are a normal part of their lives. There is clear evidence of an environment where attending the Gymnasium and subsequently going to university constitutes the norm. They struggled to think of members of their extended families who had not gone to university, and for the ones that were mentioned, sometimes a special explanation was given (for example, Alina mentions her grandmothers who were not able to study for an extended period of time because of the war and having to go to work). Ludwig explicitly talks about how important it was for his father that all his four children attended the Gymnasium because he is highly educated himself and wished the same for his children. This does not sound like cost-benefit analysis, where education is a means to an end, but rather it is an end in itself: 'Mein Vater ist ziemlich gebildet und für den war es halt glaube ich ziemlich wichtig, dass seine Kinder das auch sind und dass sie eben auch auf dem

Gymnasium sind.' ('My father is quite well educated[12] and so I think it was really important for him that his children would be the same and that they would also attend Gymnasium.')

The family habitus of the other five cases in the typical group, Daniela, Lena, Roman, Nicole and Jonas, is slightly different. Just one or neither parents is in the service class, and many do not hold degrees. Attending Gymnasium and university seems a normal and desirable thing to do here, too, but there is more evidence of variety, both with regard to educational pathways in the extended families and in the cases' own. Daniela had chosen not to attend a Gymnasium despite having had the recommendation, but went to a Gesamtschule knowing that she would be able to obtain the Abitur there provided her marks were good enough. This was indeed the case and she is now en route to obtaining the Abitur. Nevertheless, it seems likely that someone from a family like Alina, Anna or Ludwig's would have chosen the more prestigious Gymnasium rather than a Gesamtschule in her position. Nicole also had received the recommendation but her teacher and her parents were concerned that she would struggle to keep up in the Gymnasium, and therefore it would be better for her to attend Realschule initially and then to change to the Gymnasium upon completion of Realschule which is indeed what happened. Among these five cases, alternatives to university are more likely to be mentioned, although university is the preferred option. Roman for example wishes to go to university and his parents share this wish, but there was a phase when his marks weren't very good which led them to suggest that he leave school early and do an apprenticeship instead. Others keep their options open and want to make sure they find something they will enjoy and where they can earn a good living.

Jonas is the only 'typical' case whose parents do not have the Abitur themselves,[13] although his father is an accountant and therefore belongs to the service class. Educational expansion may partly explain the difference between father's and son's educational careers here: advanced secondary and higher education was not required for a stable service class position in Jonas' parents' generation, but since then, educational expansion has taken place which means that many more young people obtained more advanced educational qualifications, and that such qualifications are now more frequently a prerequisite for positions such as Jonas' father's. There is also no experience of advanced secondary or higher education in his family: he points out that he was the first in his family to enter the Gymnasium. This does not worry him; if anything, he sees it as an incentive to do well.

The aim of studying these eight typical cases in more depth was to confirm and possibly refine theory. The findings can be understood in terms of both RAT and habitus theory. It also emerged that a habitus conducive to advanced secondary and higher education seems to take more than one form: there are the most privileged cases where both parents are highly educated and in service class occupations and where such experience goes back at least one generation, but in addition, there are families where a high level of education may be a more recent phenomenon, following educational expansion, but for whom Gymnasium and university are not completely alien, either because there are some members of the extended families who have experienced them, or because the parents are in service class occupations which means that, even if they do not have a degree or the Abitur themselves, they work in an environment where this is not unusual. Obviously, there are differences among the families discussed here, but given the fact that all the cases obtain the outcome, there are clearly alternative sets of processes capable of leading to the outcome, a situation sometimes described by the term equifinality (for example George & Bennett, 2005; Ragin, 2008).

However, the discussion also showed that some important differences might be lost through QCA's summarising form of analysis (see also Cooper & Glaesser, 2012a). The eight cases in the 'typical' category are not all alike. This was true regarding differences between cases on one or the other pathway, and also regarding differences between cases on the same pathway. Accordingly, the causal mechanisms leading to their obtaining the outcome differed slightly. With Alina, Anna and Ludwig, the outcome of being in the Gymnasium seems overdetermined in the sense that even if one factor had been different, they would still have obtained this outcome. With the others, Daniela, Lena, Roman, Nicole and Jonas, a different outcome is easier to imagine, especially for Daniela and Nicole who did not attend the Gymnasium initially. It took some effort on their part to make this transition, especially for Nicole who initially attended a Realschule rather than a Gesamtschule.

5.4   Deviant cases

In this section, I discuss deviant cases falling into two categories. The first is being deviant with regard to sufficiency, that is, not obtaining the outcome despite having a quasi-sufficient configuration of factors. Samuel is the representative of this category. He attends a Realschule despite having the configuration of having at least one parent with Abitur and having received the recommendation for Gymnasium (ABI_1P*GY_REC). The second is being deviant with regard to necessity, that is, obtaining the outcome of attending a Gymnasium age 17 despite lacking the quasi-necessary condition of having received the recommendation for Gymnasium (gy_rec). The cases falling into this category are Sibel, Andreas, Julia, Christian, Aynur and Tessa. I will begin by discussing Samuel, followed by a discussion of the cases that are deviant with regard to necessity.

We have seen that habitus appears to play an important role in explaining why someone is in the Gymnasium. Why is it then that someone from the same family background as the cases discussed in the previous section and with the recommendation, which was shown to be important, does not attend a Gymnasium? Samuel is the representative of this constellation which is deviant with regard to sufficiency. His parents both hold the Abitur, though neither of them is in the service class. His father is a plumber, his mother a seamstress. His case is discussed in some detail in Cooper and Glaesser (2012a), and I will just quote the conclusion we came to in that paper (by X2 in this extract we refer to additional factors – beyond those used in the QCA – that we were looking for in the causal analysis which might help make the causal argument more detailed and more precise):

> [H]e seems to have decided, quite reflectively, early on, that this academic route, and what it led to, was not for him. He had available a model of a self-employed skilled manual working life that appealed to him and he seems to have used this in making cost-benefit (not just financial) comparisons with the alternative academic pathway he could have followed. Perhaps, then, the X2 here is the combination of a considered preference for practical activities coupled with the availability (and holiday experience) of a future job that pays enough, does not require higher education study and is enjoyable and varied. However, it may be that this could be understood, in a less specific sense, as having to do with an absence, i.e. having no immediate family experience of service class work and the opportunities it might offer for a varied working life, etc.[14]

I might add that while there is some experience in his family of the Gymnasium, there is hardly any of higher education (apart from one uncle who lives a long way away) and so it may be less clear to someone like him why he should have gone to the Gymnasium, which offers the higher education entry qualification, in the first place.

I now turn to cases who were deviant in a different way, deviant with regard to necessity: despite having lacked the Gymnasium recommendation, they find themselves en route to the Abitur aged 17. Therefore, I aim to identify conditions which act as substitutes for the missing recommendation. As noted under Table 5.3, four of the six cases who are deviant with regard to necessity attend a Gesamtschule where they are on the Gymnasium track which leads to the Abitur. The first two of those four are Julia and Aynur who are from immigrant families, having come to Germany during their primary school years. The lack of the recommendation was most likely merely due to the fact that their German wasn't good enough at that point (this is the explanation they give themselves, and it seems perfectly plausible). They are both bright, ambitious and high achieving, and, what is more, they are from families similar in habitus to those described under typical cases. This is indicated by their parents' having qualifications equivalent to the Abitur (and, in Julia's case, being members of the service class), and it also became apparent in the interviews when they talked about educational careers in their extended families and cultural activities. The other two Gesamtschule cases are Christian and Tessa. It is not so obvious why these two are on the Gymnasium track, given that their families' habitus is not so clearly conducive to advanced secondary, let alone university education, given that their parents do not have the Abitur, and Tessa's parents are not in the service class either (though Christian's father is). In their extended families and wider social circles, there are some members of their own generation who have attended or are considering university, but none of the previous generations, that is, parents, aunts and uncles, or grandparents. They both seem to be what may be termed 'late developers': while their academic performance in primary school did not allow for them to receive the highest recommendation, their performance improved subsequently, and they benefited from the fact that a relatively easy path to the Abitur exists through the Gesamtschule which provides the necessary support and also the opportunity to experience higher aspirations through teachers and peers. The latter seemed to have played a part for Tessa in particular: she talks about meeting new friends at the Gesamtschule who took school seriously, who got together to study and who took pride in doing well. This showed her that studying and learning are things that can be enjoyed, and provided her with an incentive to work hard, something, incidentally, she most likely would not have experienced had she attended a Hauptschule, as per her recommendation. This is not to say that an academically oriented peer group is sufficient on its own to help someone succeed in the Gymnasium – as can be seen from Tessa's case, individual ability and motivation are also required – but it may well be necessary, whether or not someone had the recommendation for the Gymnasium.

This leaves Sibel and Andreas who both came to the Gymnasium via the Realschule. They live in Baden-Württemberg, where there are no Gesamtschulen. In other ways though, their cases have some resemblance with Christian and Tessa: they were late developers in that their performance at the end of primary was not quite at the standard required for the Gymnasium, but they then caught up and this, together with the organisational possibility of entering the Gymnasium, provided them with the opportunity to study for the Abitur. In addition, Andreas' family's habitus is clearly conducive to his moving on to the Gymnasium, with both his parents holding the Abitur and all three siblings attending Gymnasium (for a more detailed discussion of Andreas and Sibel, see Cooper & Glaesser, 2012a).

It is worth noting that in selecting cases for interview, I had over 100 to choose from who were attending a Gymnasium at the time. Given the clear importance of the recommendation, I would have liked to select more than one case from a Gymnasium without the recommendation to explore what alternative pathways might substitute for having this necessary condition, but Sibel was the only one person attending a Gymnasium who had not received the recommendation at the end of primary school. This piece of anecdotal evidence from my experience during the sampling process for interviewees matches the necessity analysis of the SOEP data for the Gymnasium outcome where the recommendation was shown to have a consistency with necessity of 0.89.

As I suggested above, there are three reasons why the recommendation normally acts as a necessary condition for Gymnasium entry: individual, social and system. In all the cases discussed in this section, Sibel, Andreas, Julia, Christian, Aynur and Tessa, it did actually have its prohibitive effect on the system level given that none of them entered the Gymnasium straight away. Their doing so later on was only possible because the system is not completely rigid and does allow for alternative routes to the Abitur. The reason why the cases discussed here were able to make use of this after their initial deflection are to be found on the individual and social levels. On the individual level, their academic ability proved sufficient for pursuing this course of secondary study, but because of being late developers or because of their immigrant status, this had not been expressed at the end of primary school. Coupled with this, in all cases apart from Tessa, is a family background where there was some experience of the Gymnasium. With Tessa, it appears that the peer group was able to play this role, and this in turn was made possible by the institution of a Gesamtschule where there tends to be a more mixed group of pupils than would be found in a Hauptschule with regard to ability and ambition.

The alternatives to the necessary condition recommendation then appear to be individual ability[15] and ambition coupled with an environment – familial and/or peers – where this could be expressed. Obviously, an institutional arrangement offering alternative routes to Gymnasium entry at age ten is also required.

5.5   Inconclusive cases

Finally, there are some cases where it is not straightforward to predict or explain, on the basis of existing theory and of the factors considered so far, whether or not they can be expected to be in the Gymnasium. I have identified these inconclusive cases within my interview sample on the basis of rows 7 and 8 from the truth table using SOEP data, Table 5.1, which had consistencies of around 0.65, too low to be considered quasi-sufficient but high enough that experiencing the outcome of attending the Gymnasium age 17 is not unusual. It is certainly above the grand mean of 48.4 per cent. They differ in one factor only, gender, so they can be described as one configuration: having received the recommendation for the Gymnasium, but having no parent holding the Abitur and neither parent in the service class (abi_1p*sc_1p*GY_REC). In other words, their families' habitus would not seem conducive to Gymnasium attendance, but their own academic ability clearly makes this possible.[16] These cases are clearly of theoretical interest given that there seems to be the possibility of causal factors pulling in opposite directions. It is therefore not surprising that the truth table (Table 5.1) confirms this expectation, with the consistencies of around 0.65 for the relevant rows indicating that around two-thirds of cases do attend Gymnasium aged 17 and around one-third do not. There are 11 interviewees who fall into this category. As can be seen from Table 5.3, eight of them (Diana, Jessica, Magdalena, Marina, Marko, Peter, Sebastian and Vanessa) attend the Gymnasium; three (Kevin, Nadine and Patrick) do not.

To begin with, it is worth noting that even to receive the recommendation is more unusual for cases with these social background characteristics. Overall, 54.8 per cent of cases in the SOEP data received the Gymnasium recommendation, but only 36 per cent of those whose parents do not hold the Abitur and are not in the service class do. By comparison, for those who have at least one parent with the Abitur and at least one parent in the service class, this figure is 77 per cent (see also my comments at the end of Section 5.1).

Any explanation of their respective pathways can come from two angles: which factors can help overcome the potential disadvantage of growing up in a family with limited or no experience of advanced secondary and higher education, and which factors prevent children with the relevant ability from actually entering, or remaining in, the Gymnasium, which, according to rational choice theorists, should be the one to choose given the opportunity, since it offers the best chances of obtaining a high qualification and returns in the labour market (though for this particular group it is not needed for status maintenance). I start by discussing the first angle, that is, the eight cases who do attend the Gymnasium, followed by a discussion of the second, the three cases who do not.

All of the eight cases who do attend the Gymnasium may be explained, like Jonas, by educational expansion to some extent: it is much more common for their generation compared with their parents' to attend the Gymnasium, so it is to be expected that some Gymnasium pupils will be the first in their families. Diana for example talks of her mother who didn't have the chance to attend the Gymnasium because she was one of nine siblings, growing up in a small village where the only secondary school was a Hauptschule. Her mother wanted her to have opportunities she herself didn't have. The same goes for Marina and Magdalena whose parents emigrated to Germany from Russia and Poland respectively in the hope of finding better lives for themselves and their children. Peter is slightly unusual within this group because he went to a Hauptschule initially and only entered a Technical Gymnasium at the age of 16. However, according to him, the decision not to enter Gymnasium straight away was due to the fact that his uncle, to whom he had been very close, had just died. He therefore decided to stay in a familiar environment (especially in rural areas such as his, primary schools and Hauptschulen are often one school organisationally), knowing that he would be able, given adequate performance, to move to a Gymnasium later on. The existence of a Gesamtschule seems to have been particularly helpful for Vanessa: she said she always wanted to aim for the Abitur because this would make her the first in the family to obtain it, but she was too worried that she would fail the demanding Gymnasium, so she opted for the Gesamtschule which offers the same Abitur, but with the safer option of having the other streams, too. It seems, then, that adequate ambition in the family and the young people themselves coupled with institutional opportunities for obtaining a Gymnasium education may substitute for the lack of an appropriate familial habitus.

What of those cases who did not attend the Gymnasium, despite the fact that the same would apply? It is harder here to find a common factor. Specific explanations are possible, however. Patrick is straightforward: he did actually enter the Gymnasium after primary school, but in year 8 his marks were so low that he had to repeat a year. This, however, was during a phase of organisational change within Gymnasien: the years spent in a Gymnasium were reduced from nine to eight years. He had entered Gymnasium under the old system of nine years, but the year below his was under the new regime which meant that they were following a different curriculum. Therefore, the 'new' year 8 was more advanced than his 'old' year 8 and it was not possible simply to repeat year 8 in the Gymnasium. He therefore repeated year 8 in a Realschule, and at the time of the interview it was not yet certain whether he would be able to enter a Technical Gymnasium. Such reorganisation of the school system is an example of a causal process acting outside the set of causal factors under study. Nothing in Patrick's background, prior experience or individual characteristics would have allowed me to model what seems like a random factor, but in another field of interest, it would have been perfectly possible to model the causal processes that led to the reorganisation, so in that sense it is not a random event.

Nadine and Kevin were both worried that they would not be able to keep up with the work in the Gymnasium. In Nadine's case, this is because her father had had a negative experience, having been to Gymnasium but not coping with the work, and in Kevin's case, it is because he only barely achieved the marks required for the recommendation and he therefore decided that Gymnasium would be too difficult.

It seems then that for this group of relatively underprivileged young people with regard to their social class background, the decision following the recommendation is not straightforward. We see some evidence of anxiety about whether they will cope with the work (Magdalena, Kevin, Nadine, Vanessa), and more scope for critical life events to get in the way, as with Peter. While it is obviously impossible to be sure on the basis of this sample of interviewees, it seems conceivable that for someone from a family where attending the Gymnasium is the norm, even a tragic event like the death of an uncle would not have prevented the child's going to Gymnasium. In families where there is some experience of the Gymnasium, it is much more self-evident that the recommendation will lead to Gymnasium. Lena for example, whose father and brother as well as various members of her extended family all attended the Gymnasium, told me that 'ich hab mir glaub ich gar keine Gedanken drüber gemacht. Wenn ich auf's Gymnasium kann, dann geh ich ja aufs Gymnasium.' ('I don't think I thought about it much. If I get to go to Gymnasium, then of course I'll go.') This is not something most of the relatively underprivileged young people discussed in this section would have said. Most of them – including those who did decide to enter the Gymnasium – reported some anxiety and uncertainty around the decision.

5.6 Lessons from the analysis of interviews

I now use the findings from the interviews to refine the analysis of configurations of sufficient and necessary conditions based on the SOEP data. To begin with, I focus on lessons to be learnt from the analysis of typical cases. As noted, this particular analysis confirmed theoretical expectations arising from RAT and habitus theory. While consistency with sufficiency of the solution on which the selection of typical cases was based (the configuration ABI_1P*GY_REC + MALE*SC_1P*GY_REC) was high at 0.855, it also showed that some cases within this configuration do not actually achieve the outcome, and I now use the insights gained through the interviews to attempt to refine this analysis. The interviews showed that there was a subgroup of cases who seemed particularly prone to attending a Gymnasium. Alina, Anna and Ludwig are all from such families with a habitus which seemed to make attendance at anything other than Gymnasium and, later on, university, an unusual thing to do. This was less pronounced in the other 'typical' cases, despite the fact that their families also had first-hand experience of Gymnasium attendance, service class occupations or both. Alina, Anna and Ludwig share the characteristics of having both parents in the service class, and having two parents who not only hold the Abitur but a degree. In the SOEP data, the consistency with sufficiency of this configuration, GY_REC*DEGREE_2P*SC_2P at 0.951 is considerably higher than 0.855, though coverage is only at 0.203 (compared with 0.634 for ABI_1P*GY_REC + MALE*SC_1P*GY_REC). One of the limitations of the SOEP is that there are no data on the extended family. But this seemed to have some importance for the young people's pathways, judging from the interview accounts. However, having both parents holding degrees *and* both parents as members of the service class may be seen as a proxy for an extended family in which high expectations with regard to educational pathways are normal. As suggested above, the fact that QCA produces summarising solutions does entail some loss of information. The cases captured by the solution, while fairly similar, do not share all the characteristics and, accordingly, they differ slightly concerning the likelihood with which they obtain the outcome. In terms of theoretical lessons to be learnt, it seems that the closer a case is to a habitus associated with high social class occupations and high educational credentials, the more closely such a case will follow a similar route to the overdetermined cases I have described here, one where Gymnasium followed by university is the usual outcome.

The analysis of interviews with deviant cases can also be used to specify further the type of family most conducive to their children's Gymnasium attendance. Samuel was the case I discussed as being deviant with regard to sufficiency. He had received the Gymnasium recommendation and his parents both hold the Abitur, but they are not in the service class and they do not have degrees. As above, I therefore investigated the role of parental degrees as a proxy for a certain family habitus. In the SOEP data, within the configuration of GY_REC*ABI_1P, the percentage of cases obtaining the outcome whose parents do not hold degrees is 71.9 per cent, compared with 88.6 per cent of cases where at least one parent does. 71.9 per cent is below the threshold for consistency used here. We can see that were we to add this factor, then Samuel would no longer be categorised as a deviant case, since the configuration GY_REC*ABI_1P*DEGREE_0P would not be a quasi-sufficient condition for the outcome. This finding also lends further support to the conclusion I came to at the end of the previous paragraph, that a situation where both educational credentials and social class in the family are high is one that is most conducive to obtaining high qualifications for the children.

Following the analysis of cases who were deviant with regard to necessity, I investigated possible factors which can act as substitutes for the quasi-necessary condition of recommendation. Again, the role of educational qualifications held in the family was shown to be important in the cases whose interviews I discussed above, and I therefore tested the consistency with necessity of having either the recommendation *or* having at least one parent with the Abitur. This is 0.955, considerably higher than the consistency for either the recommendation (0.890) or parental Abitur (0.618) alone.

The analysis of interviews with inconclusive cases showed that there is no obviously identifiable common factor shared between them that could be investigated through analyses of the SOEP. Those who do find themselves in Gymnasium at the age of 17 are characterised by a certain amount of ambition and interest in academic work, and they also share a peer group conducive to developing such ambitions and interests. However, compared with the typical and overdetermined cases, particular life events seem to have more scope for having an impact on this group. Factors such as peer group effects and individual life events with their consequences can be difficult to investigate on the basis of survey data, though peer groups may be investigated using school and classroom level data which are available in some surveys (see Marsh, 1987, for an example of work on peer group effects based on survey data).

5.7 Conclusion

In this chapter, drawing on Bourdieu's habitus theory (Bourdieu, 1977) and on rational action theory (Breen & Goldthorpe, 1997), I analysed the role of social background to explain young people's Gymnasium attendance. The QCA analyses and the more detailed case analyses based on interview accounts showed that the family has indeed a key role in explaining Gymnasium attendance. QCA was employed to identify regularities in the data. However, as discussed in Chapter 2, regularities alone are not enough to provide causal explanations. The interview analyses were used to supplement QCA in two ways. Firstly, in analysing typical cases' accounts, it was possible to identify possible causal mechanisms more securely than would have been possible on the basis of QCA alone. Secondly, the interviews were used to probe further those areas where QCA indicated that some cases fall outside the pathways identified as quasi-sufficient and quasi-necessary for Gymnasium attendance in the analyses. In using the interviews, I tried to achieve a balance between explaining individual cases and identifying more commonly occurring patterns and regularities. For most interviewees, it is relatively straightforward to explain their particular outcome based on their individual circumstances, but there is a danger here in losing sight of the bigger picture and of a loss of generalisability; not generalisability in the statistical sense, but in the sense that causal mechanisms may be identified which are likely to be applicable to a wider range of cases. For example, the social context – whether in the form of family or peers – was shown to be important in explaining Gymnasium attendance in all cases. Thus, I have contributed to explaining the individual outcomes via a form of biographical analysis through process-tracing as well as, simultaneously, the patterns of outcomes.

As noted, survey data are useful for detecting cross-case patterns in a large data set, but the trade-off is a lack of in-depth information regarding specific factors which have been shown to be of potential interest. A particular example here concerns extended family and peer group influences which, based on the interview accounts, seem to be important, but which could not be easily analysed using SOEP data. However, I used the existence of degrees among the parents as a proxy for a family where high educational aspirations and experiences are the norm to show that the closer a family is to providing such support for a positive view of education, the closer the family environment comes to being a sufficient condition (coupled with the quasi-necessary condition of the Gymnasium recommendation) for the child's Gymnasium attendance. With decreasing conformity to such an ideal-typical family, other factors increase in importance, such as individual academic ability (as far as could be ascertained on the basis of the data used here, that is, the recommendation which was used as a proxy for academic ability despite the shortcomings of this measure, as well as the interviewees' own account of their attainment), peer group, and organisational factors such as the existence of a Gesamtschule or institutional provisions for correcting early educational decisions.

6
Secondary Schooling Careers in England

This chapter explores young people's educational careers in England. It mirrors the German analyses presented in the previous chapter to some extent, although differences between the two countries and differences in the data available to perform the analyses mean that the two chapters do not exactly map onto each other.

I begin by analysing Longitudinal Study of Young People in England (LSYPE) data (described in Chapter 4) to establish which types of cases are still in full-time education after the minimum school leaving age of 16, and which are planning to attend university later on. I then use my findings to classify interviewees as typical, deviant and inconclusive, as in Chapter 5. The subsequent analyses of interviews serve to explore further the causal processes underlying the outcomes under study, and in addition they will shed some light on how young people end up in a particular type of secondary school and the way social background factors are connected to this.

6.1 QCA findings

As noted, there are not always obvious parallels with the German analyses described in the previous chapter. England's largely comprehensive system does not have a type of school directly comparable to a German Gymnasium, except in a small number of local authorities. While selective schools exist, both in the state and independent sectors, their affordability and regional availability are much more varied than that of German Gymnasien. Instead of focussing on type of school attended, as I did for the German analyses, I therefore consider two alternative outcomes. The first one is whether the young person is still in full-time education at the age of 17. This gives an indication of likely chances of further and higher education as well as associated potential careers. The second outcome

I consider is whether someone expects that they will attend university. Some English pupils take such plans into account as early as the age of 14, when they make their option choices for GCSE subjects, and again when they choose subjects for A-level study aged 16. While a 17-year-old's expectation of university attendance is obviously at this stage an intention only, Anders and Micklewright (2013), using LSYPE data, show that expectation to apply to university and actually applying are highly correlated. In addition, this outcome of expecting to attend university is likely to be more academically and socially selective than being in full-time education at the age of 17. This is indeed the case, as I will show.

The conditions used in the German analyses were gender, whether at least one parent had the Abitur, whether at least one parent was in the service class, and whether the recommendation at the end of primary school was for the Gymnasium. Initially, I use the first three in the English analyses (with parental A-levels in place of Abitur). There is a measure of academic achievement at the end of primary schooling in the LSYPE data (performance in the key stage 2 test), but given that I do not have such a performance measure for my interviewees, I will not be able to use this to classify types of cases as the basis for the selection of interviewees. For this reason, I undertake analyses without this achievement measure initially, followed by parallel analyses with key stage 2 test results added as a fourth factor.

6.1.1   QCA without key stage 2 test, outcome 'in full-time education age 17'

Table 6.1 is the truth table setting out the configurations of conditions and their consistency with sufficiency for the outcome of being in full-time education age 17.

As is to be expected, the configurations where parents' level of education and their social class match (rows 1, 3, 5 and 8) contain more cases than those where they do not. Another point worth noting about this truth table is that the consistencies are fairly high altogether, with even the lowest well above 0.5, indicating that the majority of young people remain in full-time education beyond the legal school leaving age, regardless of social background (see also Table 4.1 in Chapter 4).

To assess which configurations are consistent with sufficiency, I have obtained Boolean solutions using three different thresholds (Box 6.1). Given that 0.8 is a commonly chosen cut-off point for quasi-sufficiency, I chose to use it as one of the thresholds, but since the consistencies of rows 3 and 4 in Table 6.1 are fairly close together, I did not think it justified not to include row 4 at all, so I obtained a third solution to cover the first four rows, effectively using a threshold of 0.79.

Each solution in Box 6.1 contains the combination of having at least one parent with A-levels and at least one parent in the service class, though at the highest level of consistency this has to be coupled with being female. However, solutions 2 and 3 have fairly high consistencies,

Table 6.1 Truth table, outcome full-time education age 17, three conditions

Row no.	Male	At least one parent with A-levels	At least one parent in the service class	Number	In full-time education age 17	Consistency
1	0	1	1	1,114		0.911
2	0	0	1	275		0.822
3	1	1	1	1,123		0.817
4	0	1	0	422		0.791
5	0	0	0	659		0.741
6	1	1	0	442		0.701
7	1	0	1	266		0.677
8	1	0	0	671		0.626

Box 6.1 Solutions for Table 6.1, outcome full-time education age 17, three conditions

Solution 1: 0.9 threshold

	Raw Coverage	Unique Coverage	Consistency
male*ALEVEL_1P*SC_1P	0.261	0.261	0.911

Solution coverage: 0.261
Solution consistency: 0.911

Solution 2: 0.8 threshold

	Raw Coverage	Unique Coverage	Consistency
male*SC_1P+	0.319	0.058	0.893
ALEVEL_1P*SC_1P	0.497	0.236	0.864

Solution coverage: 0.555
Solution consistency: 0.859

(continued)

Box 6.1   Continued

Solution 3: 0.79 threshold

	Raw Coverage	Unique Coverage	Consistency
male*SC_1P+	0.319	0.058	0.893
male*ALEVEL_1P+	0.347	0.086	0.878
ALEVEL_1P*SC_1P	0.497	0.236	0.864

Solution coverage: 0.641
Solution consistency: 0.850

too, both for the solutions overall and for the individual pathways, indicating that the combination of having at least one parent with A-levels and at least one parent in the service class is also a sufficient combination of conditions for boys. In addition, solution 3 in Box 6.1 shows that for girls it is sufficient to have just one of the two conditions related to parental education and class, although the unique coverage figures here are fairly low. This is a result of the fact that it is more common to have both conditions, parental A-levels and parental service class status, together. In other words, there is much overlap between the sets or configurations. Many cases do not just belong to one or the other pathway but to both.

6.1.2   QCA without key stage 2 test, outcome 'HE likely age 17'

In a next step, I used the same conditions to identify pathways associated with expecting to go to university. Table 6.2 is the truth table.

The numbers of cases in each row (or configuration) are the same as in Table 6.1, given that they result from the same combinations of conditions, but the order of the configurations by consistency is different. In addition, the consistency figures are lower overall. As noted above, this was to be expected given the higher selectivity of this branching point in an educational career. Again, I present solutions for different levels of consistency (Box 6.2), though only two this time instead of three given that the consistencies of rows 3–8 are too low to be considered quasi-sufficient (even my solution 2, with a cut-off point of 0.74, is below what many scholars would consider quasi-sufficient).

Table 6.2 Truth table, outcome HE expectation age 17, three conditions

Row no.	Male	At least one parent with A-levels	At least one parent in the service class	Number	HE likely age 17	Consistency
1	0	1	1	1,114		0.823
2	1	1	1	1,123		0.742
3	0	1	0	422		0.673
4	0	0	1	275		0.662
5	0	0	0	659		0.571
6	1	1	0	442		0.538
7	1	0	1	266		0.504
8	1	0	0	671		0.398

Box 6.2   Solutions for Table 6.2, outcome HE expectation age 17, three conditions

---

Solution 1: 0.8 threshold

	Raw Coverage	Unique Coverage	Consistency
male*ALEVEL_1P*SC_1P	0.284	0.284	0.823

Solution coverage: 0.284
Solution consistency: 0.823

Solution 2: 0.74 threshold

	Raw Coverage	Unique Coverage	Consistency
ALEVEL_1P*SC_1P	0.542	0.542	0.782

Solution coverage: 0.542
Solution consistency: 0.782

Again, the importance of having at least one parent educated to at least A-level coupled with at least one parent in the service class becomes clear. This is quasi-sufficient for their children to aspire to go to university. Having just one but not the other is not sufficient here, either for boys or for girls.

6.1.3   QCA with key stage 2 test, outcome 'in full-time education age 17'

I now return to the outcome of staying in full-time education after compulsory schooling, adding academic achievement as indicated by the overall result of the key stage 2 test as a fourth condition (Table 6.3). High performance here is defined as being in the top half of the distribution, that is, I split the sample at the median (see Section 4.5.1).

I noted above that 0.8 is a commonly used threshold, but in this truth table, the two rows above and below a consistency of 0.8 (rows 7 and 8 in Table 6.3) are particularly close together again, so that it did not seem justified to use this as a cut-off. Instead, as before, I took account of jumps in the consistencies of the rows to decide on cut-off points for the Boolean analyses, obtaining two solutions, one using a threshold of 0.85 and one of 0.75. Box 6.3 shows these solutions.

Box 6.3   Solutions for Table 6.3, outcome full-time education age 17, four conditions

---

Solution 1: 0.85 threshold

	Raw Coverage	Unique Coverage	Consistency
ALEVEL_1P*SC_1P*KS2+	0.398	0.189	0.912
male*ALEVEL_1P*KS2+	0.261	0.053	0.933
male*SC_1P*KS2	0.247	0.038	0.940

Solution coverage: 0.489
Solution consistency: 0.909

Solution 2: 0.75 threshold

	Raw Coverage	Unique Coverage	Consistency
KS2+	0.683	0.474	0.875
male*ALEVEL_1P*SC_1P	0.261	0.052	0.911

Solution coverage: 0.735
Solution consistency: 0.869

Table 6.3 Truth table, outcome full-time education age 17, four conditions

Row no.	Male	At least one parent with A-levels	At least one parent in the service class	High performance in key stage 2 test	In full-time education age 17	Number	Consistency
1	0	1	1	1		858	0.945
2	0	0	1	1		163	0.914
3	0	1	0	1		232	0.888
4	1	1	1	1		839	0.877
5	0	0	0	1		280	0.825
6	1	1	0	1		244	0.811
7	1	0	1	0		150	0.807
8	0	1	1	1		256	0.797
9	1	0	0	1		271	0.756
10	0	0	1	0		112	0.688
11	0	0	0	0		379	0.678
12	0	1	1	0		190	0.674
13	1	1	1	1		284	0.641
14	1	1	0	0		198	0.566
15	1	0	0	0		400	0.537
16	1	0	1	0		116	0.509

At the higher consistency level, early academic achievement features in all three pathways associated with the outcome of being in full-time education at age 17. It is not sufficient on its own, however, but has to be combined, for girls, with high levels of parental education or social class, and with both for boys (solution 1 in Box 6.3). The solution obtained using a lower cut-off level (solution 2 in Box 6.3) does contain academic achievement on its own as a quasi-sufficient condition, but it also includes a second pathway which does not contain high academic achievement at all. It is quasi-sufficient to be a girl with at least one parent with A-levels and at least one parent in the service class without high academic achievement. The unique coverage for this pathway is fairly low, however, indicating that it is not very common to have this constellation of social background factors *without* being in the top half of the key stage 2 test distribution.

In all three analyses I have presented so far (and in the fourth one which uses higher education expectations as outcome again, reported below (Table 6.4)), female gender appeared in some of the solutions, indicating that these combinations of conditions were sufficient for girls but not boys. Inspection of the truth tables also points to a particular role of gender, and I will use the analysis of staying in full-time education with four conditions (Table 6.3) to illustrate how the truth table itself can be used to explore further some relationships between factors and outcomes. The first thing that is noticeable in Table 6.3 is that the rows which contain high academic achievement are (mostly) in the top half of the table, that is, they have higher levels of consistency. This is not surprising given that high academic achievement can be expected to be associated with staying on in education. However, there is one exception: row 8 comprises girls who are *not* in the top half of the test distribution, but a higher proportion of them stay on in education than found in the next row which contains boys who are in the top half (consistencies of 0.797 and 0.756 respectively). The girls in row 8 are from the most privileged social background, with parents holding A-levels and service class occupations, whereas the boys in row 9 are from the least privileged background, with neither parent in either of these social positions. However, the difference in consistency is not large.[1]

This suggests that gender is worth exploring in more detail. If gender made no difference, we would have expected boys and girls with the same social background factors and the same academic achievement to be close together with regard to consistency, but they are not. I therefore now explore the role of gender for other parts of the truth table. To do so, I employ a procedure we have used elsewhere, the pairwise comparison of truth table rows (Glaesser & Cooper, 2012a, 2012b, see also Ragin &

Bradshaw, 1991 for a related approach). This makes it possible to explore the role of one particular factor without losing the configurational nature of the analysis. Consider rows 1 and 4, for example. They only differ on gender, but not on social background and academic achievement factors.[2] The difference is around seven percentage points between boys and girls. Differences of similar magnitudes are to be found between the other configurations that only differ on gender and where academic achievement is high. The differences between boys and girls sharing the same constellation of social background factors are greater still when academic achievement is lower. For example, the difference between boys and girls whose parents neither hold A-levels nor service class occupations and whose own academic achievement is in the bottom half of the distribution (rows 11 and 15) is 14 percentage points.[3]

As mentioned, one reason for undertaking this exercise is to focus on a particular factor without losing the advantages of the configurational approach.[4] While the QCA solutions themselves can point to important individual factors, they focus on identifying configurations that are quasi-sufficient for the outcome under study. Pairwise comparisons allow us to explore relationships between factors and an outcome at different levels of consistency. Obviously, it is interesting to find quasi-sufficient configurations conditions for some outcome, but given a change of perspective which entails an interest in a particular condition, the pairwise approach offers a useful supplement. In this particular case, I have been able to show that the same constellation of social background and academic achievement is associated with different levels of participation in full-time education for boys and girls, with the size of the gap at seven percentage points for the most privileged social background group and 14 percentage points for the least privileged.

6.1.4   QCA with key stage 2 test, outcome 'HE likely age 17'

Finally, in this section I present an analysis with academic achievement included of the outcome of whether the young person thinks it likely that they will go to university, that is, an extension of the analysis of Table 6.2 (see Table 6.4).

We can see that consistencies are, predictably, lower than for the outcome of being in full-time education at the age of 17. The case numbers are the same for each row as those in Table 6.3, but the order of the rows by consistency differs. Box 6.4 shows two Boolean solutions.

A key difference – apart from the levels of consistency – compared with the outcome of being in full-time education age 17 is that we do not find a pathway here where high academic achievement on its own is sufficient for the outcome. It has to be combined with a favourable

Table 6.4 Truth table, outcome HE expectation age 17, four conditions

Row no.	Male	At least one parent with A-levels	At least one parent in the service class	High performance in key stage 2 test	Number	HE likely age 17	Consistency
1	0	1	1	1	858		0.888
2	1	1	1	1	839		0.828
3	0	0	1	1	163		0.798
4	0	1	0	1	232		0.797
5	0	0	0	1	280		0.693
6	1	1	0	1	244		0.668
7	1	0	1	1	150		0.660
8	0	1	1	0	256		0.605
9	1	0	0	1	271		0.587
10	0	1	0	0	190		0.521
11	1	1	1	0	284		0.486
12	0	0	0	0	379		0.480
13	0	0	1	0	112		0.464
14	1	1	0	0	198		0.379
15	1	0	1	0	116		0.302
16	1	0	0	0	400		0.270

Box 6.4 Solutions for Table 6.4, outcome HE expectation age 17, four conditions

Solution 1: 0.8 threshold

	Raw Coverage	Unique Coverage	Consistency
ALEVEL_1P*SC_1P*KS2	0. 451	0. 451	0.859

Solution coverage: 0.451
Solution consistency: 0.859

Solution 2: 0.75 threshold

	Raw Coverage	Unique Coverage	Consistency
male*SC_1P*KS2+	0.276	0.040	0.874
male*ALEVEL_1P*KS2+	0.293	0.057	0.869
ALEVEL_1P*SC_1P*KS2	0.451	0.215	0.859

social background in the form of parental A-levels, service class position or, for boys, with both. This is true of both solutions in Box 6.4. On the other hand, there is now no sufficient pathway which does not contain academic achievement. Note that high academic achievement as defined here is not a very selective measure, given that it merely indicates having performed above the median at key stage 2. However, in a context where more than half of a cohort of young people attend university, it might have been expected that the requirement for academic achievement would not be very high, either, and so it is not surprising that this level of achievement is adequate, forming a part of all the sufficient pathways. In addition, the fact that it has to be combined with social background indicates that higher education aspirations are not developed merely on the basis of academic performance.

6.1.5 Necessity analyses

From the sufficiency analyses presented above, the question arises whether academic achievement above the median is a necessary condition for either of the two outcomes. In Table 6.5 and Table 6.6, I present the results of tests for necessity for all four conditions used in these

Table 6.5   Test of necessity, outcome in full-time education age 17

Condition	Consistency with necessity	Coverage for necessity
MALE	0.470	0.731
ALEVEL_1P	0.662	0.831
SC_1P	0.601	0.842
KEYSTAGE2_HIGH	0.683	0.875
wc_2p	0.907	0.796
GCSE_1P	0.901	0.794

Table 6.6   Test of necessity, outcome HE likely age 17

Condition	Consistency with necessity	Coverage for necessity
MALE	0.456	0.588
ALEVEL_1P	0.703	0.733
SC_1P	0.639	0.744
KEYSTAGE2_HIGH	0.739	0.786
wc_2p	0.922	0.671
GCSE_1P	0.909	0.655

analyses, as well as for two additional conditions, having both parents in the working class, and having at least one parent with GCSEs.

At a consistency level of 0.75 or above, none of the conditions used in the sufficiency analyses above are necessary conditions for the two outcomes on their own. Using a more lenient threshold of 0.7, we find that both having at least one parent with A-levels and having high early academic achievement are quasi-necessary conditions for the outcome of expecting to go to university. Even at this lower level, none of the conditions used in the sufficiency analysis is a necessary condition for being in full-time education age 17. This partly reflects the fact that it is fairly common for young people to stay on in education, almost regardless of social background.

I have added two additional conditions to the ones used in the sufficiency analyses in order to explore the role of coming from a lower social class background. As can be seen from Table 6.5 and Table 6.6, the *absence* of the condition of having two working-class parents, or, in other words, having at least one parent who is not in the working class, is a quasi-necessary condition for both outcomes, staying on in education and expecting to go to university. So is having at least one parent with GCSEs.

Summing up the insights gained through the four QCA analyses, parental education and parental social class both play a part in accounting for educational careers. Many of the pathways associated with the two outcomes described here contain both having at least one parent with A-levels and at least one parent in the service class. The presence of these social background measures also was part of solutions where the analysis had included the measure of prior achievement, the key stage 2 test (Table 6.3, Box 6.3, Table 6.4 and Box 6.4). An exception was one solution where having had a test result in the top half of the distribution was sufficient on its own, without being combined with either parental qualification or parental social class, for staying in full-time education at the age of 17 (Table 6.3 and solution 2 in Box 6.3).

In those analyses where I included early academic achievement (Table 6.3, Box 6.3, Table 6.4 and Box 6.4) as indicated by key stage 2 results, this achievement factor was an element of all the sufficient pathways, with one exception: for girls, coming from a privileged social background is quasi-sufficient for staying in full-time education beyond the age of 16, regardless of early academic achievement (solution 2, Box 6.3).

As was the case for the German analyses, these results fit theoretical expectations well: parents with the requisite cultural capital encourage their children to stay in education and to develop the aspirations to attend university. A rational choice approach is also compatible with this finding. While the benefits of higher educational levels are potentially the same regardless of social class, the perceived cost of attaining a level of education lower than that of one's parents can mean that children from more highly educated backgrounds are more highly motivated to continue their education. At the same time, lower educational parental levels can be associated with a greater fear of failure in a more demanding course of study.

6.2 Classification and selection of typical, deviant and inconclusive cases

The QCA analyses described above give some useful insights into the likely pathways of young people in the English education system. As with the German data, I now build on these insights to develop more detailed accounts of educational pathways and possible explanations of the phenomena established via QCA, drawing on my interviews. Typical cases can be used to assess to what extent existing explanatory theory is suitable for explaining their outcomes, while deviant and inconclusive cases will serve to develop theory. I follow the procedure for case classification and selection outlined in Chapter 5. The resulting classification is summarised in Table 6.7.

The outcome chosen for the classification of cases is whether someone at the age of 16–17 currently intends to go to university. The other outcome analysed via QCA above, being in full-time education at the age of 17, is not specific or selective enough to provide a good comparison with the outcome analysed for Germany, being in Gymnasium at the age of 17, given the high number of cases with this outcome which would mean that most cases are typical with regard to obtaining this outcome. However, I will analyse three cases (in addition to the 27 I identify as typical, deviant and inconclusive in the next section) who are *not* in full-time education at the age of 17, regardless of any condition or configuration of conditions. I decided to do so because it is fairly unusual in itself to leave education at the age of 16: in the LSYPE sample, 21.7 per cent of cases were in this group. These three interviewees are Amy, Leanne and Duncan (none of whom appear in Table 6.7).

Given that I do not have ability or achievement data for my interviewees, I draw on the analysis which was based on three conditions (gender, parental education and parental social class) as the basis for classification into typical, deviant and inconclusive. The relevant truth table is Table 6.2, and the solution I draw on for identifying sufficient configurations of conditions is solution 2 in Box 6.2. It consisted of the single pathway ALEVEL_1P*SC_1P. In addition, I draw on the necessity analysis presented in Table 6.6, though, again, I am unable to use key stage 2 test as a factor because I do not have the relevant data for my interviewees. Therefore, for the classification I draw on the other three conditions: having at least one parent with A-levels (ALEVEL_1P), not having both parents in the working class (wc_2p) and having at least one parent with GCSEs (GCSE_1P). The first of those, ALEVEL_1P, is consistent with quasi-necessity at a level of 0.703 only. While I would have preferred not to use a quasi-necessary condition with such a low level of consistency (in line with the parallel decision in Chapter 5), ALEVEL_1P is the only one of the three conditions approaching quasi-necessity that I had also used in the sufficiency analyses. The quasi-necessary condition I used for the German typology also featured in the sufficiency analyses, and I wanted to keep this aspect of the two analyses the same which is why I chose to use ALEVEL_1P for the English typology despite its low level of consistency with necessity.

27 out of 36 available interviewees are covered by the types of cases summarised in Table 6.7. The other nine did not fall into any of the categories here. The inconclusive cases are drawn from rows 4 and 7 in the truth table, Table 6.2 (males and females collapsed to give the configuration of not having at least one parent with A-levels, but having at

Table 6.7 Types of configuration with names of interviewees

Configuration	Outcome	Types of cases	Interviewees (pseudonyms)
ALEVEL_1P*SC_1P	Present	Typical with regard to sufficiency	Benjamin, Beth, Charlotte, David, Denise, Georgia, Helen, Kalvinder, Maya, Philippa, Saskia, Vicky, William ($n = 13$)
ALEVEL_1P*SC_1P	Absent	Deviant with regard to sufficiency	Deborah, Kelly, Marcus, Thomas ($n = 4$)
alevel_1p	Present	Deviant with regard to necessity	Emily, Paul, Rosie ($n = 3$)
WC_2P	Present	Deviant with regard to necessity	Lauren, Patricia ($n = 2$)
gcse_1p	Present	Deviant with regard to necessity	No cases
alevel_1p*SC_1P	Present	Inconclusive with regard to sufficiency, with outcome	Emily, Rosie ($n = 2$)
alevel_1p*SC_1P	Absent	Inconclusive with regard to sufficiency, without outcome	No cases
ALEVEL_1P*sc_1p	Present	Inconclusive with regard to sufficiency, with outcome	Alexandra, Hannah, Lauren, Matthew, Patricia, Ruth, Samantha ($n = 7$)
ALEVEL_1P*sc_1p	Absent	Inconclusive with regard to sufficiency, without outcome	No cases

least one parent in the service class, alevel_1p*SC_1P) and rows 3 and 6 in Table 6.2 (males and females collapsed to give the configuration of having at least one parent with A-levels, but not having a parent in the service class, ALEVEL_1P*sc_1p).

6.3 Typical cases

There are 13 cases in the category of typical cases with regard to sufficiency for having the outcome of higher education aspirations. These are young people who have at least one parent in the service class and at least one parent with A-levels, and who are planning to go to university. Analogous to the way I used the SOEP data for the German cases, this classification of typical cases in the interview sample was based on evidence from the LSYPE. The findings fit theoretical expectations. Bourdieu's theories on habitus and cultural capital (Bourdieu, 1977, 1986) are compatible with the finding that parental education and social class, as indicated by occupation, jointly predict university aspirations. Rational action theory (Boudon, 1974; Breen & Goldthorpe, 1997; Goldthorpe, 1996b) focusses on social class and predicts that status maintenance is an important motive, so in order to gain their parents' high social class status, these young people may be expected to opt for higher education which is seen as a route to such status maintenance.

I suggested above that there should be a connection between the nature of the school attended and whether a young person develops university aspirations. I therefore start the exploration of the typical cases discussed here by examining the type of secondary school they went to, how they came to choose their school, and their parents' role in this transition. The six school types covered by my interviewees are comprehensive with sixth form, comprehensive without sixth form, grammar school in Kent, secondary modern school in Kent, independent school, and voluntary aided comprehensive. Out of the 13 typical cases described here, just one, David, was in the comprehensive without a sixth form; the others are in the other two comprehensives (both with sixth form, one of them voluntary aided) and the two selective schools (state grammar and independent). None of these cases attended the secondary modern school.

Some interviewees talked about the transition to secondary school in terms of their own wishes and decisions, but given that they were only around ten or 11 years of age at the time it may be expected that their parents also had an influence on this transition, and possibly quite a considerable one. David is the only one whose family does not seem to have explored different secondary schools and subsequently weighed up their relative advantages and disadvantages. His school is a small comprehensive school with no sixth form in a fairly deprived area. Its academic reputation is not good, but it is his local school, his brother was already there, and most of the children from his primary school went there, too. In the other 12 cases, parents were involved in visiting different schools and using league tables as well as more informal kinds of information to choose a secondary school. For example: 'through looking at the results tables, along with my parents we came to a decision to come to this school because of the results it achieved' (Benjamin). Some of those who chose an independent school referred to local state secondary schools as not being satisfactory, whereas others made it clear that they considered the private sector generally preferable: 'it's simply because [my parents] feel [private] education is not necessarily always better but it's gonna be easier to concentrate because it's, you know, in general it's more disciplined and also because it's an all-girls school' (Kalvinder). In Saskia's parents' case, the view on private versus state schooling was based on previous experience: 'they'd also had experience from my older brothers and my sister about going from primary to a local comprehensive. So they decided that they should send me to a private school.' Saskia explained that she was given no choice in the matter: she was told that she had to move to a private school even though as a child she had been perfectly happy at her local state primary school.

Given the manner of this transition to secondary school (or even earlier in the case of some private school pupils who had attended their school from nursery), it is to be expected that similarly careful deliberations are being made with regard to plans for higher education. In accordance with rational action theory, the interviewees all mentioned hoping to gain advantages in the labour market by studying for a degree. Here's an example from Saskia's interview: 'I think that in order to get a good job that you have to go to university now. I don't think you'd, it's definitely not highly thought of in the job industry if you haven't gone to university and pursued a degree.' William explicitly undertakes a form of cost-benefit analysis: 'Tuition fees are, I really do not understand the people that say I won't be able to afford to go to university. Because it's a loan, the whole reason you go to university is so you can get a good job and pay back the loan easily.' While it might be expected that such cost-benefit analysis is undertaken regardless of social background, we have argued elsewhere (Glaesser & Cooper, 2014) that familial social background can set upper and lower boundaries within which it takes place. Reflecting this phenomenon, the interviewees in this group do not only expect to go to university, but they refer to particular courses as well as the prestige of the universities under consideration. Denise makes it quite clear that she intends to study for a 'proper' degree: 'with the fees going up I think you need to be definite about what you want to do and go and do a proper course rather than ones say like media studies or whatever.' Others mention university league tables, the Russell Group[5] and/or universities such as Oxford, Cambridge, Durham and Imperial College as possibilities.

If their parents' aim in sending them to a particular secondary school had been to develop these aspirations, the careful deliberation about secondary school choice has certainly paid off. The schools these cases attend – with the exception of David – place a strong emphasis on university applications. Help with Universities and Colleges Admissions Service (UCAS) forms and personal statements is mentioned by the interviewees as well as careers advice oriented towards university and taster courses or open days at different universities. Peers are part of this general atmosphere of academic ambition, given that they engage in discussions of subject choices, university applications, career aims and the like. Denise for example explains why most of her friends are staying on for the sixth form: 'most of the people, they are here to learn and they want to carry on and they've always had it in their head that they will stay'.

Home and school background appear to act jointly to produce university aspirations. Bourdieu's habitus theory points to the role of the family, suggesting that family environments can be more or less conducive to developing university aspirations. Consider cases such as Charlotte: 'Erm, I don't know really, I think it's just like, my parents both went to university and my brother's gone to university and to be honest I never really thought about not going. Because like, everyone in my family has, so it's just like the next step, kind of, in your education.'; or Kalvinder and Philippa who can't think of any members of their family who didn't go to university. However, it is important to bear in mind that this is not true of all cases in this 'typical' group. Some mention that they would be the first in their families to go to university. In these cases, the parental experience of some post-compulsory education, as indicated by A-levels, as well as service class occupations, coupled with a favourable school environment and a general climate of educational expansion has led to their university aspirations. It may be the case, then, that the careers of young people from backgrounds where higher education is the norm are overdetermined in the sense that more factors than required to produce university aspirations are present.

As will have become clear by now, David does not obviously fit this pattern. In his case, academic ability appears to be key, coupled with his older brother's experience who, also highly talented, is one of the very few (if not the first) pupil from their school to have secured a place at Oxford. The reason why his brother succeeded in going to Oxford appears to be his unusually high academic achievement. The teacher who had put me in touch with the young people in this school confirmed that both brothers are academically highly able, and that it is highly unusual for the school's pupils to go on to Oxbridge.

6.4 Deviant cases

Deviant cases fall into two groups: those who did not obtain the outcome despite the presence of sufficient conditions (Deborah, Kelly, Marcus and Thomas), and those who did obtain the outcome despite lacking a necessary condition, that of having at least one parent with A-levels (Emily, Paul and Rosie) or of having at least one parent not in the working class (Lauren and Patricia). Among the latter five, all but Paul are also to be found in 'inconclusive' configurations with levels of consistency with sufficiency at around 0.66. Lauren and Patricia, for example, are in the configuration of having at least one parent with A-levels coupled with not having a parent in the service class which puts them in the 'inconclusive with regard to sufficiency' category, but they are also in the category 'deviant with regard to necessity' because their parents not only are not in the service class, but they are actually both working class which makes them deviant with regard to necessity since they lack a necessary condition, but obtain the outcome nevertheless (see Table 6.7).

6.4.1 Deviant with regard to combinations of conditions and outcome – sufficiency

Deborah, Kelly, Marcus and Thomas are deviant cases with regard to sufficiency. The first thing to note is that none of them rule out going to university completely, but they are uncertain about it which is why I categorised them as not being likely to go to university. I took 'likely' to mean that someone has a fairly firm intention, akin to the way this variable is coded in the LSYPE data where the response categories are 'very likely', 'fairly likely', 'not very likely', 'not at all likely'. From the way they discussed university, it seemed to me that they were closer to the 'not very likely' than the 'fairly likely' category.

Kelly and Marcus both attend schools where university aspirations are not the norm. Kelly attends the same school as David (above), the small comprehensive with no sixth form in a fairly deprived area. Her family background is mixed: her mother left school early without gaining any O-levels (the precursor of GCSEs). Having held jobs as a cleaner, she currently works as a foster carer. Kelly's father holds a degree – though she is not sure where he went to university – and works as a local government officer. Her brother left school at 16 to get a job, and she does not know anyone apart from her father who went to university. Most people she knows 'either have jobs as cleaners, cooks or just basically working in shops'. Thus, her father's holding a degree is unusual in her wider social network. Everything else both in the school and her home is not conducive to developing university aspirations.

Marcus attends a secondary modern school in Kent where, again, university aspirations are unusual. Both his parents hold degrees and are in professional occupations. It is therefore perhaps unusual for someone like him to attend a secondary modern school, and in fact I selected him from a larger number of possible interviewees because he was the only one among my potential interviewees in this particular school with this sort of home background. It turns out that his case is not well captured by merely pointing to his parents' educational level and their occupational group or the type of school he himself currently attends. It has idiosyncratic features: he initially attended a Steiner school, but was increasingly unhappy there because of the lack of competitive sports. His parents, though keen for him and his older brother to attend a Steiner school at first, wanted him to attend a school where he was happy, regardless of the school's academic credentials, and helped him find this alternative school. He is not very interested in academic work and therefore did not attempt to enter a grammar school, unlike his brother who took his GCSEs at the Steiner school and then moved to the sixth form of a grammar school. A key to Marcus' parents' reluctance to guide him towards a more academically oriented school seems to be his father's own educational career. He attended a major public school and was unhappy there, so he wanted to spare his sons the same experience. His mother (i.e., Marcus' grandmother) paid for Marcus' brother to attend an elite preparatory school early on and would have liked to support an academically oriented elite education for her grandsons. However, according to Marcus, there was some conflict in the family, and this, coupled with liking the ethos of a Steiner school, caused his parents to choose this alternative path for their children. I will discuss Marcus in more detail in Chapter 8.

Thomas' school is a large comprehensive with sixth form where university aspirations are not unusual, but where pupils are also supported in choosing other career pathways. His parents are separated and he lives with his mother who does not hold a degree herself. She is nevertheless quite keen for Thomas to go to university because she feels that her lack of a degree made it harder for her to get work in Britain (she is from another European country). His father similarly takes a keen interest in Thomas' education, suggesting he study French for GCSE on the grounds that it would look good on his CV and help with university applications, even though Thomas finds it hard and had not really considered continuing with the language. Thomas explains that he is going to take a year out after year 11 to be home schooled because he is a year younger than his classmates:

> during primary school I went to a kind of quite deprived primary school, so my dad was very keen on raising me, like instead of doing other stuff he taught me how to read and write at a much younger age, and I knew a different type of alphabet to everybody else. So at that school they put me up a year, and then because I was coping so well with it they thought there's no point in putting me back down a year, so I'm still up a year

During his year out, he plans to continue studying subjects he enjoys at school for their own sake and also those related to possible A-level choices. On the whole, he gives the impression of being happy enough to continue his education, but university is not his only option:

> if it was something like, I'm quite interested in forestry, so if it was something to do with that I probably wouldn't need a university qualification, I'd just take courses and that, and then try and get a job. But, I dunno, I'll just have to see how I feel at the end of A-levels.

The rise in tuition fees is a clearly a concern, and he therefore does not intend to get a degree for the sake of it, but to take account of his career plans.

Deborah attends a private girls' day school. Her parents run several pubs and while they both left school with just a few GCSEs, her mother later returned to education to gain a degree because, as Deborah puts it, 'she believes in education'. This is why they have chosen private education for their four daughters (Deborah is the youngest). Deborah seems to feel ambiguous about her school. She appreciates her parents' financial sacrifices in educating her and her sisters privately, and she acknowledges the school's support, but she is not doing very well academically and finds it hard to fit in at a school which prizes academic achievement above other goals:

> Because you can just tell, you just get that like vibe from them. They just treat you different from them who yeah might be getting A*s all the time, but them people who aren't, they're developing in other ways, so why should you treat them any differently? [...] Cos we always have like showing new students around and they only pick them intelligent people and it's never any like, because I'm in like most of the bottom sets but that's only for English and science.

And none of them people ever get chosen to show them people around. And it's like, if you give us a chance, we won't always think like the school is trying to cast us out or we won't say bad things about the school because actually most of the people who come here actually enjoy the school after a while.

This feeling of not being accepted by the school is probably justified. The teacher through whom I made contact with the interviewees in this school was very dismissive about Deborah before I'd met her, saying that she was not very bright and that her parents ran a pub, implying through her tone of voice that she did not think much of this occupation.

Deborah has decided to leave her school after her GCSEs to go to a local sixth form college for a graphic design course. Her school disapproves of this decision given their academic focus, but she has made up her mind. Higher education is still unusual in her family; in addition to her mother having gained a degree, one of her sisters is at university, but the other two have either decided against it or are still unsure. Apart from that, there is no one in her family who has gone. It should be noted that while she mentions her mother's degree, she is very vague about it and it does not sound as though this has had much actual influence either on her mother's career or the family's values. Taken together, it seems that Deborah's lack of academic ability and interest and her family's orientation towards non-academic types of career are stronger than the school's ethos, especially given her sense of alienation from the school.

In summary, all four cases experience a mix of influences at home and at school, not all of which are conducive to developing university aspirations. This is coupled with the fact that while they are by no means struggling with schoolwork (with the possible exception of Deborah), their talents and interests are not obviously academic: Deborah does just about cope with schoolwork, but presumably this coping is partly as a result of intense support at her private school, and she is not particularly keen on such academic work. Kelly is still unsure about what she wants to do, Marcus is interested in sports and Thomas' interests vary but include forestry. Taken together, this combination of individual factors, social network and school ethos seems to have prevented them from developing clear university aspirations.

6.4.2 Deviant with regard to combinations of conditions and outcome – necessity

I now turn to the discussion of cases who lack one of two quasi-necessary conditions (the two conditions identified as necessary for which I have cases in my interview sample are having at least one parent with A-levels, and having at least one parent who is not in the working class), but who obtain the outcome of having developed university aspirations nevertheless (Emily, Paul, Rosie, Lauren and Patricia). Emily, Paul and Rosie lack the necessary condition of having at least one parent with A-levels, Lauren and Patricia lack the necessary condition of *not* having at least one parent who is not in the working class. In some sense, they form the opposite to the cases described just now: the former failed to develop university aspirations despite a set of seemingly favourable conditions, whereas these developed such aspirations against the odds. The first thing to note is that four out of the five young people in this category, the four girls, attend a grammar school in Kent. It seems that their academic ability, which allowed them to enter a selective school, coupled with the school's ethos, can act as a substitute for the lack of a necessary condition relating to the home background. This leaves Paul to explain. He attends a secondary modern school in Kent, and while he is not necessarily very academically minded, he has a strong interest and a talent for sports. He therefore intends to study sports science and to become a PE teacher. This is what his brother did, and what he himself has been hoping to do since he entered secondary school. He mentions wanting to inspire young people as one reason for this career aspiration, and talks about an uncle who is a youth worker – the only member of his extended family apart from his brother who holds a degree. This is how he describes his uncle:

> one of my uncles went to university. He's earning a good wage now, he's in charge of a, err, like a youth club. Obviously again, with him doing that, he's inspiring young people. Getting young people off the street, putting them into a youth club. Doing all good things really, like takes them on trips to C-Park, like obviously the best theme park in the country. So yeah, it's, he's, good man really.

These two, his brother and his uncle, seem to be role models for him, and his wish to attend university has arisen out of this very specific goal rather than a more general aspiration to attend higher education.

The coupling of individual interests and talents with a favourable school environment (for the four girls) or a clear aspiration and role models (Paul) seem to explain why these cases developed university aspirations despite lacking a condition which had been identified as necessary in the QCA analyses.

6.4.3   Deviant with regard to an outcome

Finally, there are three cases who are deviant in another respect: the LSYPE analysis indicates that 78.3 per cent of young people are in full-time education at the age of 17. Therefore, I now analyse those three in my interview sample who were *not* going to be in full-time education at that age: Leanne, Amy and Duncan. They have some characteristics in common: none of their parents hold qualifications above O-level/GCSE, none of their parents is in the service class (in fact, they are all working class with the exception of Leanne's father who is a self-employed groundworker and therefore intermediate class), and they attend schools that are not oriented towards encouraging higher education aspirations, the comprehensive without sixth form (Duncan) and the secondary modern school in Kent (Leanne and Amy), that is, schools which are vocationally rather than academically oriented. We know, on theoretical grounds and on the basis of the evidence discussed so far, that such characteristics can be associated with low educational qualifications and aspirations, but it would be too simple to conclude that this is the explanation for the outcome of these three cases, given that we also know that other cases with similar characteristics do stay on in education (the proportion of cases with parents who neither have A-levels nor are members of the service class who stay in education is 68.3 in the LSYPE data). The three young people discussed here all wish to start an apprenticeship once they leave school: Amy and Leanne would like to become hairdressers, and Duncan a car mechanic. The reasons they give for wishing to take this route rather than some form of school-based or college-based training is a mix of wanting to be independent and earn some money soon, and reasoning that this hands-on experience will give them better chances in the job market. Amy and Leanne in particular stress that they are not academic, that they do not like exams (Amy did not even take the eleven plus, Leanne took it but failed) and that while they are very positive about their current school, they do not wish to remain in a school environment. Duncan (whom I will discuss in greater detail in Chapter 8) was on the verge of being permanently excluded from school several times throughout his secondary school career, and while his behaviour is better now, he has no inclination to spend any more time in school. He currently does a placement in a garage one day a week and enjoys it much more than school.

For all three cases, we find that in addition to home and school environments which may not be strongly conducive to developing a motivation to stay on in school, there is a clear interest in an alternative route and a realistic expectation of what this will entail, based on experiences through placements or Saturday jobs, as well as informal information obtained through friendship networks. A lack of interest in academic work is perhaps not very unusual among 16-year-olds, but it seems plausible that if young people do not have the sense that a real alternative exists, they nevertheless tend to stay in education given that this is usually encouraged by schools and the wider social environment.

Bourdieu's (1977) habitus concept once again is useful to analyse the situation that Leanne, Amy and Duncan find themselves in. Their habitus is the result of family and wider social networks, and it has led to expectations for what is normal for them to do and what is not. Duncan expresses this sense of 'us' and 'them' in the following exchange:

JG: So which college have you been accepted for?

Duncan: Just X college [a vocationally oriented further education col-
         lege] in [next town]. Cos it's like, think it's the only one that
         would have us in.

JG: Right, OK, did you try others?

Duncan: Nah, I just tried that one because it's closest.
         [...]

JG: And so why did you say that they are the only ones that
         would have you, X college?

Duncan: With me qualifications and that, innit. If I got anything else,
         then like none of the high colleges would have accepted us,
         would they, like sixth form and that because, I think they're
         like, what's it called, like a smarter college. [laughs] I don't
         know how to put it.

JG: Yeah, I think I know what you mean.

Duncan: *Like the smarter people go to Y college [more academically oriented
         sixth form college] and then us lot go to X college. I'm not saying
         you as being one of us lot.*

JG: And would you have liked to go to somewhere else like Y
         college?

Duncan: Nah, not really, cos like all of me mates from last year like,
         when they left they went to X college to do mechanics and
         that. Like, some of me best mates went there and I, like, I just
         thought same as all that I'm gonna sign up for X college for
         mechanics. Like they'd probably like, help us out somehow
         like with the work. Like outside of school they could like
         tell us like bits about what they're doing and that. Like me
         older brother he did it, mechanics at X college and he, aw,

me mouth's getting all dry. And he passed his test with a distinction so like, I thought like he could probably help us with something.

In the same way as interviewees who intend to enter higher education, Duncan draws on experiences from his wider social network to guide his decision, which actually seems to be not so much a decision but a foregone conclusion. His habitus clearly is very different from theirs: his world is one where manual work rather than academic interests are the norm and where education has to be endured rather than enjoyed and/ or used to one's advantage.

I should add that there was no one among my interviewees who intended to leave school in order to take up an unskilled job. This may be a result of today's general expectation that young people should stay on in education and of the lack of such jobs in some areas, but it may also be due to a selection effect. The young people who agreed to take part in my study were approached through their schools (or former schools, in the case of some German Hauptschule pupils). Presumably, young people who do not intend to pursue any form of education are less likely to agree to participate in something that they would have associated with school.

6.5   Inconclusive cases

In the QCA analysis, there were some types of cases which did not show a clear tendency with regard to developing university aspirations. These had a mixed family background in the sense that parents either held A-levels *or* were members of the service class, but not both together. This is slightly unusual in itself since it is more common for educational attainment and occupational status to match. Theoretical expectations for these cases therefore are not clear. Among my interviewees, there are nine cases which fall into this category: Emily and Rosie who have at least one service class parent and Alexandra, Hannah, Lauren, Matthew, Patricia, Ruth and Samantha who have at least one parent with A-levels. As it happens, in this particular sample they all stated that they intended to go to university. Of course, I have already discussed Emily, Rosie, Lauren and Patricia above, because while they fall under the heading of inconclusive cases in terms of sufficient conditions, they are also deviant in terms of necessary conditions.

Among the nine cases discussed here, only three did not attend an academically selective school (Alexandra, Samantha and Matthew). For the other six who did, it seems reasonable to assume that their school, coupled with having either a parent in the service class or a parent with A-levels, was the deciding factor in swaying their outcome towards developing the intention to go to university. For Alexandra, Samantha and Matthew, there appears to be no obvious shared factor which might account for their wish to go to university, so I will discuss them individually.

Alexandra attends her local comprehensive school (a large one with sixth form) which happens to be reasonably successful academically (it is the same school as Thomas', described above), but this was not a key consideration at the time of choosing a secondary school. Both she herself and her parents were mostly concerned for her to attend a local school where her friends would be. League tables or any way of taking account of a school's academic success did not seem to enter the picture. Her family background is not obviously conducive to developing higher education aspirations: no one in her family has attended university. However, Alexandra appears to be achieving highly and to be motivated to do well. Her academic ability coupled with her school's support seem to have acted together to produce the wish in her to go to university. Here is how she herself explained this:

> No one in my family's been to university at all. So everyone was quite shocked when I said I wanted to go. I mean I think they didn't expect me to be a high achiever, I mean not in a nasty way obviously but ... They just expected me to leave school at 16, get a job and sort of do whatever they did, didn't expect me to because like all my cousins and things have just left school and got jobs

Asked why she developed other plans, she replies 'Because, well partially because my grades are high enough and I think if you have high grades you get the opportunity to do whatever you want.'

In Samantha's family, her mother is the only one with some experience of higher education, having studied for an arts degree. While she currently works as a shop assistant, she is also training to be an arts therapist, and she is keen to leave her current job. Therefore, Samantha has a model of using a university education to have a better life, even if her mother has not yet taken this step. In addition, Samantha's school is a voluntary aided comprehensive school, and while it is no longer able to select its intake on academic ability, the school's academic standard and aspirations are still very high. She herself performed well in her GCSEs, having obtained mainly As and some Bs. Taken together, this combination of factors has led to her wishing to go to university to study medicine, although she has a fallback position which would be to become a nurse – without a degree – but only if her grades would prevent her from getting a place at university (which seems unlikely).

Matthew attends the same school as Samantha. He wishes to study dentistry, and while there is no one in his family who has gone to university, his role model appears to be his GP. He had a conversation with him focussing on career plans, and he also sought out a student of dentistry whom he has asked for advice. He seems to be going about his decision in a very deliberate and rational way. His academic achievement to date should certainly enable him to follow his chosen career, given that he obtained 4 A*s and the rest As at GCSE. In his case, it seems safe to conclude that the combination of an academically ambitious school and his own considerable academic ability were sufficient to lead him to wish to attend university.

It turns out then that on closer inspection of these three cases, there are shared factors, contrary to what I suggested above. These are academic ability and a school which, while not selective in terms of policy, is clearly keen to encourage high academic aspiration in its pupils.

6.6   Lessons from the analysis of interviews

The interview analyses provided insights to supplement the cross-case QCA analyses. I used them to explore potential mechanisms which may have led to the patterns identified by the QCA. In addition, the interviews can be used to identify factors which may be used to refine the initial QCA analyses.

One factor that featured clearly in the analysis of typical, deviant and inconclusive cases was the nature of the secondary school attended. A school with an academic orientation was something that was shared by nearly all the typical cases, indicating that the combination of a favourable home *and* school environment encourages university aspirations. The analysis of the cases who were deviant with regard to necessity suggested, again, that attending a selective school may in some cases act as a substitute for a less favourable familial environment. And finally, for many of the inconclusive cases discussed here, school type seems to be what tipped the balance in favour of obtaining the outcome. The other factor which emerged was that, not surprisingly, academic ability is likely to be part of the configuration of factors which leads to a young person's developing university aspirations, and (relative) lack of ability would appear to make this less likely. Indeed, using the LSYPE data, Anders and Micklewright (2013) confirm that high academic achievement can compensate for low parental education and low parental income (they do not analyse social class, but income quintiles) as a factor affecting the expectation to go to university. This was already evident from the analyses reported above, where measured ability featured as part of all the solution pathways (see Table 6.4 and the solutions presented in Box 6.4), and, for girls, does indeed seem to compensate for low parental education or low class (solution 2 in Box 6.4) and where I showed it to be a necessary condition for having aspirations to go to university (Table 6.6). The reason for not using ability as a factor to classify cases as typical, deviant and inconclusive was simply that I do not hold any comparable information for the interviewees regarding their academic ability or achievement.

However, in the light of the interview analyses, I returned to the LSYPE data to add school type to the analyses. As noted in Chapter 4, the number of cases in selective and independent schools is disproportionately small, and this led to limited diversity in the resulting truth table, Table 6.8.

Given the nature of the selection process for selective schools, it was to be expected that configurations where parents are not in the service class, do not hold at least A-levels, or neither, would have fewer cases in selective schools. This is indeed the case, and in conjunction with the sampling problems in the LSYPE study described earlier which resulted in an underrepresentation of pupils in selective schools, some of the rows (1, 5, 6, 8 and 11 in particular) have such low case numbers that obtaining a minimised Boolean solution did not seem sensible, though inspecting the truth table itself is interesting. It shows that configurations including selective schools are mostly to be found in the top half of the truth table, that is, they are associated with higher proportions of young people wishing to go to university. For those not in selective schools, the combination of having at least one parent with A-levels and at least one parent in the service class (rows 7 and 9) also results in higher proportions with higher education aspirations compared with other combinations of parental factors.

Because of the limited diversity problem, I decided to omit gender from this particular analysis in a next step, despite my earlier findings from the analysis of the role of gender using pairwise comparison[6] (Table 6.9).

There are still some low case numbers, with the lowest *n* at just 17. As can be seen from the truth table itself (Table 6.9) and solution 1 in Box 6.5, being in a selective school at the age of 16 is clearly a quasi-sufficient condition for developing higher education aspirations, regardless of

Table 6.8 Truth table, outcome HE expectation age 17, four conditions including school type

Row no.	Male	At least one parent with A-levels	At least one parent in the service class	Attended selective school aged 16	Number	HE likely age 17	Consistency
1	0	0	1	1	11	1	1.000
2	0	1	1	1	68	1	1.000
3	1	1	1	1	129	1	0.961
4	1	1	0	1	23	1	0.870
5	1	0	0	1	15	1	0.867
6	0	0	0	1	11	1	0.818
7	0	1	0	0	1,046	1	0.812
8	0	1	0	1	16	0	0.750
9	1	1	1	0	994	0	0.713
10	0	1	0	0	406	0	0.670
11	1	0	1	1	6	0	0.667
12	0	0	1	0	264	0	0.648
13	0	0	0	0	648	0	0.566
14	1	1	0	0	419	0	0.520
15	1	0	1	0	260	0	0.500
16	1	0	0	0	656	0	0.387

Table 6.9 Truth table, outcome HE expectation age 17, three conditions including school type

Row no.	At least one parent with A-levels	At least one parent in the service class	In selective school age 16	Number	HE likely age 17	Consistency
1	1	1	1	197	1	0.975
2	0	1	1	17	1	0.882
3	0	0	1	26	1	0.846
4	1	0	1	39	1	0.821
5	1	1	0	2,040	0	0.764
6	1	0	0	825	0	0.594
7	0	1	0	524	0	0.574
8	0	0	0	1,304	0	0.476

social background in the form of parental education or social class at this level of consistency, though the level of consistency with sufficiency, among those in selective schools, is higher still for those from the most privileged social backgrounds.

It can be seen from inspection of the truth table (Table 6.9) that a similar phenomenon can be observed for cases who do not attend a selective school. Here, parental education and class again can be seen to matter, as is also evident from solution 2 in Box 6.5. It is important to bear in mind that the group of non-selective schools here is likely to be very diverse in terms of, for example, academic ethos and student intake, and this diversity is likely to explain partly some of the differences between the configurations.

Finally, one obvious reason for becoming a 'deviant' case with regard to developing higher education aspirations is simply the existence of talents and interests which can be pursued (sometimes better) without a university education. This, again, is difficult to model given the limitations of survey data.

Box 6.5   Solution for Table 6.9, outcome HE expectation age 17, three conditions including school type

Solution 1: 0.8 threshold

	Raw Coverage	Unique Coverage	Consistency
SEL_SCHOOL16	0.081	0.081	0.935

Solution coverage: 0.081
Solution consistency: 0.935

Solution 2: 0.75 threshold

	Raw Coverage	Unique Coverage	Consistency
SEL_SCHOOL16+	0.081	0.021	0.935
ALEVEL1P*SC1P	0.542	0.482	0.782

Solution coverage: 0.563
Solution consistency: 0.784

6.7 Conclusion

As noted in previous chapters (see also Chapter 9), there is a danger of explaining a particular case convincingly but without being able to use this case study to generalise to other, similar cases and without knowing whether it would have been possible, for the same case, to find an equally convincing explanation for an alternative pathway or outcome. While idiosyncrasies and salient individual life events can sometimes explain a particular historical event or pathway, they are less helpful for explaining cross-case patterns. With that proviso, it seems possible to draw some more general conclusions in addition to explaining, as I have done above, the individual cases' outcomes. These concern the roles of schools' ethos and composition as well as role models both within and outside the family. These seem to form part of the mechanisms leading to the wish to attend university, and equally to the wish not to attend university. In addition to the well-documented role of family background, schools and role models appear to be acting as substitutes in those cases where the family background would not have led an individual to developing university aspirations, and to reinforce the family's effect where it did.

Finally, it is worth pointing out that, perhaps not surprisingly, the outcome 'expecting to go to university' turns out to be very heterogeneous. For some people, it means hoping to attend a Russell Group university or Oxbridge, not necessarily with a particular degree course or career in mind but for the reputation and type of experience these institutions can offer. For others, in accordance with RAT, attending university is the most promising route to some or other good job, whereas for yet others it is a means to a particular end, as in the case of Paul who does not wish to attend university out of a general intention to gain a degree, but because it is the route to his preferred career as a PE teacher. It seems safe to assume that if the normal route into this career did not involve higher education, he would not seek it, whereas others wish to attend university regardless of career goals. This finding illustrates a general point: 'summarising' factors and solutions, whether they take the form of configurations identified via QCA or variables shown to be 'significant' in a regression-type analysis, can hide causal heterogeneity (Cooper & Glaesser, 2012a). The same goes for many outcomes, as noted at the beginning of this paragraph.[7] A further interesting topic for research therefore would be to explore whether different causal pathways are associated with attending different types of university, a finding which seems likely on the basis of the interview findings reported here.

7
What Types of Young People Are Bound for Higher Education at the Age of 17?

In this chapter, I compare England and Germany with regard to trajectories which lead to higher education. As noted in the previous chapter, while I am only able to study aspirations rather than actual transitions to higher education, these are highly correlated (Anders & Micklewright, 2013), so aspirations do give a strong indication of the likely university attendance.

I intend to explore whether and to what extent the considerable differences between the two systems in England and Germany shape young people's expectation of higher education, and whether similar or different mechanisms and processes characterise both systems. The first thing to note is that, according to the survey data, 17-year-olds' intentions in the two countries are remarkably different: in Germany, 34 per cent of Socio-Economic Panel (SOEP) respondents state that they intend to go to university (this includes Fachhochschulen ('universities of applied sciences')); in England the figure for Longitudinal Study of Young People in England (LSYPE) respondents is 65 per cent.[1] I will discuss possible reasons and implications of this finding below.

In Chapters 5 and 6, I analysed pathways through the education system in Germany and England. In both countries, I discussed the importance of individuals' social context in terms of both family and school. Doing so, I drew on the model developed in Glaesser and Cooper (2014) where we argued that habitus (Bourdieu, 1977) can help explain how upper and lower boundaries for expectations and aspirations are formed, while rational action theory (RAT) (Boudon, 1974, Breen & Goldthorpe, 1997, Goldthorpe, 1996b) contributes to an understanding of the weighing up of potential costs and benefits of certain courses of action which take place within these boundaries. In addition, the young people's class-based habitus conditions, at least to some extent, what exactly is considered to be a cost and a benefit. These broad general principles applied in both countries, so I will draw on the same theories throughout this chapter. For example, all my interviewees were aspiring to achieve some kind of qualification – a rational form of behaviour, given the associated likely benefits – but the family of origin in conjunction with the school attended by the young person created boundaries within which these aspirations fell, so that for some young people, the goal of gaining any form of qualification may be perceived to be a considerable ambition, whereas others were hoping to be admitted to a prestigious university and might even regard attending university as a failure if it wasn't their preferred highly prestigious one.

I start this chapter by discussing features of the two education systems relevant for shaping the transition to higher education, followed by a QCA analysis using SOEP data of the patterns of factors associated with higher education aspirations in Germany (for the parallel analysis for England see Chapter 6). I then draw on analyses of my interviews to illustrate the mechanisms which are likely to have led to young people's development of university aspirations or, conversely, to their not developing such aspirations.

7.1   Germany and England: system differences and similarities

Given the importance of schooling for later university entry, I will begin by discussing schools. A key difference between the two countries is the fact that the German secondary school system is formally stratified, unlike England's largely comprehensive system where forms of stratification are more varied. In some areas of England, there are grammar schools, similar to German *Gymnasien*. In addition, across the whole of England comprehensives vary enormously as a function of the socio-economic nature of their catchment areas. Some consequences of both types of school system have been described and analysed by Turner (1960). He used Britain (at the time) and the US as his exemplars to discuss prevailing 'folk norms' which had shaped the school systems and associated opportunities for mobility. *Sponsored mobility* (which, according to Turner, was the norm in Britain at the time) described a situation where an elite selects those considered suitable to join it. This selection took place early on in an individual's educational career and, subsequently, support for the developing career was offered. He compared *contest mobility*, as in the US, to a race in which everybody can expect to have equal chances of achieving highly, with the outcome kept open for as long as possible. While Germany has many features of a sponsored system (Glaesser & Cooper, 2011b), Britain today has moved away from such a system (Kerckhoff, 2001). Students have more options open to them, both when they first choose a secondary school and during their time there. Nevertheless, restrictions exist for British students, too, if they wish to continue to post-compulsory and higher education. Passing enough GCSEs at a high enough level is a prerequisite for being allowed to continue with A-level study, and A-levels in turn are a prerequisite for university entry. Subjects matter, too: some, like media studies or business studies, are considered not to be suitable for university admission, especially by prestigious universities. Subjects considered suitable usually are the more traditionally academically oriented subjects such as English, mathematics, history, biology, chemistry and physics. It seems to me, then, that some British schools effectively act as sponsors despite the system now having organisational features that are closer to a contest system. Schools can act as sponsors not only if they are academically selective but also if they have an ethos which places high expectations on their students regarding academic achievement and post-school careers, and I will discuss this in more detail below, drawing on interview data.

The higher education sectors in the two countries differ, too. While in both countries, considerable educational expansion has taken place during the second half of the 20th century, the structure of higher education provision differs. In England, formally there has been a single higher education sector since the change in status of polytechnics to universities in 1992. However, there are considerable differences between universities with regard to history, subjects, and mission (Eurydice, 2013e). They also differ in prestige, research activity and income (Ball et al., 2002). This is well known by some potential students and their parents. Ball and colleagues note that social class via cultural and social capital shapes the way in which students not only decide whether or not to go to university, but also which type of university to apply to. The notion of boundaries (which I introduced in Chapter 4 and then drew on in Chapters 5 and 6) is implicit in these authors' discussion since they show that young people's social class has an effect on both the choice the young person makes and the options he/she considers in the first place. This is true of people at any level of the social class structure: 'Embedded perceptions and expectations make certain choices "obvious" and others unthinkable, according to where you stand in the overall landscape of choice. In this respect, middle-class students in the private schools are as equally, or perhaps more, constrained than their working-class counterparts in the state sector' (Ball et al., 2002, p. 58).

Educational expansion in Germany occurred during the second half of the 20th century. People stayed in the education system for longer and more people gained degrees. Concerning the further education sector, Müller (1998, pp. 99/100) notes that the vocational training system has successfully reacted to changes in the occupational structure over this period. Another one of its successes, in his view, is the fact that, compared with other countries, there are relatively few people in Germany who enter the labour market without any form of vocational qualification. Higher education in Germany is provided by two kinds of institutions, universities and Fachhochschulen, with the latter being similar in aims and mission to the UK's former polytechnics, offering more vocationally oriented subjects such as engineering or social work. The universities are more research oriented, covering traditional academic subjects and disciplines. There is no clear hierarchy or difference in prestige within each group. Universities may differ with regard to the reputation of a particular person or research group, but to most prospective students, one university is as good as another and they are just as likely to base their choice on factors such as proximity to their home or whether the university is in a big city or smaller town. Universities do not have much say in the selection of their students, though this is beginning to change (Mayer, 2008). To be admitted to a course, a candidate has to have the Abitur. Sometimes additional specific criteria exist such as knowledge of foreign languages. Provided these criteria are fulfilled, a university is obliged to accept the prospective student. Only if there are more applicants than places will the performance at the Abitur be taken into account as well.

As is evident in the Ball et al. quote above, schools as well as families in the UK have an impact on a young person's university options and choice. This is also the case in Germany, but this impact takes a different form. The academic selection and subsequent sponsorship by the Gymnasium as an institution have the effect of creating a relatively homogeneous group of students for whom higher education aspirations are regarded as fairly normal by the school and who are actively encouraged to develop such aspirations, though entering an apprenticeship is by no means uncommon for this group of people. The other types of school in Germany, Hauptschule, Realschule and, to some extent, Gesamtschule, focus largely on various forms of vocational training. Given that they do not expect their student body to include many academically oriented and academically gifted young people, they are considerably less likely to encourage higher education aspirations, and they typically focus on other types of post-school education and/or employment as a matter of policy.

Selective and independent schools in England are similar to a German Gymnasium in this respect, but there are large differences among English non-selective state schools, with some closer in ethos and aspirations to selective schools in both countries and others more likely to cater to a wide variety of ability and interests.

Finally, a note on higher education funding in the two countries: in Germany, the individual Länder were allowed to charge tuition fees from 2005, but not all Länder did so. Where fees were introduced, they were usually set at around €500 per semester, that is, €1,000 a year. However, they were abolished again fairly soon afterwards in most places, and from 2014, tuition fees will not exist anywhere in Germany, apart from an administrative fee which is usually set at around €50–€100 per semester. Living costs still have to be covered and it is increasingly difficult to obtain a means-tested government grant (BAföG) at a level high enough to cover these costs. In England, by contrast, fees were up to £3,290 per year at the time of my interviews, but a decision had been made to allow universities to charge fees of up to £9,000 per year, with effect from 2012 (so potentially affecting my interviewees). Student loans exist to cover fees and cost of living, repayable once the recipient of the loan earns a certain income. Most of my English interviewees, and certainly those with realistic expectations to attend university, were well aware of this change in funding regime and that it was going to affect them.

7.2   University aspirations in Germany

Before using interview data from both countries to explore how young people's university aspirations are shaped, I wish to give an overview of the situation in Germany. For England, I have already done this in Chapter 6, but not yet for Germany because the outcome I analysed in Chapter 5, where Germany was discussed, was type of secondary school attended rather than university aspirations.

I initially draw on a truth table based on SOEP data to analyse factors associated with the intention of attending university. Aiming to parallel the English analyses presented in Chapter 6, I initially analysed gender, parental class, parental education as indicated by whether or not at least one parent has the Abitur, and type of school attended as factors. Perhaps not surprisingly, given the comparatively low proportion of young people (34.1 per cent) who state that they intend to go to university, there were no quasi-sufficient configurations for obtaining this outcome. This remained the case when I used parental degree instead of Abitur as the indicator for parental education. Nevertheless, it is instructive to inspect the truth table (Table 7.1), where parental education is indicated by whether or not at least one parent has a degree:

Table 7.1 Truth table, German young people's HE intention

Row no.	Male	At least one parent has degree	At least one parent in the service class	In Gymnasium age 17	Number	HE likely age 17	Consistency
1	1	1	0	1	19		0.737
2	0	1	0	1	19		0.737
3	0	1	1	1	96		0.688
4	1	1	1	1	107		0.626
5	0	0	1	1	38		0.5
6	1	0	0	1	30		0.467
7	0	0	0	1	43		0.419
8	1	0	1	1	28		0.393
9	1	1	1	0	37		0.270
10	0	1	1	0	30		0.2
11	0	1	0	0	11		0.182
12	1	0	1	0	47		0.128
13	0	0	1	0	52		0.115
14	0	0	0	0	105		0.076
15	1	1	0	0	14		0.071
16	1	0	0	0	112		0.063

Given that consistencies, as noted, are too low to undertake an analysis of sufficiency, I will not derive Boolean solutions, but instead discuss patterns in the configurations in terms of how close they are to the grand mean of 34.1 per cent. First of all, we can see that there is a marked gap between those who do (rows 1–8) and do not (rows 9–16) attend a Gymnasium at the age of 17, with those in a Gymnasium above the grand mean, and those not in a Gymnasium below. Given the institutional requirements of universities, this is as expected.[2] Among those who attend a Gymnasium, there is a considerable gap between those whose parents do and do not hold a degree themselves (the jump between rows 4 and 5). I also calculated the means for the group whose parents have degrees (rows 1–4) which is 66.8 per cent, and for the group whose parents haven't (rows 5–8) which is 44.6 per cent. Clearly, even given sponsorship via the school, young people who do not have any experience of higher education in their immediate family are less likely to develop university aspirations than those who have such an experience. Without the sponsorship offered by the Gymnasium, on the other hand, the proportion of young people hoping to go to university is considerably lower still (at 11.3 per cent overall compared with 58.4 per cent of those who attend a Gymnasium).

In the next section, I will explore reasons for and implications of these findings on the basis of interview data, along with the broader question of how young people come to develop higher education aspirations or not.

7.3   Analysis of interviews

The QCA analyses of aspirations for both countries showed the importance of parental education and school experiences for a young person's developing higher education aspirations. I will now use interview data to explore in more detail the processes which led to this pattern, focussing on three aspects: country or system differences, school influences, and individual factors. Obviously, there will be overlaps between these three aspects since they are not independent of each other, but treating the topic under these three headings will help keep things clear analytically.

7.3.1   Country and system

I described the school and university systems in both countries above. In some sense, it might be argued that the similarities are greater than the differences: higher education institutions in both countries offer academic qualifications which offer the opportunity to gain certain jobs and life chances, and in both countries the institutions select students on the basis of academic ability as indicated by qualifications held by the candidates. This process is socially as well as academically selective to some extent in both countries. In the same way, the processes leading up to the wish to apply to university in the first place are socially as well as academically selective. I will explore these processes under the headings of *school* and *individual factors* below. Here, I will focus on differences between the two countries, and whether and how they impact on the young people's experiences and expectations. The relevant differences I discuss are (1) hierarchy within the university sector: universities in the UK are more strongly differentiated in terms of their reputation and research orientation, (2) there are relatively more university places in the UK, leading to different expectations among schools, families and the young people themselves, (3) apprenticeships are more formally organised, more common and more prestigious in Germany, and (4) the route to some occupations differs: occupations such as nursing are graduate occupations in England, but not in Germany.

While the young people themselves are not necessarily aware of all these differences between countries, they are aware of their own country's characteristics, and these have shaped young people's perception of universities and their decision-making processes to some extent. Some, if not most, of the English young people are aware of the fact that universities in the UK are hierarchically ordered. Consider this exchange with Hannah, who attends an academically selective independent school. She was asked whether she thought that teachers treated students fairly, on the whole, and her reply shows clearly that she not only knows about academic rituals but that she also is aware of the differences in prestige between universities:

Hannah: I think the teachers who went to better universities, and the ones who, ... the ones maybe from a higher social class, they're definitely more lenient and respectful and they are fairer I'd say than some of the others.

JG: Right, OK. How do you know which university they went to?

Hannah: There's a list on the school website and they tell us, and at speech day when they wear their robes you can tell from the colours.

JG: Oh of course you can, yeah OK. So is that what you mean, or what do you mean by a higher social class, the ones that are from a higher social class?

Hannah: Erm ... The sort of, the ones who I would say are from a higher social class, they're, I'd say they're more, they're better educated, they've experienced more in life. They're very well spoken, whereas some of the others are maybe from the [local area], they've stayed here all their lives, maybe haven't had as many opportunities.

Her school will have facilitated Hannah's awareness of the differences between institutions. What is more, she makes a connection between type of institution and individual social class. Hannah's home background would not necessarily provide her with the relevant knowledge and way of thinking: her (single) mother holds a foundation degree from a post-92 university, and no member of her family or wider social circle has attended a prestigious university as far as Hannah knows, but she herself would very much like to go to 'Oxford or Cambridge, or Edinburgh, or St Andrews', on the grounds that 'they're really good universities and I like the areas which they're in. I think it would be lovely to study there, at one of those universities.' Other interviewees also mention specific Russell Group universities and Oxbridge, or they talk about top 10 or 20 universities. They do not specify what they actually mean by this, they merely assume a shared understanding of such categories. We find an important influence here of school attended and/ or family of origin on knowledge of system properties such as the hierarchical organisation of British universities: as we can see from Hannah's example, this knowledge of the hierarchy tends to be available to young people who attend academically selective and/or ambitious schools (on which more below), or who were from a background where there is some knowledge and personal experience of the higher education sector. By contrast, interviewees who didn't attend an academically oriented school and in whose home background university was not a common experience did sometimes mention specific universities they might want to attend, but the focus here tended to be on local universities they knew via friends or older siblings and other relatives (see also for example Ball et al., 2002, Reay, Davies, et al., 2001).

In Germany, none of the young people I interviewed gave any indication that they took a specific university's or group of universities' reputation into account in their consideration of whether they wanted to go to university and if so, where. There was no discussion of the sort found in the English interviews regarding league table position or reputation. Where German interviewees did discuss type of institution, this was in relation to whether they wanted to attend a university, Fachhochschule or Berufsakademie. As mentioned above, Fachhochschulen offer applied courses in subjects such as engineering, social work or business studies. Berufsakademien formally have the same status as Fachhochschulen and they offer similar degree types, but they differ from Fachhochschulen in that the students are employed by a company or institution during their degree course, and they alternate between college and employer on a three-monthly basis. This is attractive for potential students for two reasons: the practical experience is expected to make graduates more employable, and the fact that they are receiving a salary means that funding is not an issue. This latter point is mentioned by Diana (who has attended the same Gymnasium for all of her secondary schooling) who explains that this, for her, is the reason for preferring a Berufsakademie over other types of higher education institution. Funding is an issue for her: her (single) mother works in unskilled jobs and she cannot expect financial help from her or any other member of her family, so the Berufsakademie is an attractive option.

Another difference between the two countries I noted above is the fact that a significantly higher proportion of young people in England state that they wish to go to university. An obvious explanation for this finding seems to be the fact that in Germany, the alternatives to university are more prestigious and, especially in the case of apprenticeships, better established than in England. Pupils at any non-Gymnasium school receive information about apprenticeships as a matter of course, they are encouraged to apply for places with employers and in some cases they are taught how to write an application for an apprenticeship as part of formal lessons. Apprenticeships are in the public consciousness, too, with news of shortages or a surplus of apprenticeship places forming a regular feature in media reports (for example, here is a report in the national newspaper *Süddeutsche Zeitung*, a left-leaning, liberal paper, giving details of numbers of apprentices against places in different sectors: http://www.sueddeutsche.de/wirtschaft/bilanz-zu-nachwuchskraeften-deutschland-bildet-weniger-aus-1.1807109; an article in the tabloid *BILD* claiming that Germany is turning into 'a paradise for apprentices' due to a surplus of places: http://www.bild.de/geld/wirtschaft/auszubildende/deutschland-wird-zum-azubi-paradies-30385294.bild.html; or a report in the local newspaper *Wiesbadener Tagblatt* on a scheme by the local social work department to help young people find an apprenticeship: http://www.wiesbadener-tagblatt.de/lokales/wiesbaden/nachrichten-wiesbaden/stadt-hilft-bei-suche-nach-ausbildungsplatz_14234571.htm). It is common knowledge in Germany that an apprenticeship can be a route to a rewarding, well-paid and secure career. This is especially true of apprenticeships with large companies such as Daimler, with banks, or in the public sector. Among my interviewees, there were some who said they would prefer entering an apprenticeship over some other form of training or further schooling because it meant that they would be able to start earning money sooner. Tobias, for example, when asked why an apprenticeship would be his preferred option, replied: 'Weil dann bin ich schneller fertig, hab schneller mein Geld und alles.' ['Because then I'll be finished sooner, will have my money sooner and everything.'] Or Kevin, replying to the same question: 'Ja, bei 'ner Ausbildung kriegt man Geld und hat man endlich 'ne Arbeit. Muss man nicht mehr in die Schule und so. Es ist halt besser, find ich. Auch wenn man weniger Zeit hat, also Freizeit.' ['Well, if you do an apprenticeship, you get money and you finally have a job. You don't have to go to school any more and things. It's just better, I think. Even if you have less time, spare time.']

By contrast, university is prominent in the public discourse and therefore in young people's minds in England, as illustrated by these newspaper articles on the importance of GCSE grades in applying to university (www.theguardian.com/education/2014/aug/21/how-important-are-gcses-when-applying-to-university), numbers of disadvantaged students applying to university (http://www.thetimes.co.uk/tto/education/article 4157118.ece), or A-level results and university admission (http://www. dailymail.co.uk/news/article-2724648/A-level-results-lead-record-numbers-students-heading-university-vast-majority-accepted-choice-degree-courses.html). Not surprisingly, young people in English academically selective schools mentioned intending to go to university, but perhaps more surprisingly, some others did where this might not have been expected given their academic ability, social background and school type. For example, Kim, in a secondary modern school, mentions university as one of her options on the grounds that 'The best thing I think about going to university is that it's a whole new place, there's loads of different things that you could do and it's just all the facilities there like massive libraries. I would be really excited if I got offered to go' and, talking about the time she did work experience at the local university: 'And erm, the people there are like friendly, all the teachers there and everything and I like the place, cos it's just new and all.' No one in her family has been to university and she is not obviously academically interested or motivated. She didn't know about having to pay tuition fees. All in all, her wish to go to university does not seem very realistic or thought through, which makes it interesting that she even considers it. Some of my German interviewees also talk about the possibility of attending university in a vague way only, but the difference is that they seem more aware of what universities are for, and the uncertainty relates to whether they think they will be able to first fulfil the entry requirements and then to cope once there. Others in England seem similarly misinformed and/or ignorant of university life, so despite what I said above, it is certainly not the case that every young person in England knows or cares much about university. Harry (who attends the same secondary modern school as Kim), when asked why he thinks some people might wish to go to university replies: 'I'm not sure, cos you get a place to stay, socialise, dunno, get a really good education. Hmm, not sure.' He himself has ruled out going on the grounds that it costs a lot of money and he would spend the rest of his life paying back the loan. No one he knows is planning to go or has been to university. Duncan (attending a comprehensive school without a sixth form), when asked what he might study if he did go to university merely says: 'I haven't got the slightest idea. I don't even know what they do at university.' It could be that this lack of knowledge makes university aspirations less likely, or that talents and interests lie elsewhere and information on universities is therefore not sought and/or provided, or, indeed, that the two processes are mutually reinforcing.

Another reason for the lower proportion of higher education aspirations in Germany – and this is linked to the previous discussion of what is in people's consciousness – is the fact that some occupations do not require a degree in Germany, whereas they do in England. Nursing is a case in point. So for those young people with a particular career such as nursing in mind, their aspirations will differ depending on what the accepted training route for this career is in their own country. Sarah (from a German Hauptschule), for example, is currently training to be a nurse. She explains how she came to be interested in this profession – a combination of her father's work as a doctor, her mother's as a carer for old people and her own experiences through summer jobs and placements – but she rules out going to university, not least because she says she has problems with written German and languages more generally. By contrast, Ruth (from an English grammar school) has similar reasons for wishing to become a nurse, but it is clear for her that this is something she will pursue by going to university. She is actually worried about this because she has sometimes struggled at school due to 'having dyslexia', but given her wish to become a nurse, she will have to work hard enough to be able to go to, and succeed at, university. We can see that these two young women are fairly similar in various ways, but because of differences in the system one has clear aspirations to go to university, whereas the other has clear aspirations not to.[3]

I now turn to the differences between the secondary school systems in the two countries and the implications for higher education aspirations.

7.3.2   School influences

In order to explore the role of their school in shaping young people's aspirations, I will begin by briefly describing some of the schools attended by my interviewees. The German schools may be seen as representatives of their types, that is, the Gymnasien are able to provide sponsorship in the sense that the teaching is academically oriented, the qualification which is a prerequisite for university attendance is offered there, and there is a clear expectation that young people will be able to apply to university successfully. The Realschulen and Hauptschulen provide far more support aimed at securing apprenticeships for their students, but also some preparatory support for routes through further education which can then lead to more advanced courses of study. The Gesamtschulen have some internal stratification in the core subjects mathematics, German, English and science subjects, and in line with their aims, these schools support students in whatever is the route thought to be most suited to them by the school based on their prior attainment. In England, the *independent school* I studied (which uses an academically selective admission process) and the *grammar school* have sponsorship functions similar to a German Gymnasium's. Matters are more complicated with those English schools which do not use a formal selection process, and so I will briefly describe the four in my study here.

The *secondary modern school* in Kent is attended by pupils who either tried but failed to enter a grammar school, or who did not take the eleven plus test in the first place, or who passed it, but preferred this particular school (or their parents did). Accordingly, the school places a great emphasis on offering vocational, non-academic subjects and pathways, and supports students in obtaining skills relevant for the labour market. It is an academy[4] as well as a sports specialist college, and it offers post-16 courses in areas such as hairdressing, beauty, travel and tourism, retail and construction as well as more academic subjects in cooperation with a local grammar school.

The *comprehensive school without a sixth form* is in a former mining village in a fairly deprived area. There are no schools with a strong academic orientation in the catchment area, so pupils would have to travel to the nearby city if they wanted to attend a different kind of school. This city is also where they go if they want to continue their education after year 11 either at a sixth form college or a further education college. The school offers GCSE vocational courses and BTEC[5] courses in areas such as childcare, hair and beauty, and construction, alongside the more traditional GCSE courses such as English, maths, French and sciences.

The other two comprehensives both have a sixth form. One is a *large school* with a fairly broad curriculum, offering mainly academic subjects, but some vocational courses, too. A few pupils each year enter Oxbridge (for which the school offers interview training), and pupils are generally encouraged to apply to university, but the school also prides itself on its strong pastoral support and aims to help each pupil achieve what is 'best' for the individual pupil, including, for pupils up to the age of 16, a less academic course if that is seen to be the best fit. The sixth form does offer some BTEC courses, but the main focus there is on traditional A-levels.

The other comprehensive school in this study is a *voluntary aided comprehensive school* which recently obtained academy status. It is also fairly large. It is an academically very high-achieving school. The sixth form is particularly large because most of the school's own year 11 pupils stay on and, thanks to the good reputation of the school, pupils from other local schools join the sixth form. While the school cannot select on academic ability, it is well known locally by prospective pupils and their parents that academic achievement is valued highly. Many of its pupils go on to study at prestigious universities, including Oxbridge.

From others' work on institutional habitus (for example Reay, David, et al., 2001), it becomes clear even on the basis of these very brief descriptions that these schools may shape a young person's experience and aspirations in different ways. Institutional habitus comprises factors such as social class composition of the school, type of careers advice, curriculum and subjects, types of qualifications, and links with higher education institutions. It can be used to describe and analyse the ways in which schools shape their pupils' decisions, and it is, in that sense, comparable to familial habitus. In addition, it becomes clear that, even though the contemporary British system is formally closer to a contest than a sponsored system in Turner's classification (Turner, 1960), some schools effectively act as sponsors for their pupils once they have joined the school. This is particularly noticeable in the case of the *voluntary aided academy* where the ethos is similar to that of an academically selective school. The school expects young people attending it to do well academically and to apply to prestigious universities. This expectation is clear from the school itself and manifests itself in the types of subjects on offer, results achieved and careers advice given, but it is also amplified through peers who are observed to be behaving in accordance with the general climate of the school. By contrast, schools such as the *small comprehensive without a sixth form* will have the effect of making it much harder for their pupils to develop aspirations to apply to prestigious universities, not because they actively prevent the young people from doing so, but because they are an environment where it can be an achievement for the school leavers merely to stay in education beyond the age of 16 at all, and where the normal expectation is to pursue more practically oriented courses of study. Thus, that what is perceived to be normal tends to differ across school types.

Institutional habitus is part of a mutually reinforcing process. The schools are shaped by the young people who attend them, and they in turn respond to their pupils' needs and expectations. The *voluntary aided academy*, while not actually academically selective, has an intake of academically ambitious and academically oriented pupils, for the most part, while the *comprehensive without a sixth form* and the *secondary modern school* serve pupils who, in some cases at least, do indeed need encouragement to stay on in education post 16. Notwithstanding these general tendencies, there are, of course, exceptions where there is a mismatch between the pupil and the school. David (see also Chapter 6), who attends the *comprehensive without sixth form*, is a case in point. He is hoping to go to Oxbridge, following the example of his brother who attended the same school and who is currently studying at Oxford University. This is unusual, however, and while the school seem proud of the fact that David's brother is at Oxford and he himself might be able to go, they have not been able to offer much support to facilitate this, not least because they do not have a sixth form, but also because the careers advice they provide focusses on other types of educational and occupational careers. David's social background is perhaps slightly unusual compared with the other pupils in his school: his father is a postmaster (though his highest qualifications are O-levels), and his mother has a degree in computer science from a new university and she works as a web designer. So there is some experience of higher education in his family. Conversely, there are some young people whose own interests are less academic than those of the school. For example, Deborah, whom I also discussed in some detail in Chapter 6, was not happy with her selective independent school's preference for academic success over any other sort of goal and she left the school to do graphic design at a local sixth form college. While these two cases are examples of young people whose intentions and careers did not match the school's institutional habitus, for most others there appears to be a good fit between home background, school and personal aspirations and ability.

The school may offer an academically talented individual a way into a more ambitious educational career than his or her home background might have made likely. Grammar schools, but also schools such as the *voluntary aided academy* and the *large comprehensive school with sixth form* I described above, can effectively act as sponsors once such a child enters the school aged 11. In the case of grammar schools, this opportunity for sponsorship depends on the child's measured academic ability prior to entry, but with schools such as the other two, this is partly based on happenstance, depending on where the family lives at the time of the transition to secondary school. This was the case for Alexandra and Maya in the *large comprehensive school* or Matthew in the *voluntary aided school*. Their parents did not move to be within a particular catchment area, they just happened to live near a school which was able to nurture their talents and encourage university ambitions. The schools were able effectively to act as sponsors without being formally academically selective. As noted, I do not have any systematic data on my interviewees' academic performance, but there are some pieces of indirect evidence which led me to this view of these three cases' talents. Alexandra mentions having high grades despite not having been expected to be a 'high achiever', Maya also mentions achieving high grades, in contrast to everyone else in her family. Matthew had already taken his GCSEs by the time the interview took place, and he had gained 4 A*s and the rest As. None of these three cases' parents had been to university, and while they noted this in their interviews, they were clear that university was an appropriate route for them. It seems at least conceivable that for some such young people, things might have turned out differently if they had happened to attend a different kind of school. Matthew's sisters for example both attended a different secondary school and neither of them went to university, though without my knowing anything else about their abilities and circumstances, this reasoning is obviously not conclusive in itself.

Emily, Patricia and Rosie, all attending a grammar school in Kent, would also be the first ones in their families to go to university, but they have experienced sponsorship within an academically selective system, much like the German stratified system. In Germany, too, we find examples of young people who have developed university aspirations despite a lack of higher education experience in their families. Diana, Magdalena, Jessica, Marina, Sebastian and Marko are the cases who fit this pattern here, all attending a Gymnasium.

In my German sample, there are far fewer young people in schools other than a Gymnasium, in comparison with Gymnasium pupils, who say that they wish to go to university (they are Andreas, Nicole and Patrick from a Realschule and Aynur, Julia and Vanessa from a Gesamtschule), and among those, it is rarer still if there is no experience of higher education in the family (Patrick and Vanessa).

These cases illustrate that the discussion of institutional habitus above applies to the German schools, too, given that these schools differ in the expectations and institutional support on offer. Gymnasium pupils, if they mention any sort of careers advice at all, talk about open days at universities or mentoring programmes which introduce pupils to graduate careers. Realschule and Hauptschule pupils, by contrast, are encouraged to apply for apprenticeships or other forms of further education (which may or may not lead to qualifications allowing higher education entry), and the work experience on offer is in non-graduate fields. Gesamtschulen, in line with their more heterogeneous intake, offer a more varied range of careers advice. As with the English schools discussed above, I should note that this is a mutually reinforcing process since schools offer the type of careers advice which is most likely to be useful for their student body, and while institutional habitus and sponsorship will have had some influence on the young people's expectations and aspirations, their academic ability also affects which pathways they can enter. Since academic ability was the basis for the selection process at the end of primary school in the first place, it is not surprising that the range of academic ability within one type of school is limited, which means that there is a good match between type of careers advice and average ability within the student body. However, it is also the case that the selection process at the end of primary school is not perfect: as noted earlier, it is socially as well as academically selective, it takes place fairly early, thus potentially putting late developers at a disadvantage, and it can also be disadvantageous for recent immigrants with low levels of German language skills. Once a child has been allocated to a secondary school, however, the school's ethos is likely to have some effect on a young person's future decisions, even if their actual ability level does not quite match the school's.

7.3.3   Individual factors

Finally, whether or not a young person develops the aspiration and ambition to go to university can be linked to factors and processes relating to the individual and his/her home background, in addition to the system and school factors discussed above. Some interviewees come from families where attending university is the norm and they expect to follow this expectation. Charlotte, Kalvinder, Philippa and Georgia are examples from England for this scenario (see also Chapter 6) and Anna, Alina and Julia from Germany. In other families, it is normal not to go to university. Gabriele mentions her family explicitly to explain why she wouldn't consider university. She refers to her own and her three sisters' and two stepbrothers' educational careers when she says 'wir wollen auch alle nicht studieren oder so, wir wollen einfach nur eine Ausbildung haben.' [Also, none of us want to go to university or anything, we just want to get an apprenticeship.] Her mother, she explains, 'does not like the Gymnasium'. However, it is rare for someone to rule out university quite so categorically on such grounds, and talents and interests (on which more below) are more commonly mentioned when explaining why university is not the preferred option. The family, while an important influence, is not the only factor and some young people do not do what would be normal in their families. On the one hand, there are those who do not wish to go to university despite this being the normal thing to do in their families, though this is not very common among my interviewees. Ludwig is such a case: he does not rule out going to university, but he is not sure, not least because he'd be interested in becoming a physiotherapist which does not require a degree in Germany. Marcus likewise does not rule out going to university, but does not see himself as academically minded (see also Chapter 6 and Chapter 8). On the other hand, and much more commonly, some young people develop the wish to go to university even if there is no one in their family and wider social circle to have done so. Clearly, lacking such a role model in the family is not an insurmountable barrier to university attendance, at least not for all cases. In the context of educational expansion, this is not surprising given that more university places were made available, and so it was possible for at least some of these to be filled by people who are the first generation to attend university (Müller, 1998). As noted above, Diana, Magdalena, Jessica, Marina, Sebastian and Marko are relevant examples for Germany, all attending a Gymnasium, and so are Vanessa and Aynur, attending a Gesamtschule. In England, Emily, Paul, Rosie, Patricia, Maya and Alexandra fall into this category. These young people are of course aware that their aspiration is unusual in their family, as evident, for example, in this quote from Alexandra:

> No one in my family's been to university at all. So everyone was quite shocked when I said I wanted to go. I mean I think they didn't expect

me to be a high achiever, I mean not in a nasty way obviously but ... They just expected me to leave school at 16, get a job and sort of do whatever they did, didn't expect me to because like all my cousins and things have just left school and got jobs.
[Asked about how her family felt about her university plans:]
I think they're proud. I think so, I think they're a bit like apprehensive because they don't really know much about it. They don't know anything about university obviously not having experienced it, just stayed at like, at home and got jobs around the house.
[Asked about her own feelings:]
It makes me feel a little bit ... I'm obviously very proud. It's gonna be good but, err, it would be nice to have someone to talk to that had a bit of experience but, so I'm having to go to sort of outside the family sources for things.

Some mention that their families hope for them to improve their lives by gaining a university degree, specifically mentioning that they want something better for their children than they were able to achieve. Diana's mother for example left school with minimal qualifications and works in two jobs, as a waitress and as an unskilled worker in a factory, but she says that she wants her daughter to have opportunities she herself didn't have. Diana does not seem troubled or pressured by this; she enjoys school, describing herself as ambitious and interested in learning.

In addition to factors in their home background, the young people's academic ability affects their aspirations. As noted above, given that I had no access to school performance data or test results, I am only able to draw on what they themselves report regarding their academic achievements. Notwithstanding this constraint, there are some indicators of the importance of ability, given that it affects achievement. Young people mention academic success as well as failure in explaining their ambitions and plans. They also develop their interests in line with what they believe they can and cannot do, for example when they describe how they enjoy and do well in particular school subjects and how this has led to their plans for university. The young person in my study with the most clearly formed plan is probably Alina. She plays the French horn and has already been accepted by the music department at the university in the city where she lives to study with them on a programme for young musicians who are still at school, but who are expected to progress onto the normal degree course once they have gained their Abitur. Alina is clearly musically talented and is sure not only that she will go to university, but also exactly what she will study there.

Specific talents or interests can also lead someone to decide against applying to university. Samuel for example has known for some time that he wants to be a plumber like his father, and so he does not intend to pursue a more academic pathway even though his marks would allow this (see the more detailed discussion in Chapter 5). Other interviewees also had already secured places as apprentices based on some particular interest, or had already started their training. Sarah for example is training as a nurse and Yvonne is training as a nursery nurse. Insofar as these young people explain their non-university choices at all, it is usually with reference to lack of academic talent, or to interests which lead them elsewhere (or both). It seems, then, that at least from the perspective of the individual, talent and/or interest can at least partly explain both university and non-university aspirations. Such talents or interests seem to be considered by the young people to be necessary conditions for deciding in favour or against a particular route.

Those who have decided to apply to university, in addition to referring to interests and talents, frequently mention that they hope to have a good job and a degree is perceived to be helpful in achieving that. In England, William shows signs of rational choice-type thinking, saying 'Tuition fees are, I really do not understand the people that say "I won't be able to afford to go to university." Because it's a loan, the whole reason you go to university is so you can get a good job and pay back the loan easily.' Saskia expresses the same view: 'I think that in order to get a good job that you have to go to university now. I don't think you'd, it's definitely not highly thought of in the job industry if you haven't gone to university and pursued a degree.' Or Denise: 'I think you have a lot more opportunities if you're a graduate than if not.' In Germany, Sibel's route to the Gymnasium she now attends was not straightforward, and she says that now she has managed to get there and is on her way to gaining the Abitur, she certainly wants to go to university so as not to waste the effort but also because she wants a good job: 'Also ich will halt schon, ja einen guten Job haben später mal und ja, ich könnte mir das noch nicht vorstellen, eine Ausbildung zu machen.' [Well, I do want, well, have a good job later on and, yes, I couldn't imagine doing an apprenticeship.]

7.4 Conclusion

In this chapter, I have used theory to develop explanations of individual cases' outcomes, but also to draw more general conclusions based on the insights from the cases I have analysed. The young people themselves are not necessarily aware of the broader social processes which shape their preferences and their decision-making. To detect such patterns, both the QCA analyses for both countries and the analysis of interview data have been useful, as well as having theories to draw on which can provide potential explanatory mechanisms. Key theories here were rational action theory (RAT) (Boudon, 1974, Breen & Goldthorpe, 1997, Goldthorpe, 1996b) and Bourdieu's habitus concept (Bourdieu, 1977, Bourdieu & Passeron, 1979). I also considered specific properties of the educational system of the country the young people live in as potential influences shaping their expectations and preferences regarding their future educational careers.

While the young people themselves often explained their preferred educational pathways, whether these involved higher education or not, mainly in terms of their own talents and interests, many also engaged in some form of rational cost-benefit analysis in explaining how they came to aim for a particular educational career, explaining their preference for a degree by reference to a better job they hope to be able to obtain. I discussed the cases of William, Saskia and Sibel as examples of young people who engaged in such reasoning.

As noted above, a family's habitus defines what is considered normal for a young person, and it can impact on how well they fit in with the school's and education system's expectations and requirements. In this chapter, I showed that habitus does indeed appear to have some importance since some young people refer to what is normal in their families in explaining their preferences and decisions. The preference may be expressed for a particular job or profession, in which case the decision for an educational pathway follows from what is required for this chosen career, or it may be for a particular form of education, usually higher education, without yet having a wish for any specific occupation. This applied both to young people who did and did not wish to go to university. Cases I discussed where habitus seemed to have this role include Samuel who wishes to follow in his father's footsteps and to become a plumber, and Charlotte, Kalvinder, Philippa and Georgia from England and Anna, Alina and Julia from Germany who all consider a university career the normal thing to expect, whether or not they already have a particular occupation in mind. We saw that, for those expecting to go to university, a configuration of factors comprising home background, school ethos (or institutional habitus, Reay, David, et al., 2001), and individual talents and ambitions are conducive to developing these expectations. Habitus is not simply the presence or absence of some individual factor alone, but their combination.

Given the nature of what I have found, it might be better to conceive of habitus as constraining and enabling rather than determining. Lizardo (2009), for example, argues that the habitus concept is not inherently deterministic. While habitus clearly is important for many young people's educational careers, including those discussed in the previous paragraph, I have also shown that others follow alternative routes to those that might have been expected given their families' habitus. This applies to cases such as Marcus or Ludwig who may not go to university, contrary to what is largely the norm in their families, but also to all those cases who do aspire to go to university despite there being no such history in their families and wider social networks.

We have seen that mutually reinforcing processes are often behind the observed trajectories and outcomes. For example, children from privileged social backgrounds tend to attend academically oriented schools with a high social class composition – either because their attainment is high enough to be admitted to a selective school, or because their parents make a special effort for them to gain access to an academically oriented school, or both – and they experience teachers and peers there for whom the normal expectation is to stay in education beyond the minimum leaving age and to aspire to university as a matter of course. This expectation matches their parents' and extended families' as part of a mutually reinforcing process.

Young people are aware that other ways of life exist than that they experience at home and at school, but this is often not very clear, as is evident in Harry's reply to the question why he thought people went to university, something he has ruled out for himself. ('I'm not sure, cos you get a place to stay, socialise, dunno, get a really good education. Hmm, not sure'). Instead, they take their lead from what family, friends and peers are doing or are planning to do. All the four girls in the secondary modern school in Kent I interviewed intend to study 'hair and beauty' or do an apprenticeship as hairdressers, for example.

In the face of such mutually reinforcing processes, it is possible to draw plausible conclusions which are applicable more generally and not just to the specific cases included in the study. It is more difficult to come to such conclusions when there is a mismatch between an individual, his or her home background, and/or the school, as in cases such as Alexandra from a working-class family with no experience of higher education who achieves highly herself and who is almost certain to go to university, Marcus whose background is unusual compared with most of his peers in the secondary modern school, or Deborah who did not feel welcome in her selective, private school. I did suggest some general lessons to be learnt from such cases: individual interests may be stronger than home and/or school influences, and some schools can help overcome potential disadvantages experienced in the home. However, open questions remain and I will revisit and expand accounts of some of the cases where there is some sort of mismatch in the next chapter which develops explanations of individual cases' pathways and outcomes in greater detail.

8
Using In-Depth Case Studies to Explore Causal Mechanisms in Detail

In the previous three chapters, I drew on relevant explanatory theories to explain those patterns in the data that had been established via Qualitative Comparative Analysis (QCA). I also employed in-depth analyses of my cases to confirm and refine these theories. After initially introducing some details of the individual cases, I then moved to use these cases to draw more general conclusions regarding factors and potential underlying mechanisms that may have led to their outcomes. My goal here, in other words, was a theoretical one. In this chapter, the focus is instead on explaining individual cases' trajectories and outcomes rather than using cases to develop general theory. As well as being motivated by a substantive interest in explaining particular cases from my study, the purpose of this chapter is to illustrate, in describing my own approach, how such explanations may be undertaken. Thus, the focus now is on 'explaining' rather than on 'theorizing' (Hammersley, 2012), as I discussed in Chapter 2. I will use some of the same case studies I used in Chapters 5–7, but also additional ones.

To explain these individual cases' educational pathways and outcomes, I draw on existing theory and combine this with my knowledge of factors covered by the theory *and* knowledge of additional, specific factors characterising a particular case. Lieberson's (1997, p. 376, Lieberson & Silverman, 1965) suggestion that we combine 'underlying causal conditions' and 'immediate precipitants' in the explanation of specific events is useful here. He uses it in the context of explaining the occurrence of race riots, where underlying causal conditions make a riot more or less likely, while immediate precipitants are events which act as triggers of a riot. While these ideas are not directly transferable to my context (not least because race riots are relatively rare events, unlike most educational outcomes), they are nevertheless very helpful when the aim is to explain individual outcomes. Underlying causal conditions in my study are the individual and social background factors discussed in the previous chapters, that is, type of school system and type of school (academically selective or not, as well school's social composition), parental social class and education, and cognitive ability as indicated by the recommendation (for Germany) and prior academic achievement shown in the key stage 2 test (for England). Knowledge of the constellation of these factors helps predict for an individual case whether certain outcomes will be more or less likely. Immediate precipitants then are the presence or absence of events or idiosyncrasies which lead to an individual's either following the expected path and gaining the outcome, or deviating from this path. Timing can be important here: an event occurring immediately prior to some transition or decision point often has more potential to impact on the future career than one that falls outside a critical period. The reason I also explicitly refer to absence of events is that, for many, it is the lack of disturbing events that allows whatever is the normal course or pathway in their configurational context to proceed smoothly.

The immediate precipitants can be events that are the result of chance or contingency, as described, for example, by Bandura (1982) and Becker (1994). Becker, while not using Lieberson's language of immediate precipitants and underlying causal conditions, employs a similar model in his account of how chance encounters or events can trigger a certain outcome or change in trajectory. Again, whether this outcome or change actually occurs depends at least partly on certain preconditions being in place.

Lieberson (1997) argues that a probabilistic model of causation is helpful in explaining outcomes in the social sciences even if the underlying world is thought to be deterministic (see also Chapter 2). This is because there are usually so many potential influences on an outcome or process that it is impossible to take account of them all. Given this situation, a probabilistic model can provide a useful approximation. In addition, some factors in the world will actually be operating randomly. But any such randomness takes place within constraints and the effects the random factors or events can have usually depend on the context. Lieberson gives the example of admissions policies for highly selective universities. The most highly able and distinguished candidates are almost certain to be offered a place, and the least able ones are almost certain to be rejected, but for those who do not fall into either of these categories, chance will have some effect on whether or not they are selected for a place. This is because the criteria and the preferences of the selecting committee may vary slightly from time to time, for example.[1] Thus, it is easier to predict outcomes for very obviously qualified candidates and for very obviously unsuitable ones, but for those who, say, fulfil the formal admissions criteria but otherwise have no clearly distinguishing qualities, this is much harder.

Another angle on the issue of preconditions and precipitating events is illustrated by Lieberson's account of what may have caused the First World War. The trigger commonly cited by historians is the assassination of the Austrian heir to the throne in Sarajevo in June 1914. To answer the question of whether this is indeed a causal event, Lieberson notes:

> We can ask ourselves unknowable questions, but they help illustrate the point. Would the war have occurred anyway, even without the assassination? Would the assassination have had the same effect if it had occurred three years earlier? I have no idea. But think of the models each of these questions involve. If the war would probably have occurred anyway even without the assassination (shooting someone is no different than a penalty kick in soccer or a field goal attempt in football – you do not always succeed), this means the conditions had reached a point where a wide variety of events would trigger the war – it would be an accident waiting to happen. If that is the case, then we are interested less in the assassination and more in the condition which generates such a state in which a variety of random events will almost lead to the same outcome. If, on the other hand, the assassination is a critical event, we need to know what the probability would have been for the same consequence with an earlier assassination. In other words, the influence of a given independent variable is not constant, but depends on its timing. And its timing is presumably at least in part a random event, i.e., not totally correlated with other political events. (Lieberson, 1998, p. 142)

Educational outcomes can be the result of factors such as social background and individual ability and motivation, in the sense that these reflect causal mechanisms which make particular outcomes likely. However, as in the example of admissions to selective institutions above, it is worth noting that such factors cannot perfectly predict an outcome and specific events or experiences can trigger an outcome or a decision. Lieberson's 'accident waiting to happen' here, for example, can be a young person's situation where both parents have degrees and work in graduate level jobs, the young person is cognitively highly able, academically motivated and has received appropriate schooling. In such a situation, the young person's wish to attend university is an outcome which would seem very likely (like an accident waiting to happen). It could also be described as overdetermined (for my use of this term, see Chapters 5 and 6). For other cases, chance events and/or specific triggers are likely to be of greater importance. For example, for a cognitively highly able young person from a working-class background where both parents hold only basic qualifications, the role of a particular teacher or being a member of a particular peer group may be of much greater importance in encouraging or discouraging university aspirations than in the hypothetical 'overdetermined' case. Rutter describes such an event or experience as having the '*opportunity* to make a difference' (Rutter, 1996, p. 612, emphasis in the original). This is more likely to be the case if other experiences and factors are likely to work against the outcome (though obviously not so strongly so as to make the event irrelevant). As is evident in Lieberson's quote above, the timing can be important here, an idea which is also discussed by Shanahan et al. (2000), along with the importance of factors such as frequency of events and duration of a situation (see also Rutter, 1996).

I now apply these considerations to my aim of explaining individual cases' outcomes. To do so, I will begin by briefly revisiting *typical* cases, or cases where the outcome is *overdetermined* with regard to the constellation of potentially causal factors, in order to show that there is less possibility for contingency or unexpected events to have a significant impact on these individuals' educational pathways. The greater part of the discussion will then be devoted to cases where there is this possibility, cases whose educational pathway is *unexpected* in some way. Unexpected pathways here mean that potentially causal factors and outcome do not appear to match, either because we find a seemingly favourable factor or configuration of factors coupled with a less favourable outcome, or a combination of unfavourable factors coupled with a positive outcome. There is some overlap with cases I have described as deviant and inconclusive in Chapters 5–7, but here, as well exploring the cases in more depth, I also focus on a greater variety of outcomes. Some of the cases that I previously discussed under the label 'deviant' appear again in this chapter as 'unexpected', but, in addition, some of those I will discuss in this chapter as 'unexpected' I had previously labelled 'inconclusive'. This is because, while they may have been 'inconclusive' in relation to the QCA and truth table analyses, there are theoretical expectations that would have seemed to make a different outcome more likely than the observed outcome, as I will show.

8.1 Overdetermined outcomes

For the cases I describe under this heading, it is not necessary to look for explanations for their educational outcomes beyond the families of origin and school environment because their experiences fit a pattern we expect to find based on sociological knowledge of the underlying mechanisms. I have already discussed some of these cases under the heading of 'typical' in the previous chapters, so I will not repeat what I have said there. However, it is worth examining more closely some of the accounts of what happened at the key transition point of choosing a secondary school. I begin by discussing three cases (Vera, Zoe and Amy) who did not appear in Chapters 5 and 6 as 'typical' because the outcomes I studied there were, for the German cases, being in Gymnasium and, for the English cases, intending to go to university, but these academic pathways are not 'typical' outcomes for cases such as these three, as will be seen.

Vera in Germany is from a family where both parents have low qualifications and working-class jobs. She received a recommendation for the Realschule, but her primary teacher informally suggested to her parents that she might be better off in a Hauptschule, and since her sister also went there, she and her parents were happy to accept this piece of advice. While she herself doesn't comment on her family's background in relation to this decision (neither spontaneously nor on prompting), it is possible to fill in the gaps, as it were, and use existing sociological knowledge of typical processes and the role of social background in educational decision-making to get some idea of why a family would choose Hauptschule, a route presumably perceived as less risky and more familiar than the Realschule, even though a Realschulabschluss would offer better opportunities later on. In England, we find similar cases in Zoe and Amy who live in Kent but did not even attempt to take the eleven plus which, if they had passed it, would have given them the opportunity to attend a grammar school. Neither their parents nor their teachers in primary school seem to have argued very strongly that they should take the test. Zoe doesn't know much about her parents' educational careers, but it seems that they left school with no or with minimal qualifications, and she also hints at health and/or mental health problems. Her father works as a porter, her mother has never worked, as far as Zoe knows. Her parents are separated and she lives with her father, but sees her mother regularly. Again, it is not hard to see how a lack of educational experience in her family may have contributed to the lack of interest in possible grammar school entry for Zoe. This is possibly coupled with not very high academic ability. While I do not have any independent evidence of Zoe's level of ability, she says about herself: 'I'm not that smart' when explaining why she does not wish to go to university. Vera, Amy and Zoe all intend to leave school with some qualifications and to enter occupations such as hairdressing or interior decorating.

These are just three examples of cases where a lack of educational credentials in the family coupled with working-class occupational experience and no obvious signs of a high level of academic ability seem sufficient to explain educational decisions to follow routes which are unlikely to lead to high qualifications. At the opposite end of the scale, we find young people who aspire to study at university, and whose family background and educational experience to date seem to offer a straightforward explanation of such an aspiration. Again, it is worth exploring key transitional points, and I will do so for two cases I have already discussed as 'typical' in Chapter 6 (Charlotte and Philippa). For Charlotte, who attends an independent, selective school in England, the only other option she considered at the end of primary school was a different independent school. She and her parents ruled out her attending a state school because they lived too far from a 'good' state school. Both parents hold degrees; her father is a solicitor, her mother is a science teacher at Charlotte's school. Philippa's parents also both hold degrees; her father works as a medical physicist, her mother is a teacher. Since she lives in Kent, she had the option of attending an academically selective secondary school via passing the eleven plus, which is what she did. The way she talks about this transition to secondary school makes it clear that both she and her family as well as teachers and friends expected her to go on to grammar school, presumably because of her ability, but also because this was clearly the 'normal' thing for someone like her to do: 'most people expected me to go to a grammar school anyway.[...], like the teachers and friends and stuff.' When asked why she thought people expected this, she referred to her ability: 'Because I've always been quite clever.' Her sister already attended her grammar school when Philippa took the eleven plus.

Thus, it seems to be the case, that, as I said at the beginning of this section, the cases under this heading may be explained satisfactorily by referring to the configurations of social background and individual factors, and that it is not necessary to look beyond family and school experiences. It is of course possible that the young people described here did experience specific life events or situations which in principle might have had the potential to change their pathways and outcomes, but the

young people did not think to mention such experiences because no
such change actually did take place.

8.2 Unexpected constellations and the role of contingency

In this section, I draw on the ideas concerning contingency and chance
described in the introductory section to this chapter, showing how
chance interacts with configurations of background factors to produce
particular pathways and outcomes in selected cases. I focus on cases
where there is some unexpected element in their particular constellation and outcomes are less easily predicted than in the cases discussed
in the previous section since contingency has more scope to be of
importance here, in other words, as noted above, it has an *'opportunity*
to make a difference' (Rutter, 1996, p. 612, emphasis in the original).
I will conduct thought experiments to analyse the role of the contingent event or situation in question, drawing on relevant comparison
cases where possible. The rationale for such counterfactual reasoning[2] is
that using additional insights wherever possible to show that some life
event or particular situation is indeed the cause of some outcome can
serve to strengthen the case for a particular explanation of a potential
causal mechanism. For example, if someone unexpectedly does not
obtain some outcome, then a comparison with another case or other
cases which are as similar as possible in as many ways as possible but
which do obtain the outcome can point to the one factor, event or constellation of factors which led to the unexpected lack of the outcome.
Lieberson (1998) uses such counterfactual reasoning in trying to deter-
mine whether the assassination of the Archduke of Austria was indeed a
trigger for the First World War, whether other triggers could have played
the same part, and, if not, whether the assassination was only able to act
as a trigger at this particular point in time, given the particular constellation of factors (see quote above).

I begin by discussing cases where an unfavourable configuration of
factors is coupled with a positive outcome, followed by cases where a
favourable factor or configuration of factors is coupled with an unexpectedly low educational outcome.

8.2.1 Unfavourable factors and positive outcome

The first set of cases I discuss in this section are those with the unexpectedly positive outcome of Gymnasium attendance aged 17, notwithstanding that we should not have expected this theoretically,
given their social background of no parental Abitur combined with

no parental service class occupation. While Germany's academically selective secondary school system is likely to be detrimental to some children, it can be particularly beneficial to those from such a family where there is no experience of higher education or service class occupations provided they are cognitively highly able and can therefore gain sponsorship via a selective school. This applies to various cases in my interview sample (Diana, Jessica, Magdalena, Marina, Marko, Sebastian), and I will discuss Marko in some detail by way of example. The Gymnasium recommendation came as no surprise to him given his good performance throughout primary school. His academic ability is also evident, for example, in the fact that he always gains top marks in science subjects without having to study at home, or his physics teacher's suggestion that he move to a school for people with a special gift for physics. His mother is a hairdresser, his stepfather works as a carer in a sheltered workshop. His father – whom he is in contact with – last worked as a construction worker, but currently does not work because of ill health. There is no one in Marko's family or among his family friends he can talk to about studying at university. However, he seems to know whom to approach and what to ask regarding how to apply to university, what to apply for, and what possible career routes there are, in particular talking to teachers, but also others such as a client of his mother's. He spends a lot of time away from home, taking part in activities such as volleyball, extracurricular Spanish and drama, and running a youth group for the church. He is very aware of the difference between himself and some of the other pupils at his schools with regard to support from home and money (or lack of it), but does not seem to feel particularly aggrieved about this. If anything, he stresses that he thinks of himself as much more independent and capable of organising his everyday life than 'rich' children who, unlike him, do not have to help out at home, who get driven to school, and who have never earned their own money, something he does for example by tutoring other pupils or delivering leaflets. This is how he describes a rich classmate's life compared with his:

> Der hat schon vor Ewigkeiten ein iPhone gehabt, wo es noch ganz neu war und richtig teuer. Und der spielt Golf und trägt Tommy Hilfiger. OK, das tragen viele jetzt grad, aber der ist halt schon ziemlich ..., der wird jeden Tag in die Schule gefahren und abgeholt. [...] ich kenn ihn jetzt nicht gut genug, aber wenn ich jetzt denk, dass der mal später im Leben selber bügeln muss oder irgendwie so was, der kriegt das ja nicht auf die Reihe. Die haben eine Putzfrau

daheim, der muss sein Zimmer nicht selber aufräumen. Ah ja, wenn ich denk, meine Mutter ist selten daheim, früher schon, bevor mein Stiefvater, also bevor die zusammen waren, da war ich ja fast immer allein nach der Schule, hab ich alles selber gekocht und mit der Zeit kriegt man es rein. Bügeln tu ich eigentlich schon immer selber.' ['He already had an iPhone ages ago when they were still new and really expensive. And he plays golf and wears Tommy Hilfiger. OK, lots of people wear that now, but he is quite ..., he is driven to school every day and gets picked up again. [...] I don't know him well enough, but if I imagine that he'll have to do his own ironing later in life or anything like that, he won't manage it. They have a cleaner at home, he doesn't have to tidy his own room. And if I think, my mother is hardly ever at home, already I used to, before my stepfather, so before they were together, I was almost always by myself after school, cooked everything and with time you work it out. I've always done my own ironing.

A relevant thought experiment here is to imagine that Marko lived in England instead of Germany with its selective secondary school system. It seems plausible that whether someone like him living in England would succeed academically would depend much more on whether he or she happened to live in the catchment area of a 'good' school such as the voluntary aided comprehensive or the comprehensive with sixth form some of my interviewees attend, or whether their default secondary school would be one such as the small comprehensive without a sixth form. Indeed, as I have shown in the previous chapter, the evidence bears this out: while young people in either of the first two schools mostly wish to gain A-levels and attend university, regardless of their social background, none of those whose social background is comparable to Marko's who attended the small comprehensive without sixth form developed such ambitions. For many individuals, school type clearly matters. In Germany, for someone like Marko who is considered academically able enough to attend the Gymnasium, place of residence matters much less given that there will always be a Gymnasium within reach, so the type of secondary school is not determined by place of residence as much as academic ability in primary school (which, as we know, is itself not completely independent of social background, of course, but this is another matter). Marko's academic ability had the *'opportunity* to make a difference' (Rutter, 1996) because he happened to live in a part of the world where academically selective schools offer sponsorship (Turner, 1960) to those considered suitable for entering them.

However, as I suggested in Chapter 7, certain comprehensive schools in England may act as sponsors for those lucky enough to live nearby. Obviously, this is not purely luck: some parents make an active effort to live near a 'good' school, and/or have other ways of ensuring that their children attend those. But my focus here is on cases where parents do not make such an effort, and where they live really is a matter of luck. Alexandra (previously discussed in Sections 6.5 and 7.3.3) is a case in point. Her social class background is similar to Marko's. Like him, she attends an academically oriented school (the comprehensive with sixth form), and she is planning to attend university to study medicine, hoping, incidentally, that she will be able to gain a scholarship to attend the sixth form at a local independent academically selective school instead of her current comprehensive school. Arguably, as with her university aspirations, it seems possible that it would not have occurred to her to aim to attend such a school if the secondary school she attended initially had not been so academically oriented.

I now turn to a rather different type of outcome. Throughout this book, I mostly discuss outcomes that are a sign of academic success, such as attending Gymnasium and expecting to go to university. However, it is worth bearing in mind that for a significant number of young people, university aspirations are out of reach and it may be considered an achievement – indeed, an unexpected outcome – merely to stay in education and to gain some qualifications. I shall briefly describe two such cases (Duncan and Katja), with the aim of identifying some factor or configuration of factors which contributed to their staying on in school. They may be characterised, briefly, by a configuration of factors comprising parental non-service class occupations, a broken home, attending a non-academic type of secondary school, and behaviour problems especially in the earlier part of secondary schooling. Despite this set of problematic factors, they have obtained the unlikely outcome of completing or being about to complete secondary schooling with some qualifications.

Duncan (see also Chapter 6) attends the comprehensive without sixth form. His mother was permanently excluded from school when she was 14 years old. His father left the family when Duncan was born, and he lives with his mother, an older stepbrother and a younger half-brother. His maternal grandfather left school at 14 to work in the mines. Duncan himself was temporarily excluded from school numerous times and, for most of his time in secondary school, was on the verge of being excluded permanently, but things had become much better by his current year 11, according to him. Asked what it was that helped him turn things around, he points to a friend's experience: 'And then I think, I think the last time that I got excluded I just, I went over the top. Me and Gordon, like he went absolutely mental, he got permanent [exclusion], but we went mental together, but like I think when he got permanent I just realised that I really don't wanna be like that. I just, I just don't wanna get excluded to be honest, like I've just had enough of it. Like I know for a fact that I'm on me last chance now and if I get excluded again then that would be it for me and like it's really too late to find a new school, innit.' In addition to this realisation triggered by the incident with his friend, two people seem to have been crucial in supporting him and strengthening his resolve to stay in school now. One is his grandfather (the one mentioned above): 'I've been kicked out a few times, but like, since like I dunno, I think it's probably like something me granddad's said to us. Cos like me granddad's been like the most supportive since I was little, he's been like the one person I've just really wanted to make happy with all of me qualifications and that. I think I'm just doing it for him to be honest.' The thought of working in the mines[3] from the age of 14 like his grandfather horrifies him and this seems to have been contributing to his wish to finish school and gain some qualifications. It is clear throughout the interview that he is close to his grandfather, and that his grandfather's experience has affected him. The other person is one particular teacher who apparently did everything he could to keep him in the school: 'Mr Harris he's a star really. He's definitely been there since I was in year 7. He's excluded so many people he's told me that, even all the teachers have said, "Do you know how hard Mr Harris has been trying to keep you in this school?" He's like really canny, you can get on with him really well. He goes to me "I don't really say this often, right, but when I exclude someone I don't really think about it. Like if I excluded you I think you're like one of the only students that I would miss". Champion. Yeah, so I think like that person has been trying really hard to keep us in.' While he is not out of the woods yet – he still has to pass some exams and take up his place at a further education college – it seems that these three factors, the incident with his friend, his grandfather's experience and his teacher's support, have contributed to keeping him in school.

The second case I wish to discuss is that of Katja. She currently attends year 10 of a Hauptschule scheme which will allow her to gain a Realschulabschluss (that is, the intermediate qualification which is formally sufficient for any form of apprenticeship), since her Hauptschulabschluss qualification was good enough for her to be admitted to this scheme. She had a troubled upbringing in various respects: her mother moved to

Germany from Russia, though Katja herself was born in Germany. Her father died when she was one year old. Katja lives with her mother, but very unhappily, as she does not get on with her. She describes herself as having been an aggressive child, not having any friends in primary school and falling out with teachers. From the age of 12, she stayed out until midnight occasionally, hanging out with friends who had gone off the rails, were truanting and were taking drugs. She came to close to taking drugs herself, but this was when she decided to put a stop to things. Asked about how she managed to achieve this, she is not really sure: 'Ich weiß es nicht, ich hab gedacht, so weit muss ich nicht sinken. Ich hab schon geraucht und das hat mir gereicht. Dann hab ich gesagt, mehr muss, ich muss mir nicht noch mehr kaputt machen und nachdem ich mich da irgendwie ja, nachdem ich da raus bin, hat mich mein Trainer dann aufgebaut.' [I don't know, I thought I don't have to sink as low as this. I was smoking in any case and that was enough already. Then I said to myself, I shouldn't mess things up any more, and after I somehow, well, after I got out of this, my coach then supported me.] This is her table tennis coach, and he appears to be an important figure in her life, acting as a mentor and also supplying her with a surrogate family. As well as enjoying the sport itself and the sense of community in the table tennis club, she spends more time at her coach's house than at home, helping out round the house as well as with his business which is in insurance. The latter led to her developing an interest in insurance as a possible occupation, and she is currently trying to get an apprenticeship in this field. Her other idea for a career is to join the criminal investigation department (Kriminalpolizei). This came about because a friend of hers was murdered not long ago and she and other friends were interviewed as witnesses by the police, clearly a chance event which had the effect of broadening her ideas for a possible career. Apparently one of the police officers suggested that she might do well as a police officer, making her waver between this as a possible career and insurance. However, all these plans depend to some extent on how well she does in her current year 10 which she finds more of a struggle than the previous Hauptschule, but she is determined to work hard, having asked her mother to pay for extra tuition to help her improve her marks. Like Duncan, then, she is not yet clearly on track for sufficient qualifications and a settled career, but she does seem to have managed to turn her life around following the difficult childhood years.

It is tempting to conclude that I have identified the specific triggers that helped move these two young people towards gaining the unexpected outcome of successfully completing secondary education: for Duncan, it would be that his grandfather and the teacher he mentions coupled with the final event of his friend being excluded for good led to his resolve to make an effort to stay on and gain some qualifications and an apprenticeship, and for Katja that it was the supportive influence her coach had in her life. However, it is difficult to draw any firm causal conclusions when explaining individual cases. A more modest claim would be that both of them had the potential for staying in – or rather returning to becoming committed to – education despite the difficult circumstances of their growing up and early secondary schooling, but they needed some specific trigger (in the form of an event or a particular person's influence) such as those mentioned. However, other triggers could potentially have fulfilled the same role, as in Lieberson's (1998) discussion of what caused the First World War. Staying on in school, for both of them, may have been 'an accident waiting to happen', and the precise nature of the trigger may then have been less important. Put differently, given Duncan's and Katja's potential, these triggers had the opportunity to make a difference, to use Rutter's (1996) phrase again. However, it is also worth emphasising again that there is no guarantee that these two will not have difficulties staying on track again later, especially if they were to encounter adverse circumstances such as not gaining a place for training in their desired occupations, a spell of unemployment, personal problems or similar.

8.2.2   Favourable factors and unexpectedly low educational outcome

The cases in this section contrast with those I discussed in the previous section in the sense that they combine (seemingly) favourable factors with an unexpectedly low educational outcome.

The *unexpected* element in Julia's case is that she did not obtain a recommendation for the Gymnasium despite the fact that both her parents hold degrees and both are in the service class. She had a recommendation for the Realschule instead. This is unusual: among the 790 Socio-Economic Panel (SOEP) cases, 92 have Julia's constellation of parental education and class, and only 11 (12 per cent) of them did not receive a recommendation for the Gymnasium. The most obvious explanation here is the fact that Julia emigrated to Germany from Russia at the age of ten, and her German at the time of the recommendation was not good enough for a Gymnasium recommendation. This is indeed the explanation Julia herself gives: 'Damals war ich erst seit zwei Jahren in Deutschland und meine Sprachkenntnisse waren auch nicht so toll.' [I had only been in Germany for two years at the time, and my language skills weren't that great, either.] To corroborate this subjective account, the first obvious check is a comparison with young people from a comparable social background. Julia's explanation seems plausible because, given the high proportion of cases from her background receiving the recommendation, some external force seems likely to be required to explain exceptions, and lack of language proficiency fits this. In addition, it would be useful to compare her history with that of a similar young person in terms of social background who had immigrated at an earlier age, but there is no one in the sample. The closest comparison case is Roman who, unlike Julia, does not have a parent in the service class, but whose parents, like hers, do hold the equivalent of the Abitur. This family emigrated from Poland before Roman was born, which meant that all his schooling took place in Germany and his language skills were on a par with those of someone of German origin, and he duly received a recommendation for the Gymnasium. Looking to England, there are two cases of young people whose parents were immigrants and who come from a similar social background as Julia. Kalvinder's parents came to England from Pakistan before she was born, and so did William's from Russia. Both followed educational pathways indistinguishable from those of English young people from similar backgrounds, Kalvinder going to an academically selective private school and William to an oversubscribed voluntary aided comprehensive. Obviously, the English system does not lend itself to an immediate comparison with the tripartite German system, but the experience of these second generation immigrants is relevant to explaining Julia's case. A final check is Julia's own subsequent educational pathway: she entered a Gesamtschule instead of a Realschule on the grounds that the Abitur was on offer at this school and her mother in particular was keen for her to have this opportunity. Indeed, she was on the pathway to Abitur at the time of the interview, showing many of the characteristics young people of her social background show in terms of habitus and reasoning about educational decisions. Taken together, these various forms of evidence do suggest that it is indeed her immigration experience which prevented her from obtaining the recommendation for the Gymnasium straight away. The existence of a Gesamtschule where she lives was probably helpful in keeping her on track for the Abitur, but it seems likely that this would not have been essential. Given her parents' social and educational background, she would have been likely to obtain her Abitur, even if this would have involved a slightly less straightforward route such as attending a Realschule to begin with and then, through hard work and adequate performance, moving to a Gymnasium later on.

A similar case is Aynur who came to Germany from Turkey as a child. Again, the unexpected element is her not having obtained a recommendation for the Gymnasium despite having parents with a favourable social background (father's service class occupation and both parents' Abitur). The main difference from Julia is that her parents do not hold degrees, merely the Turkish equivalent of the Abitur, and that she actually spent all her schooling in Germany. Nevertheless, like Julia, her lack of German at the time is the reason she gives for having received a recommendation for the Hauptschule initially. She then entered the same Gesamtschule as Julia, and, like her, is on the Gymnasium track within the Gesamtschule. It seems plausible therefore that it was indeed her lack of language skills that prevented her from entering a Gymnasium straight after primary school. It is worth noting that she speaks Kurdish (and sometimes Turkish) with her parents and German with her siblings, though presumably when she was younger, she spoke Kurdish with her siblings, too. The existence of a Gesamtschule is likely to have been beneficial for her, too, especially given the fact that she merely had a recommendation for Hauptschule, since it is relatively common to move up from the Realschule to a Gymnasium, but comparatively rare to achieve this after attending Hauptschule initially.

The unexpected outcome for Peter is that he attended a Hauptschule despite having received a Gymnasium recommendation. In his case, a specific negative event can be identified as trigger. He grew up with his mother, his father having left her while she was pregnant. However, he was very close to his uncle who lived next door and was a 'father figure' (his words) to him. This uncle died around the time when the decision for a secondary school had to be made, and Peter – with his mother's support – decided to go to Hauptschule even though he had received a recommendation for the Gymnasium, on the grounds that the Hauptschule was part of the same school as his primary school and he wanted as little change as possible during this difficult time. His cousin, the uncle's daughter, made the same decision at the time. At the time of the interview, Peter was attending a Gymnasium, having taken the extra year 10 after doing well in Hauptschule, so it might be said that his earlier decision did not in the end prevent him from getting on track for the Abitur. However, this was an uncertain path to take – not many pupils make the transition from Hauptschule to Gymnasium (his cousin for example had lost interest in the Gymnasium by the time she left Hauptschule and did not even try to enter it) – and he also notes that he is struggling with certain subjects, especially French which is a completely new subject for him, and mathematics where the demands are much higher than at the Hauptschule. The reason for describing these aspects of Peter's educational career briefly here is that I want to raise, yet again, the issue of how social background and specific events may come together to shape an individual's experience. Peter's mother's highest qualification is the Realschulabschluss, and she works as a masseuse. A thought experiment here is to consider what the effect of a tragic event such as that experienced by Peter would have been on someone from a different background, one where degrees, service class occupations and a Gymnasium career are the norm. It seems likely that given such a background, he would have entered the Gymnasium straight away despite his uncle's death. For his mother, however, it was more important that he stayed in a familiar environment despite the potential risk this implied for his educational career. I do not have any comparison cases to draw on because tragic events such as the one experienced by Peter are relatively rare, so the reasoning here rests on the mainly theory-informed counterfactual claim of how the habitus in a service class family with highly educated parents usually results in expectations, actions and decisions leading to advanced secondary education for the children being the norm, regardless of any particular circumstances.

The last case I wish to discuss here is that of Marcus where the unexpected element is, again, a mismatch between family background and outcome (with respect to both school type attended and aspirations for further study). He is one of the 'deviant' cases in Chapter 6. The configuration of his social background factors is favourable, with both parents holding degrees (his mother has a PhD) and service class occupations, but his outcomes are attending a non-academic type of school (a secondary modern school in Kent) and not having firm intentions of attending university. In some sense he could be described as being the opposite to Marko, discussed above. His older brother initially attended a prestigious independent prep school, while Marcus himself went to a Steiner school around the same time. His paternal grandmother did not approve of the Steiner system which is why she paid for Marcus' brother to attend the other school. However, then 'something happened in the family', as Marcus puts it, and his brother came to the Steiner school with him. He explains his parents' preference for the Steiner school by referring to his father's own educational experience:

> He went to [a major public school] at a young age, boarding school, all boys, and he didn't see his parents at all really and that affected him. And he, he's one of three brothers, he's in the middle and he was the one that was picked to do well. So he was sent to [the major public school], two other brothers were sent to a local boarding

school in Oxford, and I don't think it really worked out the way that Nan thought it would. Because my Dad, erm ... he was very strict on us when he was young like his father was to him when he was young, and then during my early education at Steiner he kind of changed and just became, 'well, it's your life, I'll support you in whatever you want to do.' And he had various fallings out with his mum, mother about various things.

The Steiner school worked out well for Marcus' brother who took his GCSEs there and then went on to a local grammar school to take A-levels, doing very well academically, according to Marcus. But the Steiner school was not ideal for Marcus himself once he reached the age of about 13, he 'grew out of it', as he puts it, mainly citing his interest in sports as the reason for not fitting in. He was excluded from the school for kicking a ball 'and I can't be anywhere where that happens'. His parents supported him in his wish to attend a different school, and he likes his current secondary modern school a lot, not only the sports side of things but also the way lessons are taught. The grammar school would have been an option, assuming he could have passed the entrance exam, but he would have had to wait for three months to take this exam and did not want the delay, having made the decision to leave the Steiner school. He also describes himself as not particularly academically minded or interested. His intention for the sixth form is to do a BTEC sports course and an electronics course, ideally at his current school. University seems a long way off to him, and he is not at all sure that he would like to go, since he does not like academic work.

For some of the cases I discussed at the beginning of this section, such as Julia and Marko, the additional insights gained by considering the details of their life stories and educational experiences concern generalisable factors such as the school system and its interaction with cognitive ability, or an immigration experience interacting with social background. With Marcus, the situation is different: his particular trajectory seems to have been shaped by the particular constellation of his own individual interests and talents as well as parental histories including changes of heart and family conflict, rather than more general factors such as social background. He is the only one in the group of English interviewees who had two parents with degrees and in service class occupations who did not express a clear wish to attend university. In Germany, among cases with this configuration of parental educational and social class background, there is only Ludwig who is not certain as to whether he wishes to attend university, and in fact his case has some parallels with Marcus. Ludwig also has experienced conflict in the family – in his case, a complete lack of contact with his educationally very ambitious father, following his parents' divorce two years before the interview – and this, coupled with an interest in a non-graduate career,[4] may have produced this outcome. These individuals' experiences serve to illustrate the fact that educational outcomes are not merely a direct product of social background and school system characteristics. Within these parameters, there is a considerable amount of scope for individual differences (including among the parents), as well as individuals' experiences and ambitions, even in cases which appear, on the face of it, overdetermined. Achieving a high level of qualification is not everyone's key aim in life, regardless of their social background, and occasionally this will produce slightly unexpected outcomes. Lieberson's (1997, p. 376, Lieberson & Silverman, 1965) notion of 'immediate precipitants' is perhaps better suited to capturing the underlying causal processes here than chance events: applied to Marcus, the factors that might be seen as immediate precipitants of his unexpected educational career, given his privileged family background, are family conflict and the disillusionment on his father's part with a traditional academic education, and Marcus' own non-academic interests and talents. For Ludwig, likewise, we find (presumably prolonged) family conflict and a loss of contact with his educationally ambitious father.

8.3   Conclusion

In this chapter, I have used a combination of theoretical knowledge, knowledge of background factors in individual cases, and knowledge of specific life events and/or circumstances to explain outcomes, the latter especially in the case of outcomes that were unexpected given known background factors. I have aimed to illustrate that the role of chance and how it affects people partly depends on their particular constellation of individual and social background factors, using thought experiments and comparisons with other cases from the interview sample as sources of additional insight. However, beyond the general point that chance and constellation of specific factors act jointly to produce outcomes, it is difficult to generalise from the cases' experiences. Some of the experiences or situations discussed in this chapter are relatively uncommon and it is therefore unlikely that they are characteristic of the general population. However, this is not to say that they are not of great importance to the individual concerned. An example is Peter's loss of his father figure, something which is fairly unusual, but in his case it was the one thing that had a big impact on his educational career (see also Rutter, 1996, pp. 616/617).

Finally, a note of caution: for most, if not all, cases, it is possible to create plausible accounts to explain an outcome based on existing information obtained through the interviews, combined with relevant theoretical knowledge. However, it is important to bear in mind that the interviewees themselves select the information they wish to share, and that this may be at least partly driven by a wish to give an account which makes sense to themselves and the interviewer. Duncan for example mentioned the incident with his friend as the reason for deciding that he had to pull himself together in order to be able to stay in school, but it is hard to tell to what extent this was prompted by the interview process, a point we also stress in Glaesser & Cooper (2014) where we note that social pressure may exist on interviewees to account for their decisions in a 'rational' manner.

George and Bennett (2005) note the importance of avoiding confirmation bias (where the researcher only seeks evidence that fits the original hypothesis). I have attempted to deal with this issue by drawing on additional evidence and on my comparative thought experiments wherever suitable comparator cases were available among my interviewees. However, there always remains uncertainty in such 'historical' accounts.

9
Summary and Conclusions

Following the detailed analyses and findings reported in the previous chapters, in this final chapter I summarise both substantive and methodological conclusions, as well as raising some issues that might be of possible relevance to policymakers.

9.1 Substantive conclusions

Rational action theory (RAT) (Boudon, 1974, Breen & Goldthorpe, 1997, Goldthorpe, 1996b) and Bourdieu's concepts of habitus (Bourdieu, 1977) and cultural capital (Bourdieu, 1986) (see Chapter 4) have formed the theoretical background to the sociological analyses throughout this book. Both theories have been developed to address a range of social phenomena including the link between an individual's educational outcome and his/her parental social class and parental education. RAT explains this link by referring to cost-benefit analyses that are undertaken with the aim of at least maintaining the family of origin's social status (for example Goldthorpe, 1996b). Habitus, which refers to durable dispositions, is formed in the family of origin and shapes the ways in which decisions are made and what kind of course of action is considered normal or expected. Cultural capital comprises material and immaterial goods and values present in the family which can be converted into educational advantages.

Throughout this book, my aims have been, first, to describe, in a conjunctural manner, educational pathways and outcomes, in other words, to 'establish the phenomenon' (Merton, 1987) of the link between background and outcomes, and, second, to identify generative mechanisms (Pawson, 1989) which generated these empirical regularities, but also exceptions to them. I used cross-case Qualitative Comparative Analysis

(QCA) analyses of large survey data sets mainly for the first task, and a combination of theoretical knowledge, the QCA results and within-case analysis, that is, the analysis of process-tracing in-depth interviews, for the second. The findings from the QCA analyses I undertook confirmed the broad theoretical expectations briefly outlined above (explained in detail in Chapter 4), and the in-depth interview analyses showed that these theories were indeed fruitful in supplying plausible explanations for individuals' outcomes. The interviewees described their families and their school experience in ways which point to explanations of why they considered certain educational and occupational careers, but not others. At the same time, there was evidence of some cost-benefit analysis, but what exactly is considered to be a cost (and how high a cost) and a benefit (and how great a benefit) are also shaped by the family background as well as school environment and peer group. My findings serve as further confirmation of the predictions of these well-established theories. It is not commonly argued that the different theoretical strands work well together, but in my view, this approach captures the whole picture better than an attempt to explain these processes by reference to one or the other theory alone.

I hope to have contributed to theoretical development by showing that the joint presence of many advantageous factors is the surest route to educational success. If fewer advantageous factors are jointly present, the lack of some can be substituted for by others, but those cases are more prone to deviate from an expected pathway if unexpected life events interfere. Such exposure to contingency is less likely to affect those whose educational trajectories are 'overdetermined' by the joint presence of advantageous factors. While a regression-based method can model interaction effects, QCA is particularly well suited for showing the difference it makes to have factors jointly or individually (or not at all) present. To use an abstract example, a combination such as $A*B + A*C + B*C$ may have been found to be sufficient for an outcome, with consistency levels for the individual parts of around 0.85. The combination $A*B*C$ may well have a higher consistency of around 0.9 and in that sense might be described as overdetermining the outcome. While a lack of just one of the three conditions A, B and C would still mean a sufficient combination of conditions existed, the presence of all three is sufficient at a higher level of consistency. Examples from my analyses illustrating this may be found in Box 5.1 and Box 6.3 and the associated discussions.

In addition, my use of interview analysis to uncover the details of the supposed generative mechanisms was helpful in showing that summarising factors and combinations of factors can sometimes fall short of describing the social reality they are intended to represent. In some sense, though, this is a data problem rather than a theoretical insight. For example, a parental degree can be an indicator of a family where education is highly valued, where higher education is the norm and where occupations match the educational level, or, conversely, it can be an isolated characteristic of one parent, possibly obtained at a not very prestigious institution, with no other family experience of higher education or service class occupation and without the degree having translated into a matching professional career. Parental degrees – and any other such summarising factor – therefore can indicate very different things, and, accordingly, their effects are likely to be different. Quite frequently, this was the reason for 'deviant' cases following a seemingly unexpected pathway: on closer analysis, these cases' pathways were not as unexpected as they first appeared. In some cases, however, idiosyncrasies concerning individual talents and interests as well as family history and experience seemed the most likely explanation of the cases' deviation from some expected pathway.

The comparison of two different countries was theoretically fruitful in showing that many social processes appear across school systems. The effects of familial habitus, cultural capital and RAT-type reasoning were present in both countries. However, the system shapes the particular form the relevant social processes take. German parents of service class origin and with certain educational credentials and cultural capital might encourage and support their child in entering and attending the Gymnasium where he or she can experience academic rigour and sponsorship by the school, whereas English parents of a similar type can either opt for private schooling for their child to enable them to experience this sort of environment or they can carefully choose a state secondary school which can offer it, for example by moving into the catchment area of a prestigious comprehensive school, effectively buying a certain form of education through a larger mortgage, or, to use Bourdieu's language, converting their economic capital into cultural capital for their children (Bourdieu, 1986). I have argued that the role of certain formally non-selective secondary schools in the comprehensive English system can be very similar to that of a German selective Gymnasium. Academically oriented, ambitious and supportive comprehensive schools with an intake of ambitious and talented pupils can act as sponsors much in the same way as a selective school (Turner, 1960). Such schools tend to be located in catchment areas with a higher than average social class composition. Given this, in some ways it can be easier for a working-class child from a home lacking cultural capital to enter a school where he or she has a chance of experiencing encouragement to stay in education and aim for university in Germany than in England, provided that he or she is cognitively able. As noted in Chapters 4 and 5, this is not to say that the selection for Gymnasium is free from social class bias. On the contrary, children from working-class families are less likely to reach the required level, and less likely, even if they do reach this level, actually to be selected. However, if a child from a working-class background does gain access to a Gymnasium, he or she has the chance of attending a school which can provide sponsorship, regardless of place of residence, whereas in England more depends either on being lucky enough to live near such a school or on having parents who will ensure attendance at such a school.

9.2 Methodological conclusions

As noted in Chapter 2, the goal of social science research often is to provide causal explanations. My key methodological aim in this book was to discuss and apply non-experimental methods oriented to reaching this goal.

One of my specific aims was to demonstrate how the use of QCA with survey data can offer a way of supplying sophisticated descriptions of social processes and structures which can form the basis for subsequent causal analysis. Configurational models, I have argued, have a greater affinity with social reality given that they analyse configurations of conditions (instead of net effects of variables), alternative pathways to some outcome, and the relationships of necessity and sufficiency which sometimes, though not always, are to be found in the social world (for examples of sociological theories consistent with this view taken from Cooper and Glaesser (2012b), see Section 2.4).[1] The QCA solutions I developed support this view given that they are compatible with existing theory and that, in addition, subsequent interview analyses largely confirmed the findings and were able to point to likely generative mechanisms that led to the pattern observed in the survey data.

QCA was originally developed for use with small to medium sized samples to help researchers working with such case numbers to analyse them in a more systematic way. However, this history is no reason not to use it with large *n*. The key criterion for choosing an analytic method is the underlying causal model: if the assumption is that this is best described by a conjunctural method of analysis, and/or one that can take account of relationships of sufficiency and necessity, then QCA can and should be used regardless of sample size. This applies to other methods, too. Obviously, it is not always possible to follow this principle since in some cases there can be practical limitations. For example, statistical methods need a minimum sample size to perform analyses adequately, and in-depth case studies cannot be conducted with samples that are too large for one's given resources.

Another specific methodological aim was to show how the integration of survey data analyses and in-depth case studies via QCA can enhance causal understanding. There were two aspects to this aim: one was the use of QCA to obtain a typology of cases to be interviewed and analysed; the other was the use of the resulting in-depth case studies to supplement large *n* cross-case analyses in order to uncover causal mechanisms. QCA is most commonly used to undertake Boolean analyses of truth tables, as I have done, but in addition it can be very useful to map out what Lazarsfeld (1937) has termed the 'property space', or 'attribute space', which is defined by the factors under study (see also Becker, 1998, Chapter 5). I made use of this idea by drawing on the truth table itself as well as Boolean solutions to identify types of cases of interest for further study. My aim, then, was to use an approach where the different methods are not simply used one after the other to study different aspects of the research topic, but where they are well integrated in a way relevant to a particular goal. I have also occasionally returned to the survey data following interview findings in order to test some hypothesis arising out of the interview analysis. In doing so, I loosely followed Goldthorpe's (2001) suggestion of developing and testing hypotheses following large *n* analyses, though he refers to testing via statistical modelling used in conjunction with theoretical knowledge rather than testing via a combination of QCA, insights gained from interviews and theoretical knowledge.

Overall, I aimed to collect as comprehensive a body of evidence as possible (Freedman, 1991) to provide convincing causal explanations of educational processes and outcomes. The QCA truth tables and solutions were part of this body of evidence, as were the analyses of interview data, but existing theoretical knowledge was also brought to bear on the task. For the aim of explaining individual cases' outcomes in Chapter 8, an additional tool was the use of counterfactual reasoning and thought experiments, to corroborate my interpretation of a specific case's pathway.

Another important element was my comparative use of two countries. The key point here is that the comparative design enabled me to show that the broad theories concerning the sociological analysis of educational pathways are valid in more than one societal context, though the social forces expressed themselves in different ways.

I do not wish to suggest that my approach be used as a general template for conducting research. Research problems are too varied for there to be any one 'right' or 'best' way to proceed. In Hammersley's words: 'How much evidence is required, and of what kinds, varies according to the nature of the knowledge claim made, both in terms of its type (descriptive, explanatory, or theoretical) and its own degree of plausibility and credibility' (Hammersley, 2001, p. 547). Hopefully, I have been able to demonstrate in practice an approach that readers might find useful to adapt to their own problem, with its specific demands and challenges.

I will end this section by noting some observations concerning the interviewing process itself. I was able, for each of the individual cases I discussed, to provide a – hopefully convincing – account of how their educational pathway came to be the way I found it. With the 'deviant' and 'inconclusive' cases, this involved drawing on additional evidence over and above the theoretically plausible explanations that were possible for the typical cases, as identified by their particular configurations of factors based on my QCA models. Clearly, this additional evidence was solely based on what the interviewees chose to tell me. I have no reason to expect that they were trying to mislead me in any way, but it is possible, for example, that some of the reasons they gave for their educational decisions were post-hoc rationalisations, triggered by my questions. They may not have been aware of making a conscious decision at the time, but faced with my questions they may have felt that they had to justify their course of action, whether to me or to themselves (or both). They may have been motivated both by the wish to tell a coherent story and by social desirability. This then begs the question of whether my own interpretations were also partly motivated by the former, that is whether they involved constructing accounts which, on the face of it, seem plausible, but which leave open the possibility that either the reality lacked such coherence or that an equally plausible alternative account might have been missed (see also Hammersley, 2008, Chapter 5). However, the various strategies I described – using a combination of large *n* survey analysis via QCA with in-depth interview-based case studies, drawing on several relevant sociological theories, and analysing the case studies by various means including counterfactual reasoning – were intended to safeguard, as far as possible, against this danger.

9.3 Implications for policy

There are several perspectives that drive policy making in education. They can be linked to the perceived purposes of education. Ball (2008) notes that these can usefully be summarised into economic and social purposes (though these may partly overlap). The social purpose of education is, broadly speaking, to increase fairness, social mobility and people's quality of life via education, while the economic purpose is to increase productivity and competitiveness, both the individual's and society's. The latter seems to have received more attention from policy-makers and in the public discourse lately, according to Ball: education is seen to be key to developing knowledge and skills which can then be traded in some marketplace. In other words, both the individual and the state regard education as an investment which is expected to yield a benefit in the form of a rewarding job (for the individual) and a skilled workforce which will aid economic development (for the state). However, policymakers do also recognise the social purpose of education, and given the focus of this book, I will comment only on this. In the introductory chapter, I mentioned issues such as social mobility, discussed in England, and the Programme for International Student Assessment (PISA) shock, discussed in Germany, as indicators of a public interest in equity and fairness in education. The secondary school system is sometimes thought to influence social inequality in education: proponents of a comprehensive school system expect this to be particularly helpful for children from underprivileged backgrounds given that it offers – or is supposed to offer – the same educational opportunities for everyone regardless of social background. However, there are also those who argue that a selective system is particularly beneficial to able children from underprivileged backgrounds given that it can offer an academically oriented form of education to those who otherwise, given their background, might not seek out and receive such an education. The empirical evidence, however, is mixed at best: while this question is not easy to analyse given that there are always many factors in addition to the type of secondary school system that can potentially have a bearing on equity in the education system, it seems that no system can claim to be 'fairer' than the other (Boliver & Swift, 2011, Goldthorpe, 2013). We have come to a similar conclusion (Glaesser & Cooper, 2012a, see also Chapter 4) following a QCA analysis of National Child Development Study (NCDS) data. The analyses in this book have confirmed this view of the relative unimportance of school system. Social advantage finds a way of expressing itself, whether this is by supporting a child in gaining admission to a selective school in a selective system, or, in a comprehensive system, by choosing a suitable 'comprehensive' school, or by paying for private tutoring or for private education outside the state system (see also Lieberson, 1985, for example his discussion of school segregation, pp. 53–60). One particular feature of the German selective system seems to be important with regard to equity though: this is that there is the opportunity to enter advanced forms of secondary education later on if the initial placement was for a less academically oriented track or school type. The importance of such opportunities was evident in findings reported previously (Glaesser, 2008, Glaesser & Cooper, 2011b, for a summary of the latter see Chapter 4), where we showed that a considerable proportion of young people change track following their initial placement, and that this is more commonly in an upward rather than downward direction (though it also became clear that upwards mobility is socially selective again: in addition to a recommendation for a school above Hauptschule, higher parental educational and occupational levels were part of the configurations linked to such mobility).

The importance of institutional arrangements allowing fluidity in the system also became apparent in the analyses presented in this book. Among my interviewees, a number of young people who initially attended a Realschule and one who first went to a Hauptschule intended to continue their education in a Gymnasium, and similarly some who had gone to a Gesamtschule without a recommendation for the Gymnasium were now on track to obtain their Abitur. The reasons why these young people did not receive a Gymnasium recommendation or, if they did receive it, chose not to attend a Gymnasium, vary. Some were what might be termed 'late developers' who at the age of ten would not have coped with the more demanding content and workload of a Gymnasium but who are capable of doing so now, and some were immigrants whose German language skills were not good enough to follow the more demanding course of study in a Gymnasium, but who, with support, were able to flourish in the Gesamtschule.

In any school system, organisational features clearly are something that is put in place by policymakers. In addition, it is important for teachers to be aware of these features and to direct pupils accordingly wherever appropriate. This is why I mentioned teacher education in my introductory chapter as a potentially policy-relevant area: a teacher's task is not only to impart knowledge, important though this obviously is, but also to guide and support a pupil's development as best they can. To do this, knowledge of the relevant organisational procedures is essential. The same goes for careers advisors and other professionals involved at any stage in this process.

There is another reason why I suggested that my findings might be relevant to teacher education. While teachers obviously cannot influence what happens in the home, it is important that they are aware of the processes influencing young people's and their parents' expectations and decision-making. It would also be beneficial for teachers to be aware of the differences in habitus and cultural capital among their pupils. While certain forms of knowledge and thinking about the world will come naturally to some of these pupils, others will never have come across these in their home or wider social network because their parents lack the relevant resources and/or knowledge themselves. If teachers are aware of this, they can take action in various ways. For example, they can direct a child towards certain books and/or activities if it seems that these are not offered at home but the child might be interested. Awareness of the differences in upbringing and experience can also help teachers not to take certain forms of knowledge or skills for granted but to try to adapt teaching so that children are able to learn what they have not had access to at home. Finally, when it comes to further education and career choices, teachers can help counteract what is normal in the home and school if they feel that a young person would be better suited to an alternative route. This can mean encouraging university aspirations in a bright young person from a disadvantaged background who attends a school where university plans are not the norm, but it can also mean suggesting alternatives to higher education to someone who feels under pressure from home and school to enter higher education but who may not have the talent for and/or interest in a university degree.

For these reasons – the importance of home background and wider social network – it is also important to note the limitations of the potential impact any education policy might have. Neither schools nor universities or further education providers can fully compensate for all the shortcomings and difficulties a young person might experience in their upbringing. Any policy aimed at improving social mobility therefore needs to take account of the wider social context in order to be successful. According to Goldthorpe, this is borne out by the evidence:

> In sum, attempts at increasing equality of opportunity, in the sense of a greater equality of mobility chances, would seem unlikely to be effective, whether made through educational policy or otherwise, unless the class-linked inequalities of condition on which class mobility regimes are founded are themselves significantly reduced.

It is notable that in discussion of Scandinavian societies, in which increased social fluidity can be most persuasively claimed as a political accomplishment, the emphasis has fallen less on educational policy per se than on the reduction of class differences in incomes and levels of living through redistributive fiscal and welfare policies and, further, on strong trade unionism and employment protection that help maintain the security and stability of incomes, of wage-earners especially, and on models of political economy that, again to the advantage of wage-earners, prioritise full employment. (Goldthorpe, 2013, p. 446)

Finally, I would like to comment on one feature of QCA analyses which can be particularly beneficial with regard to informing policy. This is the potential for identifying necessary conditions. Knowledge of necessary conditions can be particularly useful for policymakers given that without these being present, an outcome is unlikely to be achieved. The necessary conditions I identified in the analyses in this book were mostly factors relating to parental background, and while this is useful to know, it is not something that can be changed easily by policy interventions. However, I also identified having had a recommendation for the Gymnasium at the end of primary school as a quasi-necessary condition for attending a Gymnasium at the age of 17. If a policymaker's aim was to have more children enter the Gymnasium at the end of primary school, an obvious conclusion might be to abolish the recommendation altogether, given that it clearly does not predict perfectly who will and will not succeed in a Gymnasium. In addition, receiving the recommendation is linked to social background as well as academic ability. However, this in itself is not to say that the recommendation does not have an important predictive function, generally matching children to an appropriate curriculum. It is crucial to take a policy's wider context into account. At the time of my interviewees' transition from primary to secondary school, the recommendation was largely binding, it was not easy to overturn it (and of course this partly accounts for its predictive power). In a bid to overcome the recommendation's social selectivity, some reform was undertaken so that the recommendation was still given, but made not binding in some German Länder. However, Ditton and Krüsken (2009) have shown that the transition to secondary school became more socially selective in Länder where the recommendation was not binding than in those where it was. This is because more highly educated parents were more likely to send their child to a Gymnasium even if the child lacked the appropriate recommendation, whereas less well educated parents were less likely to follow a recommendation for the Gymnasium.

This finding reminds us that any policy decision has to take account of likely unintended consequences. However, while this would be desirable, policymakers do not always seem to take account of potential unintended consequences of their policies, even if – as is the case here – there is clear empirical evidence to indicate the likelihood of such consequences. More and more Länder now do not have a binding recommendation. In Baden-Württemberg, for example, this was changed in 2012 with the explicit aim of reducing the social selectivity at the transition to secondary school, even though the Ditton and Krüsken paper had already been published. An understanding (and a willingness to take account of the knowledge provided by researchers) of the underlying causal mechanisms would have been helpful here, since it would have enabled these consequences to be predicted (see also Lieberson, 1985, in particular his example concerning the income gap between blacks and whites, pp. 191–194).

Cartwright and Hardie (2012) stress the general importance of taking account of the context in which a policy is to be implemented and of having an understanding of underlying causal mechanisms. They note that the kind of evidence favoured by policymakers is frequently obtained through conducting randomised controlled trials (RCTs). These can provide useful evidence, but the danger is that they only show that some policy or intervention is effective in one context. It may not be effective in another context. For this reason, they stress the importance of understanding causal mechanisms. It is not enough to show that something worked somewhere, once, but we also need to know why it worked in order to be able to predict whether it will work again, somewhere else. They argue that various forms of evidence should therefore be used together. This can be RCTs, but also econometric analyses, process-tracing and others.

Cartwright and Hardie's book is specifically concerned with the effectiveness of policy and how this can be established. Their suggestion to use evidence from multiple sources, not just that established via RCTs, has some affinity with my own approach throughout this book. I have used theoretical knowledge, findings from previous research (both my own and others'), a cross-country comparison, large *n* analyses of survey data via some descriptive analysis and QCA, and in-depth analyses of process-tracing interviews. For the latter, I employed thematic analysis and counterfactual analysis. This combined approach has proved fruitful first, to 'establish phenomena' (Merton, 1987), and, second, to establish potential generative mechanisms and causal explanations of individuals' pathways.

9.4 Concluding remarks

This book is intended to contribute to the fields of sociology of education and social science research methodology. I hope that the substantive findings are of interest to sociologists as well as education practitioners, and that the methodological insights will be of benefit to social science researchers in substantive fields other than the sociology of education. My methodological approach has combined the use of cross-case and within-case analysis in order to develop causal understanding. This has involved respectively the analysis of both survey and interview data. I aimed to develop configurational explanations of educational outcomes, and for this purpose first employed the set-theoretic method QCA to undertake cross-case analyses, but subsequently combined this with within-case work, something also recommended by Charles Ragin. There is no reason why the integrative approach I have used in this book should not be applied more widely. For example, Dirk Berg-Schlosser (2012) has also fruitfully combined QCA with other methods in the field of political science. QCA is also being applied in fields such as sociology, business studies, organisational studies, evaluation, education and public health and there is scope for an integrative approach that combines QCA with other methods to be used within all of these.

In the light of my comments on policy evaluation above, and taking note of Cartwright and Hardie (2012), Hammersley (2001) and Pawson (2006) on policy evaluation and systematic reviews, I believe that another area where such an integrated approach might usefully be employed is policy studies where knowledge of causal mechanisms is important in order to avoid implementing policies that are unlikely to succeed.

Above all, my intention was not to write a recipe book on how to implement a particular research approach, but to encourage thinking about ways to approach a research problem and, more generally, ways of thinking about the social world. Social relations are complex, and influences on any individual's educational pathway and outcome originate from a multitude of sources. This is clear from the analyses presented in this book, where I show a possible way of tackling such complexity. Social science's aim is to reduce complexity so that an understanding of patterns, regularities and mechanisms becomes possible. At the same time, there is a balance to be struck between undertaking summarising analyses that may be used as a basis for generalising, and detailed analyses that contribute to in-depth understanding of mechanisms (for a discussion of these issues see Hammersley, 2008, pp. 44–46). Using different sources of insight, as I have done (and as proponents of the 'mixed methods' movement advocate), can be helpful here. Currently, policymakers and many academics see RCTs and other forms of experimental methods as the best, if not the only, method to establish causation and to inform policy decisions. By contrast, throughout this book, I intended to show that non-experimental methods can form a key component of the set of approaches available to social researchers wanting to understand and explain social processes. Such understanding can then provide the basis for policy decisions.

Finally, some comments on the substantive focus of this book. Young people today live in a world where they are well aware, as we have seen, that formal qualifications matter because of the way they influence future careers. The individual and social circumstances in which they gain their qualifications differ widely, and accordingly young people vary in the goals they pursue. Gaining the highest possible qualifications is still not an important goal for every young person; some value other things in life. It is worth bearing this in mind, so as not to regard young people's lives as failures if they do not attain or strive for the highest qualifications they might in principle obtain. We have also seen that individuals make their decisions within the framework of the constraints and opportunities they experience. They are not always aware of the multiple influences on their lives. As social researchers, we are able to take a wider view and to analyse the social forces acting upon individuals as well as their subjective accounts and interests. It is for this reason that a vibrant social science will always have something to offer both to citizens and to those politicians and policymakers who are aiming to improve their constituents' lives.

Notes

1 Introduction

1. Some of the discussion of England might be seen to apply to all of the United Kingdom, but there are some important differences between England, Scotland, Wales and Northern Ireland. Therefore, I have chosen to focus just on England.
2. All else being equal, this would also seem to imply the opposite, that is, people from the top should be able to move down if they do not have the requisite qualifications and/or skills to stay at the top, but, not surprisingly, this is less frequently mentioned explicitly.
3. Goldthorpe (2013) discusses a number of misconceptions regarding both the analytic concept and empirical support for social mobility.
4. This pessimistic view might appear to be contestable in the light of my Hauptschule interviewees who were in further education or some form of vocational training at the time of the interview (with the exception of one young woman who dropped out of a course of study in a vocational school because she had a child during that time. At the time of the interview, she was caring for her then one-year-old child, but intended to start an apprenticeship the year after). However, it seems likely that this is at least partly due to a selection effect: the young people were contacted via their former school, and presumably only those agreed to be interviewed who did not feel any animosity towards their old school or a general dislike of education.
5. Others still of course argue that observational data cannot ever provide causal models, and that randomised controlled trials (RCTs) and other forms of experimentation are the only way of obtaining causal understanding. I discuss RCTs briefly in Section 2.4.

2 Description and Explanation: Methodological Rationale

1. However, class itself is just a shorthand for possible causal mechanisms. It has explanatory value because of what we know it stands for: a higher social class background is often linked to a higher income, which makes it easier for young people from such backgrounds to delay entering the labour market. It is also linked to higher education, allowing parents to recognise the value of a degree for their children, and so on.
2. There is a view that regularity accounts of causation have advantages over other versions of causal analysis such as counterfactual or probabilistic accounts (for example Baumgartner, 2008). I do not share this view, as will become clear throughout. While it is my view that regularities are an important element in the attempt to establish causal relationships, they are not sufficient in themselves.
3. Hammersley (1985) also discusses this piece of work as one of just a few examples of theory-focussed ethnography undertaken in the sociology of education.

3   Qualitative Comparative Analysis

1. This is true in the crisp context, where a case is either completely in or completely out of a set. With fuzzy sets, cases can have partial membership in sets, considerably complicating the measurement of consistency. See Ragin (2000, 2005, 2006b, 2008), also Cooper (2005).
2. Again, this applies in the crisp context.
3. Readers concerned that such threshold-setting seems arbitrary should bear in mind that much decision-making in the social sciences involves the researcher's judgement and/or convention. An example is the use of a 5 per cent level in significance testing.
4. In solution 3, raw coverage of the term A*B is 0.26, its unique coverage is 0.211. The latter is the same as the solution coverage in solution 1, where the solution term is A*B*C. This is not a coincidence: the unique coverage figure describes that part of a pathway which is not covered by the other pathway. In solution 3, the two pathways are A*B and B*c. B*c comprises the configurations A*B*c and a*B*c. A*B comprises the configurations A*B*C and A*B*c. We can see that the part of the solution not covered by A*B*c is A*B*C which is therefore the same as the solution term in solution 1.
5. Matters can be more complicated when fuzzy sets are employed.
6. Strictly speaking, only two dummy variables are needed for a factor with three possible values. If, in the example used here, service class and working class are used as the two dummies, then the absence of *both* would indicate that the case belongs to the intermediate class.

4   Overview of the Project

1. This is usually at the age of ten, but in some Länder children attend primary school for six years which means they enter secondary school at the age of 12.
2. This is another instance of a difference between Länder, with a school leaving age of 18 in some and 19 in others. In addition, around the time of the study there was a move towards the eight-year-Gymnasium (i.e., a school leaving age of 18) in the majority of Länder, although at the time of writing (2014) a counter-reform movement is gaining momentum, with some Gymnasien changing back to nine years.
3. This is yet another instance of differences between Länder, and of a policy that is subject to reform. At the time of writing, the recommendation is not binding in most places, but it was still common for it to be binding during the period at which my interviewees experienced their transition to secondary school.
4. A comparison of my sample on the variables I used with the full data set showed that my sample appears to be slightly skewed towards higher educational credentials and aspirations (both parents and young people) and higher parental social class.
5. The data were made available to me by the SOEP study at the German Institute for Economic Research (Deutsches Institut für Wirtschaftsforschung; DIW), Berlin.

6. Again, my sample is slightly skewed towards higher educational credentials and aspirations (both parents and young people) and higher parental social class, compared with the full sample.

7. While the SOEP is a representative panel study by design, some groups deemed to be of particular interest were oversampled, high income households among them (Haisken-DeNew & Frick, 2005).

8. 'Voluntary-aided (VA) schools are maintained schools and often, but not always, have a religious character' (https://www.gov.uk/voluntary-aided-schools-capital-funding).

9. Ideally, I would have selected interviewees from the samples used for the QCA. However, since the SOEP and LSYPE are large anonymised surveys not conducted by me, this was obviously not possible. Instead, I matched types of cases from SOEP and LSYPE to those I was able to interview.

10. However, it is worth making a point concerning possible measurement error: in row 5, two out of three cases have the outcome. If it transpired that the case without the outcome had been inaccurately recorded in the data set and should have been allocated the outcome, then, on recoding, the consistency for this row would become 1, putting it above the consistency threshold. The same point applies to row 6 where, again, the recoding of a single case would put this row above the threshold. Clearly therefore, when there are only a small number of cases in a row, the potential problems caused by even small errors in coding might be considerable.

5 Which Young People in Germany Are in a Gymnasium at the Age of 17? A Typological Analysis

1. Given that the recommendation, while based on performance, is also linked to social background, Ditton and Krüsken (2009) point out that it might have been expected that those Länder where the recommendation is not binding would have less social selectivity in the transition to secondary school. However, they found the opposite to be the case: there is more social selectivity in Länder without a binding recommendation since more parents from highly educated backgrounds enrol their children in a higher school type than that recommended, while, conversely, not highly educated parents are more likely to enrol their children in a lower school type than that recommended.

2. I have also analysed the negation of the outcome, that is, the question of who does not attend a Gymnasium at the age of 17. This resulted in rows 12–16 of Table 5.1 being entered in the Boolean minimisation process, using a consistency threshold of 0.85. The resulting solution is abi_1p*gy_rec + MALE*sc_1p*gy_rec. Interestingly, leaving aside details of consistency and coverage, this is almost an exact mirror image of solution 3 for the original outcome (Box 5.1). However, it is important to note that this outcome is far more heterogeneous than the original outcome of attending Gymnasium, given that it comprises attending any other school type, that is, Hauptschule, Realschule and Gesamtschule. This makes the finding harder to interpret since the underlying mechanisms that lead to attending each of these school types may well differ.

3. There are in fact just 39 cases in the configurational component of the pathway that doesn't overlap (MALE* abi_1p*SC_1P*GY_REC, i.e. 1011), with 31

of these achieving the outcome. In total 382 cases achieve the outcome and these 31 represent 0.081 of these, thus providing the figure in Box 5.1 for the unique coverage of MALE*SC_1P*GY_REC.

4. The coverage for necessity of the recommendation is 0.785. This is equivalent to its being quasi-sufficient for the outcome with a consistency of 0.785. It is important to stress, however, as we know from our analysis of the truth table (Table 5.1), that in the cases of rows 6–8, fewer than 75 per cent of the cases obtain the outcome.

5. Regression equations can, of course, document multiple paths to an outcome, insofar as, for example, high values on one independent variable can compensate, additively, for low values on another. In a simple case with two independent variables, the relevant equation might be $Y = 6X + 8Z$. Then a case with the values of $X = 4$, $Z = 3$ and a case with the values of $X = 8$, $Z = 0$ would each have an outcome of $Y = 48$. However, the multiplicity of such alternative paths is not usually related to any notion of types of cases, as it is in QCA.

6. I should note that necessity analyses can be unstable depending on the relative case numbers in the condition under study, regardless of the underlying relationship of necessity (Cooper & Glaesser, 2015).

7. The point here is not that these conditions were quasi rather than perfectly sufficient, but that they were sufficient rather than necessary. Even in the case of perfect sufficiency, there will be cases obtaining the outcome without having the sufficient condition, simply because it is sufficient but not necessary.

8. In the SOEP, 21.5 per cent of cases who had the recommendation do not attend a Gymnasium aged 17.

9. Their other types of cases, chosen for different purposes, are diverse, extreme, influential, most similar, and most different cases. Rohlfing (2008) also discusses the use of residuals analysis in case selection. Noting the increasing tendency to combine regression with case study under the banner of mixed methods, he undertakes nested case analysis (as he calls the combination of large and small *n* analysis, following Lieberman, 2005) specifically to improve the model fit of a regression. For my view of the 'mixed methods' concept, see my comments at the end of Chapter 2. For case selection on the basis of fuzzy QCA, see also Schneider and Rohlfing (2013, 2014).

10. Habitus theory is obviously also relevant for such key points in a career – and I will discuss it in relation to them – but it was developed in a different context.

11. These three cases form part of the sample discussed in Glaesser and Cooper (2014). That paper uses all those interviews with young people whose parents are either both members of the service class or are both working class because we wished to obtain types of cases which are 'pure' in terms of social class background.

12. The word Ludwig uses, *gebildet*, is usually not only meant to imply a person holding formal qualifications, but also more generally someone who is intellectual, sophisticated, cultured.

13. Ludwig is listed against the same configuration in Table 5.3 as Jonas because this part of the solution, MALE*SC_1P*GY_REC, does not specify parental education. However, because Ludwig's parents do hold the Abitur, he also appears in the row above, ABI_1P*GY_REC.

14. We could ask whether, *given* ABI_1P*GY_REC, it is then quasi-necessary to be SC_OP [= neither parent is in the service class] in order to be deviant in the way Samuel is. If we do, we find SC_OP a consistency with necessity of 0.242 for ~GY_17 (where the ~ indicates not GY_17). This (within-configuration) necessity hypothesis needs to be discarded. On the other hand, a parallel test for the necessity of neither parent having a degree does approach the 0.75 threshold (reaching 0.727) [this is footnote 24 in Cooper & Glaesser (2012a)].

15. While the recommendation itself is supposed to be an indicator of individual ability and potential, it does also reflect social background, as discussed in Section 5.1. This might be one reason why someone with high enough cognitive ability may not receive the recommendation; another is lack of language skills, as in the case of recent immigrants.

16. As noted, I do not have an ability measure for my interviewees, but the fact that they received the recommendation for the Gymnasium despite their relatively unfavourable social background makes it safe to assume that their academic ability is comparatively high.

6 Secondary Schooling Careers in England

1. The mean on the key stage 2 test is 25.03 for these girls from the most privileged social background and 29.66 for these boys from the least privileged background. Classification into high and low attainment in this test appears justified in this instance, despite the fairly crude indicator which merely split the sample at the median: these girls did indeed perform less well in the key stage 2 test than the boys, but the girls appear higher up in the truth table nevertheless.

2. They do not differ on the binary factors. The mean for the key stage 2 test is 30.52 for the cases in row 1 and 30.68 for those in row 4, so it is appropriate to say that they do not differ on academic achievement either.

3. The mean key stage 2 test performance is 23.93 for these girls and 23.99 for these boys.

4. In Glaesser and Cooper (2012a, 2012b), the factors were secondary school policy (selective or comprehensive) and gender.

5. The Russell Group is an association of 24 research-intensive universities in the UK. Their reputation for academic excellence attracts highly achieving, ambitious students. See http://www.russellgroup.ac.uk/.

6. Adding academic achievement to this analysis as a fourth factor instead of gender results in the problem of limited diversity again. In particular, as expected, the configuration of not highly able in selective schools is practically non-existent, with just two cases overall.

7. Lindesmith (1981) actually argues that it may not be appropriate to conceive of causation in the social world as complex, with multiple causes and effects, and to leave it at that. Instead, sociology is not yet advanced enough clearly to differentiate phenomena which appear to belong to the same group but are actually different. This, in his opinion, is one of the reasons why we think that multiple causes exist for the same phenomenon. While I do not agree entirely – in my view, causation in the social world *is* complex – it is

important to pay close attention to the phenomena under study and their potential causes in order to be able to refine analytical categories.

7   What Types of Young People are Bound for Higher Education at the Age of 17?

1. These proportions are close to those in my interviews: 34.9 per cent of the German interviewees and 63.9 per cent of the English interviewees say they are hoping to go to university. While this is useful to know, it is important to bear in mind that my interview samples are not representative in other ways. For example, I have oversampled students attending selective schools in England. This is because my case selection strategy was to choose theoretically interesting cases (see Chapter 4) rather than to achieve an interview sample that was representative of the survey sample.
2. It is also worth noting that consistency with necessity of being in Gymnasium is 0.829.
3. The fact that nursing is a graduate occupation in Britain but not in Germany may well have implications for salary, career progression and so on, but this topic is beyond the scope of this book.
4. Academies are described by the Department for Education as follows: 'Academies are publicly funded independent schools. Academies don't have to follow the national curriculum and can set their own term times. They still have to follow the same rules on admissions, special educational needs and exclusions as other state schools. Academies get money direct from the government, not the local council. They're run by an academy trust which employs the staff' (https://www.gov.uk/types-of-school/academies).
5. BTEC stands for Business and Technology Education Council. This is a vocational qualification broadly equivalent to academic qualifications such as GCSE and A level.

8   Using In-Depth Case Studies to Explore Causal Mechanisms in Detail

1. It might be argued that the composition of a selection committee is not a chance event either, but could be explained given enough information about the general context and specific factors. The same applies to events such as illnesses: whether they are genetic or caused by contagion, etc., there will be an identifiable causal path that led to them. But in the context of a different causal field, that of educational outcomes, such events or factors may be indistinguishable from a chance event.
2. Ragin (2008, Chapters 8 and 9) outlines how counterfactual thinking can help understand causal processes in the case of limited diversity in QCA. See also Collier et al. (2004).
3. Since the time of Duncan's grandfather, coal mining in Britain has all but ceased. There is none in Duncan's area now, so obviously he would not do this particular job, but the thought of a job like it motivates him to stay in education.

4. It is worth noting that the profession he mentions is physiotherapy which in England is a graduate occupation. This example serves to reinforce, yet again, the difference between the two systems and the difficulties in undertaking comparisons of this kind. Does Ludwig's wish to become a physiotherapist make him more like the other cases with his constellation of social background factors, i.e. his ambition is 'really' a higher education aspiration, or, taking a German perspective, is he really an outlier in his wish not to pursue a university degree?

9 Summary and Conclusions

1. In cases where the truth table does not contain configurations of high enough consistency levels to justify a claim of quasi-sufficiency, picking out combinations of conditions associated with proportions of cases achieving the outcome well above the grand mean provides an alternative form of analysis.

References

Ambler, J.S. & Neathery, J. (1999). Education policy and equality: Some evidence from Europe. *Social Science Quarterly*, 80, (3), 437–456.

Anders, J. & Micklewright, J. (2013). *Teenagers' Expectations of Applying to University: How do they Change?* London: Institute of Education, Department of Quantiative Social Science, Working Paper No. 13–13.

Ball, S.J. (2008). *The Education Debate*. Bristol: Policy Press.

Ball, S.J., Davies, J., David, M. & Reay, D. (2002). 'Classification' and 'judgement': Social class and the 'cognitive structures' of choice of Higher Education. *British Journal of Sociology of Education*, 23, (1), 51–72.

Bandura, A. (1982). The psychology of chance encounters and life paths. *American Psychologist*, 37, (7), 747–755.

Baumert, J. & Schümer, G. (2001). Familiäre Lebensverhältnisse, Bildungsbeteiligung und Kompetenzerwerb. In: Deutsches PISA-Konsortium (ed.), *PISA 2000. Basiskompetenzen von Schülerinnen und Schülern im internationalen Vergleich*. Opladen: Leske + Budrich, 323–407.

Baumert, J., Watermann, R. & Schümer, G. (2003). Disparitäten der Bildungsbeteiligung und des Kompetenzerwerbs. Ein institutionelles und individuelles Mediationsmodell. *Zeitschrift für Erziehungswissenschaft*, 6, (1), 46–72.

Baumgartner, M. (2007). *Complex Causal Structures. Extensions of a Regularity Theory of Causation*. Bern: PhD thesis Bern University, retrieved from http://www.unige. ch/lettres/baumgartner/publications.html (accessed 16th September 2014).

Baumgartner, M. (2008). Regularity theories reassessed. *Philosophia*, 36, 327–354.

Becker, H.S. (1994). 'Foi por acaso': Conceptualizing coincidence. *The Sociological Quarterly*, 35, (2), 183–194.

Becker, H.S. (1998). *Tricks of the Trade. How to think about your Research while you're doing it*. Chicago: University of Chicago Press.

Berg-Schlosser, D. (2012). *Mixed Methods in Comparative Politics. Principles and Applications*. Basingstoke: Palgrave Macmillan.

Bertaux, D. (1981). From the life-history approach to the transformation of sociological practice. In: Bertaux, Daniel (ed.), *Biography and society*. Beverly Hills: Sage, 29–45.

Bertaux, D. & Bertaux-Wiame, I. (1981). Life stories in the bakers' trade. In: Bertaux, Daniel (ed.), *Biography and society*. Beverly Hills: Sage, 169–189.

Boliver, V. & Swift, A. (2011). Do comprehensive schools reduce social mobility? *British Journal of Sociology*, 62, (1), 89–110.

Boudon, R. (1974). *Education, Opportunity, and Social Inequality*. New York: Wiley.

Bourdieu, P. (1974). Cultural reproduction and social reproduction. In: Brown, Richard (ed.), *Knowledge, education and cultural change*. London: Tavistock Publications, 71–112.

Bourdieu, P. (1977). *Outline of a Theory of Practice*. Cambridge: Cambridge University Press.

Bourdieu, P. (1986). The forms of capital. In: Richardson, J.G. (ed.), *Handbook of theory and research for the sociology of education*. New York: Greenwood, 241–258.

Bourdieu, P. & Passeron, J.-C. (1977). *Reproduction in Education, Society and Culture.* London: Sage.

Bourdieu, P. & Passeron, J.-C. (1979). *The Inheritors. French Students and their Relation to culture.* Chicago: University of Chicago Press.

Breen, R. & Goldthorpe, J.H. (1997). Explaining educational differentials. Towards a formal rational action theory. *Rationality and Society, 9,* (3), 275–305.

Breen, R. & Goldthorpe, J.H. (2001). Class, mobility and merit. The experience of two British birth cohorts. *European Sociological Review, 17,* (2), 81–101.

Buchmann, C. & DiPrete, T.A. (2006). The growing female advantage in college completion: the role of family background and academic achievement. *American Sociological Review, 71,* (August), 515–541.

Buchmann, C., DiPrete, T.A. & McDaniel, A. (2008). Gender inequalities in education. *Annual Review of Sociology, 34,* 319–337.

Bynner, J. & Joshi, H. (2002). Equality and opportunity in education: evidence from the 1958 and 1970 birth cohort studies. *Oxford Review of Education, 28,* (4), 405–425.

Cartwright, N. & Hardie, J. (2012). *Evidence-based Policy. A Practical guide to doing it better.* Oxford: Oxford University Press.

Centre for Longitudinal Studies (2008). *National Child Development Study: Childhood Data, Sweeps 0–3, 1958–1974, Sweep 5, 1991, Local Authority Data, 1958–1974: Special Licence Access.* 2nd Edition. National Birthday Trust Fund, National Children's Bureau, [original data producer(s)]. Colchester, Essex: UK Data Archive [distributor], August 2008.

Collier, D. (2011). Understanding process tracing. *PS: Political Science and Politics, 44,* 823–830.

Collier, D., Seawright, J. & Munck, G.L. (2004). The quest for standards: King, Keohane, and Verba's *Designing Social Inquiry.* In: Brady, Henry and Collier, David (ed.), *Rethinking social inquiry. Diverse tools, shared standards.* Lanham: Rowman & Littlefield, 21–50.

Cooper, B. (2005). Applying Ragin's crisp and fuzzy set QCA to large datasets: social class and educational achievement in the National Child Development Study. *Sociological Research Online, 10,* (2), http://www.socresonline.org.uk/10/2/cooper.html.

Cooper, B. & Glaesser, J. (2008). How has educational expansion changed the necessary and sufficient conditions for achieving professional, managerial and technical class positions in Britain? A configurational analysis. *Sociological Research Online, 13,* (3), http://www.socresonline.org.uk/13/3/2.html.

Cooper, B. & Glaesser, J. (2011). Paradoxes and pitfalls in using fuzzy set QCA: Illustrations from a critical review of a study of educational inequality. *Sociological Research Online, 16,* (3), http://www.socresonline.org.uk/16/3/8.html.

Cooper, B. & Glaesser, J. (2012a): Qualitative work and the testing and development of theory: Lessons from a study combining cross-case and within-case analysis via Ragin's QCA. *Forum Qualitative Sozialforschung/Forum: Qualitative Social Research, 13,* (2), Art. 4.

Cooper, B. & Glaesser, J. (2012b): Set theoretic versus correlational methods: the case of ability and educational achievement. In: Cooper, Barry, Glaesser, Judith, Gomm, Roger and Hammersley, Martyn (ed.), *Challenging the qualitative-quantitative divide: explorations in case-focused causal analysis.* London & New York: Continuum, 170–207.

Cooper, B. & Glaesser, J. (2015). Analysing necessity and sufficiency with Qualitative Comparative Analysis: how do results vary as case weights change? *Quality and Quantity*, DOI 10.1007/s11135-014-0151-3.

Cooper, B., Glaesser, J., Gomm, R. & Hammersley, M. (2012). *Challenging the Qualitative-Quantitative Divide: Explorations in Case-Focused Causal Analysis.* London & New York: Continuum.

Department for Education and National Centre for Social Research (2012). *Longitudinal Study of Young People in England: Waves One to Seven, 2004–2010 [computer file]. 12th Edition.* Colchester, Essex: UK Data Archive [distributor].

DfE (2011). *LSYPE User Guide to the Datasets: Wave 1 to Wave 7.* Department for Education.

Ditton, H. & Krüsken, J. (2009). Bildungslaufbahnen im differenzierten Schulsystem – Entwicklungsverläufe von Laufbahnempfehlungen und Bildungsaspirationen in der Grundschulzeit. *Zeitschrift für Erziehungswissenschaft,* Sonderheft 12 (edited by Jürgen Baumert, Kai Maaz and Ulrich Trautwein), 74–102.

Duşa, A. & Thiem, A. (2013). *QCA: Qualitative Comparative Analysis.* R package version 1.0–5.

Erikson, R. & Goldthorpe, J.H. (1993). *The Constant Flux. A Study of Class Mobility in Industrial Societies.* Oxford: Clarendon Press.

Eurydice. (2013a). 'Germany. Organisation of Private Education', from https://webgate.ec.europa.eu/fpfis/mwikis/eurydice/index.php?title=Germany:Organisation_of_Private_Education&oldid=75839.

Eurydice. (2013b). 'Germany. Overview', from https://webgate.ec.europa.eu/fpfis/mwikis/eurydice/index.php?title=Germany:Overview&oldid=75693.

Eurydice. (2013c). 'United Kingdom (England). Organisation of General Lower Secondary Education', from https://webgate.ec.europa.eu/fpfis/mwikis/eurydice/index.php?title=United-Kingdom-England:Organisation_of_General_Lower_Secondary_Education&oldid=82008.

Eurydice. (2013d). 'United Kingdom (England). Organisation of Private Education', from https://webgate.ec.europa.eu/fpfis/mwikis/eurydice/index.php/United-Kingdom-England:Organisation_of_Private_Education.

Eurydice. (2013e). 'United Kingdom (England). Types of Higher Education Institutions', from https://webgate.ec.europa.eu/fpfis/mwikis/eurydice/index.php/United-Kingdom-England:Types_of_Higher_Education_Institutions.

Fiss, P.C. (2011). Building better causal theories: A fuzzy set approach to typologies in organization research. *Academy of Management Journal,* 54, (2), 393–420.

Freedman, D.A. (1991). Statistical models and shoe leather. *Sociological Methodology,* 21, 291–313.

Freedman, D.A. (1997a): From association to causation via regression. In: McKim, Vaughn R. and Turner, Stephen P. (ed.), *Causality in Crisis? Statistical methods and the search for causal knowledge in the social sciences.* Notre Dame, Indiana: University of Notre Dame Press, 113–161.

Freedman, D.A. (1997b): Rejoinder to Spirtes and Scheines. In: McKim, Vaughn R. and Turner, Stephen P. (ed.), *Causality in Crisis? Statistical methods and the search for causal knowledge in the social sciences.* Notre Dame, Indiana: University of Notre Dame Press, 177–182.

Freedman, D.A. (2005). Linear statistical models for causation: A critical review. In: Everitt, Brian S. and Howell, David C. (ed.), *Encyclopedia of Statistics in Behavioral Science.* Chichester: John Wiley & Sons, 1061–1073.

Galindo-Rueda, F. & Vignoles, A. (2005). The declining relative importance of ability in predicting educational attainment. *The Journal of Human Resources*, 40, (2), 335–353.

Geertz, C. (1973). Thick description: toward an interpretive theory of culture. In: Geertz, Clifford (ed.), *The interpretation of cultures*. New York: Basic Books, 3–30.

George, A.L. & Bennett, A. (2005). *Case Studies and Theory Development in the Social Sciences*. Cambridge, Massachusetts: MIT Press.

Glaesser, J. (2008). Just how flexible is the German selective secondary school system? A configurational analysis. *International Journal of Research and Method in Education*, 31, (2), 193–209.

Glaesser, J. & Cooper, B. (2010). *Employing Ragin's Configurational methods to Undertake case Selection from a Large Dataset for in-depth Study in order to test and Develop Theory*. Paper presented at the BSA Annual Conference in Glasgow.

Glaesser, J. & Cooper, B. (2011a): Selecting cases for in-depth study from a survey dataset: An application of Ragin's configurational methods. *Methodological Innovations Online*, 6, (2), 52–70.

Glaesser, J. & Cooper, B. (2011b): Selectivity and flexibility in the German secondary school system: A configurational analysis of recent data from the German Socio-Economic Panel. *European Sociological Review*, 27, (5), 570–585.

Glaesser, J. & Cooper, B. (2012a): Educational achievement in selective and comprehensive local education authorities: a configurational analysis. *British Journal of Sociology of Education*, 33, (2), 223–244.

Glaesser, J. & Cooper, B. (2012b): Gender, parental education, and ability: their interacting roles in predicting GCSE success. *Cambridge Journal of Education*, 42, (4), 463–480.

Glaesser, J. & Cooper, B. (2014). Using rational action theory and Bourdieu's habitus theory together to account for educational decision-making in England and Germany. *Sociology*, 48, (3), 463–481.

Goldthorpe, J. (1985). On Economic Development and Social Mobility. *British Journal of Sociology*, 36, (4), 549–573.

Goldthorpe, J. (1996a): Problems of 'meritocracy'. In: Erikson, Robert and Jonsson, Jan O. (ed.), *Can education be equalized? The Swedish case in comparative perspective*. Boulder: Westview Press, 235–287.

Goldthorpe, J. (2013). Understanding – and misunderstanding – social mobility in Britain: The entry of the economists, the confusion of politicians and the limits of educational policy. *Journal of Social Policy*, 42, (3), 431–450.

Goldthorpe, J.H. (1996b): Class Analysis and the Reorientation of Class Theory: The case of Persisting Differentials in Educational Attainment. *British Journal of Sociology*, 47, (3), 481–505.

Goldthorpe, J.H. (2001). Causation, statistics, and sociology. *European Sociological Review*, 17, (1), 1–20.

Goldthorpe, J.H. (2003). The myth of education-based meritocracy. Why the theory isn't working. *New Economy*, 10, (4), 234–239.

Goldthorpe, J.H. (2005). *Education-Based Meritocracy: The Barriers to its Realisation*. Paper presented at the in Center for Policy Research, Maxwell School of Syracuse University.

Goldthorpe, J.H. (2007a): Intergenerational class mobility in contemporary Britain: Political concerns and empirical findings. *British Journal of Sociology*, 58, (4), 525–546.

Goldthorpe, J.H. (2007b): *On Sociology. Second Edition. Volume One: Critique and Program*. Stanford: Stanford University Press.

Goldthorpe, J.H. (2007c): *On Sociology. Second Edition. Volume Two: Illustration and Retrospect*. Stanford: Stanford University Press.

Haisken-DeNew, J.P. & Frick, J.R. (2005). *DTC. Desktop Companion to the German Socio-Economic Panel (SOEP)*. Berlin: DIW. http://www.diw.de/english/soep/services_amp_documentation/compendium_dtc/27925.html.

Halsey, A.H., Heath, A.F. & Ridge, J.M. (1980). *Origins and Destinations. Family, Class, and Education in Modern Britain*. Oxford: Clarendon Press.

Hammersley, M. (1985). From ethnography to theory: A programme and paradigm in the sociology of education. *Sociology*, 19, (2), 244–259.

Hammersley, M. (1991). A myth of a myth? An assessment of two ethnographic studies of option choice schemes. *British Journal of Sociology*, 42, (1), 61–94.

Hammersley, M. (2001). 'Systematic' reviews of research literatures: a 'narrative' response to Evans & Benefield. *British Educational Research Journal*, 27, (5), 543–554.

Hammersley, M. (2008). *Questioning qualitative inquiry. Critical essays*. London: Sage.

Hammersley, M. (2012). Troubling theory in case study research. *Higher Education Research & Development*, 31, (3), 393–405.

Heath, A.F. & Jacobs, S. (1999). Comprehensive reform in Britain. In: Leschinsky, Achim and Mayer, Karl-Ulrich (ed.), *The comprehensive school experiment revisited: evidence from Western Europe*. Frankfurt/Main: Peter Lang, 101–130.

Johnson, R.B. & Onwuegbuzie, A.J. (2004). Mixed methods research: A research paradigm whose time has come. *Educational Researcher*, 33, (7), 14–26.

Kerckhoff, A.C. (2001). Education and social stratification processes in comparative perspective. *Sociology of Education*, 74, (Extra Issue), 3–18.

Lacey, C. (1970). *Hightown Grammar. The school as a social system*. Manchester: Manchester University Press.

Lareau, A. (2003). *Unequal childhoods. Class, race, and family life*. Berkeley: University of California Press.

Lazarsfeld, P.F. (1937). Some remarks on the typological procedures in social research. *Zeitschrift für Sozialforschung*, 6, (1), 119–139.

Lieberman, E.S. (2005): Nested analysis as a mixed-method strategy for comparative research. *American Political Science Review*, 99, (3), 435–452.

Lieberson, S. (1985). *Making It Count. The Improvement of Social Research and Theory*. Berkeley, Los Angeles, London: University of California Press.

Lieberson, S. (1997). The big broad issues in society and social history. Application of a probabilistic perspective. In: McKim, Vaughn R. and Turner, Stephen P. (ed.), *Causality in Crisis? Statistical methods and the search for causal knowledge in the social sciences*. Notre Dame, Indiana: University of Notre Dame Press, 359–385.

Lieberson, S. (1998). Causal analysis and comparative research: what can we learn from studies based on a small number of cases? In: Blossfeld, Hans-Peter and Prein, Gerald (ed.), *Rational choice theory and large-scale data analysis*. Boulder: Westview Press, 129–145.

Lieberson, S. & Silverman, A.R. (1965). The precipitants and underlying conditions of race riots. *American Sociological Review*, 30, (6), 887–898.

Lindesmith, A.R. (1981). Symbolic interactionism and causality. *Symbolic Interaction*, 4, 87–96.

Lizardo, O. (2009). *The Cognitive Origin of Bourdieu's Habitus*. http://nd.edu/~ olizardo/papers/jtsb-habitus.pdf.

Mackie, J.L. (1974). *The Cement of the Universe*. Oxford: Oxford University Press.

Mahoney, J. (2012). The logic of process tracing tests in the social sciences. *Sociological Methods & Research*, 41, (4), 570–597.

Mahoney, J. & Goertz, G. (2006). A tale of two cultures: Contrasting quantitative and qualitative research. *Political Analysis*, 14, (3), 227–249.

Mahoney, J., Kimball, E. & Koivu, K.L. (2009). The logic of historical explanation in the social sciences. *Comparative Political Studies*, 42, (1), 114–146.

Marsh, H.W. (1987). The big-fish-little-pond effect on academic self-concept. *Journal of Educational Psychology*, 79, (3), 280–295.

Mayer, K.-U. (2008) (Completely rev. ed.): Das Hochschulwesen. In: Cortina, Kai S., Baumert, Jürgen, Leschinsky, Achim, Mayer, Karl-Ulrich and Trommer, Luitgard (ed.), *Das Bildungswesen in der Bundesrepublik Deutschland: Strukturen und Entwicklungen im Überblick*. Reinbek bei Hamburg: Rowohlt, 599–645.

Merton, R.K. (1987). Three fragments from a sociologist's notebooks: Establishing the phenomenon, specified ignorance, and strategic research materials. *Annual Review of Sociology*, 13, 1–28.

Ministry of Education (1954). *Early Leaving. A Report of the Central Advisory Council for Education (England)*. London: HMSO.

Morris, P. (2012). Pick 'n' mix, select and project; policy borrowing and the quest for 'world class' schooling: An analysis of the 2010 schools White Paper. *Journal of Education Policy*, 27, (1), 89–107.

Müller, W. (1998). Erwartete und unerwartete Folgen der Bildungsexpansion. In: Friedrichs, Jürgen et al. (ed.), *Die Diagnosefähigkeit der Soziologie*. Opladen: Westdeutscher Verlag, 81–112.

Ofsted (2003). *Boys' Achievement in Secondary School*. London: HMI.

Pawson, R. (1989). *A Measure for Measures. A Manifesto for Empirical Sociology*. London, New York: Routledge.

Pawson, R. (2006). *Evidence-based Policy: A Realist Perspective*. London: Sage.

Pawson, R. (2008). *Causality for Beginners. NCRM Research Methods Festival 2008*. Available at http://eprints.ncrm.ac.uk/245/1/Causality_for_Beginners_Dec_07. doc, accessed 5th September 2013.

Pearl, J. (1999). *Reasoning with Cause and Effect*. IJCAI Award Lecture: http:// bayes.cs.ucla.edu/IJCAI99/ijcai-99.pdf.

Phillips, D. (2000). Learning from elsewhere in education: some perennial problems revisited with reference to British interest in Germany. *Comparative Education*, 36, (3), 297–307.

Ragin, C.C. (1987). *The Comparative Method. Moving Beyond Qualitative and Quantitative Strategies*. Berkeley, Los Angeles, London: University of California Press.

Ragin, C.C. (2000). *Fuzzy-Set Social Science*. Chicago and London: University of Chicago Press.

Ragin, C.C. (2004). Turning the tables: How case-oriented research challenges variable-oriented research. In: Brady, Henry and Collier, David (ed.), *Rethinking social inquiry. Diverse tools, shared standards*. Lanham: Rowman & Littlefield, 123–138.

Ragin, C.C. (2005). From Fuzzy Sets to Crisp Truth Tables. http://www.compasss. org/files/WPfiles/Raginfztt_April05.pdf.

Ragin, C.C. (2006a): The Limitations of Net-Effects Thinking. In: Rihoux, Benoît and Grimm, Heike (ed.), *Innovative Comparative Methods for Policy analysis.* New York: Springer, 13–41.

Ragin, C.C. (2006b): Set Relations in Social Research: Evaluating Their Consistency and Coverage. *Political Analysis,* 14, (3), 291–310.

Ragin, C.C. (2008). *Redesigning Social Inquiry: Fuzzy Sets and Beyond.* Chicago: University of Chicago Press.

Ragin, C.C. & Bradshaw, Y.W. (1991). Statistical analysis of employment discrimination: a review and critique. *Research in Social Stratification and Mobility,* 10, 199–228.

Ragin, C.C., Drass, K.A. & Davey, S. (2009). *Fuzzy-Set/Qualitative Comparative Analysis 2.0.* Tucson, Arizona: Department of Sociology, University of Arizona. Website: http://www.u.arizona.edu/%7Ecragin/fsQCA/software.shtml.

Ragin, C.C. & Sonnett, J. (2005). Between Complexity and Parsimony: Limited Diversity, Counterfactual Cases, and Comparative Analysis. In: Kropp, Sabine and Minkenberg, Michael (ed.), *Vergleichen in der Politikwissenschaft.* Wiesbaden: VS Verlag für Sozialwissenschaften, 180–197.

Reay, D., David, M. & Ball, S.J. (2001). Making a difference?: Institutional habituses and Higher Education Choice. *Sociological Research Online,* 5, (4), http://www.socresonline.org.uk/5/4/reay.html.

Reay, D., David, M. & Ball, S.J. (2005). *Degrees of choice. Social class, race and gender in Higher Education.* Stoke on Trent: Trentham Books.

Reay, D., Davies, J., David, M. & Ball, S.J. (2001). Choices of degree or degrees of choice? Class, 'race' and the Higher Education choice process. *Sociology,* 35, (4), 855–874.

Rohlfing, I. (2008): What you see and what you get: Pitfalls and principles of nested analysis in comparative research. *Comparative Political Studies,* 41, (11), 1492–1514.

Rutter, M. (1996). Transitions and Turning Points in Developmental Psychopathology: As applied to the Age Span between Childhood and Mid-adulthood. *International Journal of Behavioral Development,* 19, (3), 603–626.

Saunders, P. (1997). Social mobility in Britain: an empirical evaluation of two competing explanations. *Sociology,* 31, (2), 261–288.

Schneider, C.Q. & Rohlfing, I. (2013). Combining QCA and process tracing in set-theoretic multi-method research. *Sociological Methods & Research,* 42, (4), 559–597.

Schneider, C.Q. & Rohlfing, I. (2014). Case studies nested in fuzzy-set QCA on sufficiency: formalizing case selection and causal inference. *Sociological Methods & Research,* Online first, DOI: 10.1177/0049124114532446.

Seawright, J. & Gerring, J. (2008). Case selection techniques in case study research: A menu of qualitative and quantitative options. *Political Research Quarterly,* 61, (2), 294–308.

Shanahan, M.J., Sulloway, F.J. & Hofer, S.M. (2000). Change and Constancy in Developmental Contexts. *International Journal of Behavioral Development,* 24, (2), 421–427.

Statistisches Bundesamt (2012). *Bildung und Kultur. Private Schulen.* Wiesbaden: Statistisches Bundesamt. https://www.destatis.de/DE/Publikationen/Thematisch/BildungForschungKultur/Schulen/PrivateSchulen2110110127004.pdf?__blob=publicationFile.

Swartz, D. (1981). Classes, educational systems & labor markets. *European Journal of Sociology*, 22, (2), 325–353.

Tarrow, S. (2004). Bridging the quantitative-qualitative divide. In: Brady, Henry and Collier, David (ed.), *Rethinking social inquiry. Diverse tools, shared standards.* Lanham: Rowman & Littlefield, 171–179.

Turner, R.H. (1960). Sponsored and contest mobility and the school system. *American Sociological Review*, 25, (6), 855–867.

Tymms, P. & Coe, R. (2003). Celebration of the success of distributed research with schools: the CEM centre, Durham. *British Educational Research Journal*, 29, (5), 639–653.

Vester, M. (2006). Die ständische Kanalisierung der Bildungschancen. Bildung und soziale Ungleichheit zwischen Boudon und Bourdieu. In: Georg, Werner (ed.), *Soziale Ungleichheit im Bildungssystem. Eine empirisch-theoretische Bestandsaufnahme.* Konstanz: uvk, 13–54.

Index

Academic ability   9, 21, 22, 40, 43,
   44, 45, 48, 49, 56, 60, 61,
   63–64, 68, 80–83, 88, 106, 110,
   111, 115–117, 129, 132, 137,
   138, 140, 146, 150, 152–153,
   161, 173, 181
Achievement (*see also* Attainment)   1, 2,
   11, 17, 23, 40–41, 43, 44, 48, 53,
   90, 94, 96–97, 99–101, 106, 109,
   116–117, 124, 135, 140, 146, 181
Apprenticeship (*see also* Education,
   further, *see also* Education,
   vocational)   3, 46, 75, 77, 112,
   125, 129, 131–132, 134, 138,
   139, 141, 143, 155, 156–157, 177
Aspiration   10–11, 40, 43, 80, 88, 99,
   101, 103–121, 122–123, 125–126,
   128, 133–141, 148, 150, 154,
   160, 172, 178, 179, 183
Attainment   8, 9, 22, 27, 33, 40, 41,
   46, 61, 88, 114, 134, 143, 181
Attribute space (*see under* Property
   space)

Becker, Howard S.   56, 146, 168
Boolean algebra   4, 7, 22
Boolean minimisation (*see under*
   Minimisation)
Boolean notation   7, 22, 29, 33
Boolean solution (*see under* Solution)
Boudon, Raymond   8, 23, 40, 42, 68,
   104, 122, 142, 164
Bourdieu, Pierre   8, 12, 23, 40, 41–43,
   48, 68, 74, 76, 87, 104, 106,
   113, 122, 142, 164, 166
Boys (*see also* Gender)   9, 23, 26–27,
   43, 60–61, 92, 93, 96–97, 99, 181
Brothers (*see under* Siblings)

Cartwright, Nancy   24, 25, 174, 175
Case selection   4, 8, 9, 25, 50, 67,
   69–70, 74, 81, 85, 90, 101, 108,
   151, 179, 180, 182

Case study   4, 10, 17–18, 19, 24, 39,
   48, 50, 67, 70, 74, 121, 145,
   168, 169, 180
Causal condition (*see also* Necessary
   condition, *see also* Sufficient
   condition)   7–8, 11–12, 23, 29,
   30, 32–38
Causal model   4, 15, 20, 21, 167, 177
Causal pathway   18, 29–30, 36–37,
   58, 59, 60, 61, 64, 67, 68, 69,
   70, 73–74, 78, 81, 83, 87, 92,
   96, 99–102, 117, 121, 151, 175,
   178–179
Causation (*see also* Deterministic
   (view of) causation,
   see also Probabilistic (view of)
   causation, *see also* Regularity
   view of causation, *see also*
   Explanation, causal)   1, 16, 20,
   23, 25, 146, 176, 177, 181
CEM centre data (*see under* Survey
   data, CEM centre)
Centre for Evaluation and Monitoring
   (*see under* Survey data, CEM
   centre)
Chance (*see also* Contingency)   146,
   148, 151, 156, 162, 182
Classification of cases   9, 53, 68,
   69–73, 89, 101–104, 117
Cognitive ability (*see under* Academic
   ability)
Comparison   5, 19, 151, 157–158,
   160, 162
   of countries   4, 12, 166, 174,
   183
   pairwise comparison   62, 96–97,
   117
Comprehensivisation   45, 48, 61
Condition (*see under* Causal
   condition)
Configuration   4, 7–8, 15–16, 23, 33,
   167, 175
Confirmation bias   18, 163

Consistency
  with necessity 31
  with sufficiency 30, 37, 38
Constellation (configuration and
  outcome) 11, 71, 148, 151, 162
Constraints 43, 146, 176
Contest mobility (*see under* Mobility,
  sponsored and contest)
Context 4, 16, 22, 23, 25–26, 41, 87,
  122, 146, 169, 172, 173–174
Contingency 12, 146, 148, 151–162,
  165
Cooper, Barry 5, 7, 8, 16, 23, 28, 29,
  34, 38, 43, 48, 57, 60, 61, 67,
  71, 74, 76, 78, 79, 81, 96, 105,
  121, 122, 124, 163, 167, 170,
  171, 178, 180, 181
Cost-benefit analysis (*see also* Rational
  Action Theory (RAT)) 40, 43,
  48, 75, 79, 105, 142, 164, 165
Counterfactual 151, 160, 168, 169,
  174, 177, 182
Coverage 31–37, 38
  raw 33–37
  unique 32–37
  solution coverage 35
Crisp sets 34, 37, 38, 178
Critical realism 16
Cross-case analysis (*see also* Within-
  case analysis, *see also* Large n
  analysis) 1, 4, 7, 10, 11, 16,
  23, 24, 29, 39, 48–49, 87, 121,
  164, 168, 175
Cultural capital 8, 12, 23, 40, 41–43,
  48, 56, 61, 68, 76, 101, 104,
  124, 164, 166–167, 172

Decision-making 3, 11, 40, 41, 43,
  76, 129, 142, 149, 172
Description 4, 6–7, 13–16, 17, 20, 21–24,
  25, 27, 57, 74, 167, 169, 174
Deterministic (view of) causation 20,
  146
Deviant case (*see also* Classification
  of cases) 9, 10, 25, 53, 69–73,
  78–82, 86, 89, 101–103,
  107–114, 116, 120, 148, 160,
  166, 169, 181
Dummy variable 38, 178

Education
  comprehensive (*see under* School
    system, comprehensive, *see also*
    School type, comprehensive)
  further (*see also* Apprenticeship,
    see also Education, vocational)
    10, 89, 113, 125, 132, 134, 138,
    155, 172, 177
  higher (*see also* University) 4, 9, 10,
    11, 14, 38, 45, 75, 77, 78, 79, 83, 89,
    104, 106, 110, 115, 121, 122–144,
    152, 166, 172, 177, 182–183
  private (*see also* School types,
    English, Independent) 44, 45,
    47, 48, 105, 109, 124, 166, 171
  secondary 3, 4, 6, 8, 43, 44–48, 49,
    61, 75, 77–78, 104–106, 115,
    116, 123, 134, 137, 138, 149,
    150, 152, 153, 154, 160, 166,
    170, 171, 173–174, 178, 179, 181
  selective (*see under* School systems,
    selective)
  vocational (*see also* Apprenticeship,
    see also Education, further) 46,
    125, 134, 135, 177, 182
Eleven plus 26, 44–45, 112, 134,
  149, 150
Environment (*see also* Context) 10, 23,
  41, 76, 78, 82, 88, 106, 111, 112,
  113, 116, 136, 149, 165, 166
ESRC (Economic and Social Research
  Council) study 1, 5, 8, 39–62
Event (*see under* Life event)
Evidence 6, 12, 16, 18–19, 22, 24,
  26–28, 158, 163, 168–169, 174
Experiment (*see also* Randomised
  controlled trial) 6, 15, 25,
  176, 177
Explaining (*see under* Explanation,
  see also Theorising)
Explanation
  Causal 1, 4, 6–7, 13–15, 16–21, 22,
    24, 26, 39, 40, 70, 76, 87, 121,
    141–142, 145, 146, 151, 167,
    168, 175
  Historical 18, 24, 121, 163
  Individual (*see also* Explanation,
    Historical) 18, 39, 74, 87, 121,
    141, 145–163, 165, 168, 169, 175

Family   23, 27, 40, 42, 49, 60, 75–88,
    105, 106, 108, 110–111,
    113–116, 121, 123, 125, 128,
    130, 132, 136–140, 142–143,
    149–150, 152, 160, 162,
    164–166
  extended   76–78, 80, 84, 85, 88,
    111, 143
Fluidity (in the education
    system)   171, 173
Freedman, David A.   15, 19, 24, 26, 168
Friends (*see also* Peers)   80, 106, 113,
    115, 130, 143, 150, 152, 155,
    156, 157, 163
Fuzzy sets   37–38, 178, 180

Gender (*see also* Boys, *see also*
    Girls)   8, 40, 43, 50, 56, 57,
    60–61, 63, 90, 96–97, 126
Generalisation   4, 25, 87, 121, 162, 176
Girls (*see also* Gender)   43, 60–61, 64,
    69, 92–93, 96–97, 101, 117, 181
Glaesser, Judith   5, 7, 8, 16, 23, 29,
    38, 43, 48, 57, 60, 61, 67, 71,
    74, 76, 78, 79, 81, 96, 105, 121,
    122, 124, 163, 167, 170, 171,
    180, 181
Goldthorpe, John H.   2, 7, 8, 15, 16,
    17, 19, 37, 40, 49, 50, 87, 104,
    122, 142, 164, 168, 170, 172,
    173, 177

Habitus   8, 12, 40–41, 43, 48, 68, 74,
    76–87, 104, 106, 113–114, 122,
    142, 143, 158, 160, 164, 166,
    172, 180
  institutional habitus   135–136,
    138, 142
Hammersley, Martyn   17, 18, 22, 25,
    26, 28, 145, 169, 175, 176, 177
Higher education (*see under*
    Education, higher)
Higher education aspiration (*see under*
    Aspiration)

Immediate precipitants (*see also*
    Underlying causal conditions)
    11–12, 145–146, 162
Immigrant   3, 80, 81, 138, 158, 171, 181
Immigration   3, 158, 161

In-depth case study (*see also* Case
    study, *see also* Within-case
    analysis)   1, 4, 7, 10, 39, 70,
    145–163, 165, 168, 169
Inconclusive case (*see also* Classification
    of cases)   9, 10, 53, 69–74,
    82–85, 86, 89, 101–103, 107,
    114–116, 148, 169
Institutional habitus (*see under*
    Habitus, institutional habitus)
Insufficient but necessary part of
    a condition which is itself
    unnecessary but sufficient
    (*see under* INUS condition)
Interests   11, 75, 86–87, 108–114, 120,
    126, 132–133, 136, 139–144,
    156, 161, 162, 166, 172, 176
INUS condition   30

Kent test (*see also* Eleven plus)   44
Key stage   9, 51
Knowledge, theoretical (*see under*
    Theoretical knowledge)

Large n analysis (*see also* Cross-case
    analysis)   1, 5, 16, 24, 29, 39,
    50, 57, 70, 168, 169, 174
Lazarsfeld, Paul F.   56, 168
Lieberson, Stanley   11, 20, 69, 145, 146,
    147, 148, 151, 157, 162, 171, 174
Life event   11–12, 21, 84, 87, 121,
    146–148, 150, 151, 156, 157,
    159–160, 162, 165, 182
Limited diversity   34, 37, 56–58, 117,
    181, 182
Longitudinal Study of Young People in
    England (*see* survey data, LSYPE)
LSYPE (*see* survey data)

Mechanism   4, 6–7, 9, 10, 15–20, 21,
    24–27, 43, 48, 68, 70, 78, 87,
    116, 121, 142, 145–163, 164,
    165, 174–176, 177, 179
Merton, Robert K.   7, 13, 16, 39, 164, 174
Minimisation   34–35, 57–58, 62, 179
Mixed methods   27, 176, 180
Mobility, sponsored and
    contest   123–124, 135
  social (*see under* Social mobility)
Model (*see under* Causal model)

National Child Development Study
(*see under* Survey data, NCDS)
NCDS (*see under* Survey data, NCDS)
Necessary condition 31, 32
Norm 76, 84, 88, 106, 107, 113–114,
136, 139, 142–143, 150, 160,
164, 166, 172

Organisational features of school
systems (*see under* School
systems, organisational
features)
Overdetermined cases 78, 86, 106,
148, 149–151, 162, 165
Oxbridge (*see under* University,
England)

Parental class (*see also* Social class, *see
also* Social background) 8–9,
10, 33, 40, 43, 47, 49, 50, 53,
54–56, 57, 58–60, 63, 64–66,
68, 70–71, 74–83, 85–86, 90–93,
95–103, 106–120, 126–128,
146–152, 154, 157–161, 164,
166, 171, 180, 181
Parental education (*see also* Social
background) 8–9, 10, 21,
33, 40, 43, 49, 53, 54–56,
57, 58–60, 61, 63, 64–66, 68,
70–71, 74–83, 85–86, 88, 90–93,
95–103, 106–120, 126–128,
137, 146–152, 157–161, 164,
166, 171, 173–174, 179, 180
Pathway (*see under* Causal pathway)
Pattern 7, 17, 20, 70, 87, 116, 121,
128, 142, 167, 175
Pawson, Ray 7, 15, 16, 19, 28, 164,
175
Peers (*see also* Friends) 21, 80–82,
87–88, 106, 136, 143, 148, 165
Phenonemon (*see also* Regularity) 7,
13, 16, 22, 26–27, 39, 40, 70,
74, 164, 181
PISA 3, 170
Policy 1, 3, 5–6, 12, 25–26,
170–176
Population (*see also*
Generalisation) 14, 25
Preferences 11, 77, 79, 105, 121,123,
131–132, 134, 139, 142, 160

Private education (*see under*
Education, private,
see also School types, English,
Independent)
Probabilistic (view of) causation 20,
146, 177
Process-tracing 5, 18, 24–25, 50, 70,
87, 165, 174
Property space 56, 168

QCA (*see under* Qualitative
Comparative Analysis)
Qualifications
English
O-level 107
GCSE 49
A-level 49
German
Hauptschulabschluss 46
Realschulabschluss 46
Abitur 46
Qualitative Comparative Analysis
(QCA) 29–38
Quasi-necessary condition (*see also*
Consistency, *see also*
Coverage) 31
Quasi-sufficient condition (*see also*
Consistency, *see also*
Coverage) 30

Ragin, Charles 4, 7, 14, 15, 21, 29,
30, 31, 32, 35, 37, 38, 56, 57,
78, 96, 175, 178, 182
Randomised controlled trial (RCT) 6,
25–26, 174, 176, 177
Randomness (*see also* Contingency,
see also Chance) 20, 21, 69,
146
RAT (*see under* Rational Action
Theory)
Rational Action Theory (RAT) 8, 40,
48, 74, 87, 104, 105, 122, 142,
164
RCT (*see under* Randomised controlled
trial)
Recommendation (at the end of
German primary school) 8–9,
46–47, 53, 59–60, 63–64, 67,
68, 70, 73, 80, 81, 82, 84, 86,
88, 173–174, 178, 179, 180, 181

Regression analysis   7, 15–16, 21, 22, 29, 67, 70, 180
Regularity   7, 13, 16–19
Regularity view of causation   177
Russell Group (*see under* University, England)

School systems
  English   44–45
  German   45–48
  comprehensive   3, 5, 12, 44–45, 48, 49, 53, 61–62, 89, 123, 166, 170–171, 181
  selective   3, 5, 12, 44, 48, 53, 56, 61–62, 137, 138, 152–153, 170–171, 181
  organisational features of school systems   4, 44, 124, 171
School types
  English
    Comprehensive   44
    Selective (*see under* School type, English, Grammar)
    Grammar   44
    Secondary modern   45
    Academy   134, 182
    Voluntary aided   53, 179
    Independent (*see also* Education, private)   45
  German
    Hauptschule   3, 46
    Realschule   46
    Gymnasium   46
    Gesamtschule   46
Set theory   4, 7, 29
Siblings   75, 84, 104, 105, 106, 107, 108, 111, 113, 136, 139, 154, 160, 161
Sisters (*see under* Siblings)
Social background (*see also* Parental class, *see also* Parental education, *see also* Social class)   1–3, 11, 40, 43, 48, 60, 63–64, 87, 105, 143, 146, 147, 149–150, 160, 162, 170, 173, 179, 181
Social class   2, 14, 18, 23, 40–43, 45, 61, 68, 76, 84, 86, 101, 104, 122, 124, 135, 143, 164, 166–167, 172–173, 177

Social inequality in education   1, 8, 40, 45, 170
Social mobility   2, 19, 75, 170, 172, 177
Socio-economic panel (*see under* Survey data, SOEP)
SOEP (*see under* Survey data, SOEP)
Solution   8, 21–22, 34–37
Sponsored mobility (*see under* Mobility, sponsored and contest)
Sponsorship   10, 124–125, 128, 134–135, 137, 138, 152–154, 166–167
Sufficient condition   30–31, 32
Survey data
  CEM centre data   49, 60
  LSYPE   49, 51
  NCDS   49, 61
  SOEP   50, 52

Talent (*see also* Academic ability)   9, 10, 11, 42, 106, 110, 111, 120, 133, 137, 139, 140, 141, 142, 161–162, 166, 172
Teachers   6, 12, 47, 64, 77, 80, 110, 129, 132, 143, 148, 149, 150, 152, 155, 171–172
Theoretical knowledge   4, 24, 162–163, 165, 168, 174
Theorising   19, 20, 27, 70
Theory   4, 8, 11, 16–20, 23–27, 39, 74, 78, 82, 101, 141, 145, 160, 167, 177
Thick description   22
Thought experiment   151, 153, 160, 162–163, 168
Trajectory   74, 75, 122, 143, 145, 146, 165
Transition   75, 104–105, 123, 137, 146, 149
Trigger   145–148, 151, 156–157, 159
Truth table   8, 33–35, 37, 56
Type of case   9, 25, 56, 67, 68, 70, 72, 74, 89, 90, 102, 103, 114, 168, 179, 180
Typical case (*see also* Classification of cases)   9, 10, 12, 53, 67, 69–73,

74–78, 85, 87, 89, 101–106,
116, 148, 149–150, 169
Typology of cases (*see also*
Classification of cases) 102,
168

Underlying causal conditions
(*see also* Immediate
precipitants) 11–12, 145–146
Unexpected pathway 12, 70, 148,
151–162, 165–166
University
England
Hierarchy 129, 130
Oxbridge 106, 121, 130, 135,
136

Russell Group 105, 121, 130, 181
Polytechnic 124, 125
Germany
Hierarchy 125, 129
University 125, 130
Fachhochschule 122, 125, 130,
131
University aspiration (*see under*
Aspiration)

Vocational training (*see under* Education,
vocational)

Within-case analysis (*see also*
Cross-case analysis) 50, 69,
70, 165, 175

Printed and bound by CPI Group (UK) Ltd, Croydon, CR0 4YY